SOCIAL CHANGE AND
ECONOMIC LIFE INITIATIVE

This volume is part of a series arising from the Social
Change and Economic Life Initiative—a major interdisciplinary programme of research funded by the Economic and
Social Research Council. The programme focused on the
impact of the dramatic economic restructuring of the 1980s
on employers' labour force strategies, workers' experiences
of employment and unemployment, and the changing
dynamics of household relations.

SOCIAL CHANGE AND
ECONOMIC LIFE INITIATIVE

Series Editor: Duncan Gallie

SOCIAL CHANGE AND
THE EXPERIENCE OF UNEMPLOYMENT

SOCIAL CHANGE
AND THE EXPERIENCE
OF UNEMPLOYMENT

Edited by

DUNCAN GALLIE, CATHERINE MARSH

and

CAROLYN VOGLER

OXFORD UNIVERSITY PRESS
1994

Oxford University Press, Walton Street, Oxford OX2 6DP
Oxford New York Toronto
Delhi Bombay Calcutta Madras Karachi
Kuala Lumpur Singapore Hong Kong Tokyo
Nairobi Dar es Salaam Cape Town
Melbourne Auckland Madrid
and associated companies in
Berlin Ibadan

Oxford is a trade mark of Oxford University Press

Published in the United States
by Oxford University Press Inc., New York

British Library Cataloguing in Publication Data
Data available
ISBN 0–19–827782–2
ISBN 0–19–827917–5 (pbk.)

Library of Congress Cataloging in Publication Data
Social change and the experience of unemployment / edited by
Duncan Gallie, Catherine Marsh, and Carolyn Vogler.—
(The Social change and economic life initiative)
1. Unemployment—Great Britain—Psychological aspects.
2. Unemployed—Great Britain—Psychology. 3. Great Britain—
Social conditions—1945– . 4. Great Britain—Social conditions—1945–
5. Social change. I. Gallie, Duncan. II. Marsh, Catherine.
III. Vogler, Carolyn M., 1950– . IV. Series.
HD5708.S65 1994 331.13'7941—dc20 93–14377
ISBN 0–19–827782–2
ISBN 0–19–827917–5 (pbk.)

Set by Hope Services (Abingdon) Ltd.
Printed in Great Britain
on acid-free paper by
Bookcraft (Bath) Ltd.
Midsomer Norton, Avon

FOREWORD

This volume is part of a series of publications arising from the Social Change and Economic Life Initiative—a programme of research funded by the Economic and Social Research Council. The major objectives of the programme were to study the nature and determinants of employer labour force policies, worker experiences of employment and the labour market, the changing dynamics of household relations and the impact of changes in the employment structure on social integration and social stratification in the community.

The research programme focused on six local labour markets: Aberdeen, Coventry, Kirkcaldy, Northampton, Rochdale, and Swindon. These were selected to provide contrasting patterns of recent and past economic change. Three of the localities— Coventry, Kirkcaldy, and Rochdale—had relatively high levels of unemployment in the early and mid-1980s, whereas the other three experienced relatively low levels of unemployment.

The data collected by the Initiative give an exceptionally rich picture of the lives of people and of the operation of the labour market in the different localities. Three representative surveys were carried out between 1986 and 1987, providing fully comparable data across the localities. The first—the Work Attitudes/Histories survey—was a random survey of the noninstitutional population aged between 20 and 60, involving interviews with about 1,000 people in each locality. It provides information on work histories, current experiences of employment or unemployment, and attitudes to work. This was taken as the point of departure for the other two surveys, focusing respectively on the household circumstances of respondents and on the policies of their employers. In the Household and Community Survey approximately a third of the original respondents were reinterviewed to develop a picture of their household strategies, their organization of domestic work, their leisure activities, their friendship networks, and their attitudes towards welfare provision. Where people had partners, interviews were carried out both with the original respondents and with their partners. The Employers' Survey was based on telephone interviews with senior management in the establishments for which respondents in the original Work Attitudes/Histories survey worked. A further non-random follow-up survey was carried out involving 180 of the establishments that had taken part in the initial survey. The details of the research design and sampling for the different phases of the programme are provided in an Appendix at the end of this volume.

In addition, related studies were carried out in individual localities, focusing in greater depth on issues that had been covered in the common surveys. These included studies of the historical context of employment practices, current processes of technical change, managerial employee relations policies, industrial relations, gender segregation, the relationship between employer and employee perceptions of employment conditions, and household strategies with respect to labour market decisions and the organization of work within the household.

The team that implemented the programme consisted of thirty-five researchers drawn from fourteen different institutions. It brought together sociologists, economists, geographers, social historians, and social psychologists. The major common research instruments were collectively constructed through a series of working groups responsible for particular aspects of the study. The programme involved, then, a co-operative interdisciplinary, research effort for which there are few precedents in British social science.

DUNCAN GALLIE
National Co-ordinator and Series Editor

MA

PREFACE

The chapters in this book are based upon a number of data sets that emerged as the result of an extended period of co-operative effort by the multidisciplinary team involved in the Social Change and Economic Life Initiative. Many of those who made important contributions to the design of the survey and the format of questions are not authors in this particular volume, although they are writing chapters for other publications in the series. We would like, however, to underline the fact that this book would not have been possible without the wider collective effort.

We also owe a good deal to a number of people who assisted us in the various phases of the collection, preparation, and analysis of the data. The fieldwork was carried out by Public Attitude Surveys Ltd., under the direction of Barry Lee, Ruth Lennox, Stuart Robinson, and Eileen Sutherland. We were very impressed by their ability to cope with a quite exceptionally complex organizational structure for the development of the survey instruments. Our subsequent work has shown that the fieldwork was carried out to a very high standard. Martin Range and Jane Roberts played a central role in setting up the data tapes, and Martin Range also gave invaluable assistance with the programming of the work history data. Sarah McGuigan was responsible for the word processing of a number of the chapters of the book and she also gave a great deal of administrative help with the overall volume. Finally, we would like to thank the staff of Oxford University Press for their work in the preparation of the book.

An earlier version of Chapter 10 has been published in the *European Journal of Sociology* (vol. xxi, 1990, no. 1) and Chapter 5 has been published in the *Oxford Bulletin of Economics and Statistics* (vol. 54, 1992, no. 2). We are grateful in both cases for permission to use the relevant material.

Finally, we note with great sadness the very early death of our co-editor Catherine Marsh. Cathie had a burning concern for the issue of unemployment and she ensured that it remained a central preoccupation in the Initiative. In characteristic fashion, she carried on her work as editor until the last days of her life: indeed letters were still arriving from her, containing notes and recommendations about the book in the days following her death. We dedicate this book to her memory.

DUNCAN GALLIE
CAROLYN VOGLER

CONTENTS

LIST OF FIGURES

LIST OF TABLES

NOTES ON THE CONTRIBUTORS

BRENDAN BURCHELL is a Lecturer in the Faculty of Social and Political Sciences and Fellow of Magdalene College, University of Cambridge.

RICHARD B. DAVIES is Professor of Social Statistics and Director of the Centre for Applied Statistics, University of Lancaster.

PETER ELIAS is Professorial Fellow at the Institute for Employment Research, University of Warwick.

DUNCAN GALLIE is an Official Fellow, Nuffield College, Oxford.

JONATHAN GERSHUNY is Professor of Sociology and Director of the ESRC Research Centre on Micro-social Change, University of Essex.

RICHARD LAMPARD is a Lecturer in Sociology at the University of Warwick.

CATHERINE MARSH was Professor of Quantitative Methods in the Faculty of Economics and Social Studies at the University of Manchester.

ROGER PENN is a Reader in Economic Sociology at the University of Lancaster.

CAROLYN VOGLER is a Lecturer in Sociology at the City University, London.

£2⁴

1

The Experience of Unemployment

DUNCAN GALLIE AND CATHERINE MARSH

1. THE CONTEXT

In the 1980s unemployment in Britain rose to levels that were unprecedented since the great inter-war recession of the 1930s. Levels of unemployment were historically low in the 1950s and 1960s, began to rise in the early 1970s, and, then climbed very steeply after the second 'oil shock' of 1978–9. Since the mid-1980s a period of decline in the official rate was followed by another sharp upturn in unemployment. While the underlying similarity of pattern between many of the advanced societies suggests that global forces were at work, making unemployment an issue over which market economies may not have full control, the rise in unemployment in Britain during the early 1980s was particularly steep. Britain moved from being a country with one of the lowest unemployment rates in the OECD to one with among the highest rates in a very short period of time.

An intriguing mythology has grown up around unemployment as a political issue. Unlike inflation, it is argued, the burden of unemployment falls on the shoulders of relatively few people, and is therefore tolerable politically to the vast majority. However, the picture this suggests of relative unconcern by the majority for the plight of the minority bears no comparison to reality. Gallup interviewers ask a monthly quota sample of adults in Britain what they think is the 'most urgent problem' facing the country today. Unemployment dominated the replies throughout the 1980s, being the issue most frequently named as either the most urgent or the second most urgent problem. Other political events such as the Falklands War barely dented the prominence of unemployment as an issue. Furthermore, the time-course of concern over unemployment tracked the time-course of the official unemployment figures remarkably closely during the 1970s and 1980s, as Figure 1.1 shows. It was only at the end of the 1980s that the two time trends seemed to be moving apart, with concern falling more sharply than the decline in the official figures.

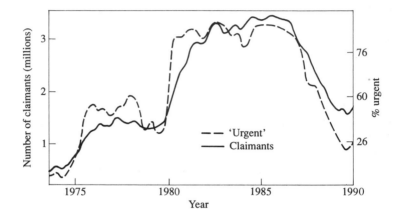

FIG. 1.1. The problem of unemployment, actual and perceived. The unemployment series is the GB total unadjusted, as reported each month; it is therefore not a consistent series. The percentages on the right-hand axis represent those who answered 'unemployment' in response either to the question 'What would you say is the most urgent problem facing the country at the present time?' or to a probe for the next most urgent problem. Both series have been smoothed using the resistant smoothing algorithms in Minitab. *Source*: *Department of Employment Gazette* and Gallup Political Index, monthly 1973–90

There can hardly be another political issue about which the public has proved so sensitive. There is nothing like the same public awareness and concern about inflation for example, the issue by which the Conservative administration asked to be judged. The sincerity of the concern of the general public for the plight of the unemployed comes through in every major survey there has been of the topic during the 1980s.

Unemployment may not have won or lost elections, but it dominated the agenda of the 1980s as Britain struggled in response to world recession. It was natural, therefore, that a major programme of research into changing labour market conditions conducted in the mid-1980s should make unemployment one of its central concerns. Any lessons we can learn about the causes and consequences of unemployment seem likely to remain of relevance for the 1990s, as unemployment returns to the forefront of the political and economic agenda.

However, there are severe limitations on the progress that can be made in the investigation of the issues surrounding unemployment on the basis of available official statistics. The range of issues covered is relatively narrow, the meaning of such statistics is often open to very diverse interpretations and there are serious problems of comparability across time. To take one case in point, analyses comparing the level of demand as reflected in the job vacancies series with the level of registered unemployment showed a mirror image relationship until the 1980s, which then disappears (see Fig. 1.2). But, given the numerous changes in the way in which the unemployed are counted, resulting from changes in the system of administering unemployment benefits, together with the acute uncertainty about the extent to which the

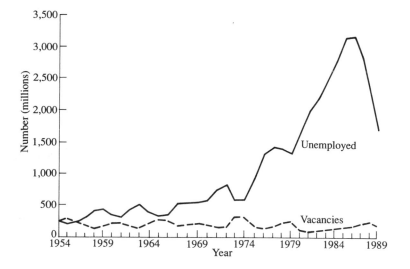

FIG. 1.2. Unemployment and vacancies, 1954–1989. *Source*: annual averages from Ministry of Employment and *Department of Employment Gazettes*

vacancy series undercounts job opportunities, we cannot be sure whether this reflects a change in the world out there or problems in the quality of data that social scientists have available.

If we want to ask any searching questions about the causes and consequences of unemployment, particularly during the 1980s, we need to turn to sources other than administrative statistics. In this volume, researchers report the result of a series of analyses conducted upon an integrated body of survey data, documenting the experiences of a representative sample of employed and unemployed people in six labour markets in Britain in 1986.

2. THE SOCIAL CHANGE AND ECONOMIC LIFE INITIATIVE

In 1986 the UK Economic and Social Research Council undertook a major research initiative into Social Change and Economic Life (SCELI). During the early 1980s, there had been widespread debate about the extent to which Britain's industrial and social structure was developing in similar ways in different localities. The conclusions from a series of small locality studies seemed to point in different directions, and it was unclear whether this was because of genuine differences, or because of variations in the questions being asked, in the research methodologies, or in the research interests of the investigators concerned. It was timely to conduct a series of controlled labour market studies in which systematic comparisons could be made between experiences in different localities. Research teams from ten different universities came together to collaborate in this research initiative (see the Methodological Appendix at the end of this book).

In order to study the processes of economic restructuring, the programme of research aimed to focus on the interaction between labour supply and demand in different concrete situations. This research design was not undertaken in the belief that local labour markets were autonomous from wider national and international forces. On the contrary, available evidence seemed to suggest that as capital had become increasingly international, different areas had been drawn into an international division of labour in which their vulnerability to outside economic forces had grown. As we shall see in the next chapter, the job losses in two of the most devastated areas studied were initiated by multi-nationals which were simultaneously taking decisions to expand production in other parts of the world. The point was rather to select a set of different labour markets and to subject them to similar scrutiny.

A key aim of the study was to collect information on the inter-action between household and formal economy, and to know something of the way in which key economic actors, employers, employees, self-employed, homeworkers, and unemployed, under-stood the parameters of the situation in which they found them-selves. Since much of the debate about the causes of Britain's economic distress during the 1980s turned on interpretations of the beliefs and attitudes of these economic actors, a considerable research effort was made to measure these carefully and to enable systematic comparisons in these more subjective variables to be made across localities.

2.1. The Selection of Study Towns

An early decision was taken to restrict the number of localities studied to six, for practical purposes. Some attempt was made to select areas which differed in their economic history and profile, and, in perhaps the most important indicator of economic difficulty, in their rates of unemployment. However, the interests and geography of participating teams of researchers were also factors affecting the choice of locations to be studied. The six areas finally selected were Aberdeen and Kirkcaldy in Scotland, Northampton and Coventry in the Midlands, Rochdale in the North-west, and Swindon in the South-west (see Fig. 1.3).

The general design objectives were achieved. The areas selected were very different in their industrial history, their traditional occupational structure, their mix of public and private sectors, and their tradition of female participation in the formal eco-nomy, as we shall see in more detail in the next chapter. Three of the areas had relatively low unemployment rates and three rela-tively high. However, as we shall see, the trajectories to the levels of unemployment recorded in 1986 differed between localities and so did the individuals affected.

They also had to be areas which had relatively self-contained

FIG. 1.3. Location of SCELI towns

labour markets in order to facilitate the comparison of the demand side and the supply side of the labour market. In fact, the areas were defined in terms of the Department of Employment's Travel to Work Areas, based on information about place of residence and place of work in the 1981 census. As a result, most of conurbation Britain was ruled out: there would have been no way to draw boundaries around areas small enough to provide feasible research settings. At the other extreme, very small towns and rural areas were not brought into the study as they could not supply a sufficiently concentrated set of employment experiences for study. It is then a study of processes of economic and social change in six middle-sized urban labour markets.

Intensive focus on a small number of localities with very different economic experiences enables us to ask the important question of the extent to which responses to economic difficulty and unemployment are common across areas or are importantly structured by the experience of very diverse labour market conditions. We can begin to untangle some very important issues: how far does living in an area of high or low unemployment affect people's perceptions of the labour market and their experiences within it, or are these better explained by broader sociological factors such as class and gender?

2.2. The Surveys

In each of the six areas, three major surveys were undertaken. One thousand adults between the ages of 20 and 60 were interviewed in each locality, giving an overall sample of some 6,111. A representative sample of 300 employers were also interviewed in each locality and information collected from them about the demand side of the local economy (see Rubery and Wilkinson forthcoming). Further, 300 of the original 1,000 adults interviewed in each locality were followed up between six and nine months after their initial interview, and more information was also collected at that point from the partners of the original interviewees. Finally, there were a number of intensive studies specific to individual localities, which formed an integral part of the overall research programme.

2.3. Defining the Unemployed

The unemployed are not just people without work but people who would participate in the formal economy if there were jobs available for them. They are considered part of the labour force and are distinguished from the economically inactive who would not want to work even if a job was offered to them. However, one of the consequences of economic change during the 1980s has been that it has become very hard to make clean distinctions between these different economic categories.

There are traditionally two approaches to the identification of the unemployed. Since the modern sense of the term 'unemployed' has come into being alongside the system of social security designed to give workers insurance against periods of unemployment, one approach is to deem unemployed anyone whom the social security system recognizes as unemployed for the purposes of obtaining benefits. The problem with this method was highlighted earlier: the result is a series that follows the institutional and political history of the system of social security, rather than providing a picture of the real demand for

employment among people currently without work. Most industrialized countries have therefore adopted a second approach,
which is to ask a random sample of adults on a continuous survey about their labour market behaviour, to try to establish if
those without work would accept a job if one were offered to
them. Many countries use these estimates in their tallying of the
numbers unemployed, rather than counting those receiving
benefits.

One of our major research interests was precisely to explore
the significance of these different definitions of unemployment. In
classifying a person as unemployed, either definition of unemployed was accepted. If someone was receiving benefit on
grounds of unemployment, they were routed through the questionnaire as if they were unemployed, regardless of their inten-
tions to work in the future. Similarly, if anyone without a job
said that they had looked for work in the last four weeks, they
were treated as unemployed, regardless of whether or not they
were eligible for benefit. This, then, is a broader definition of
unemployed than conventionally used, although our data can be
easily converted to any particular definition of unemployment
that is of interest. It is, however, still restrictive in some respects;
most significantly, it meant that the survey categorized as 'inactive' any non-claimant discouraged workers who had stopped
looking for work because they did not believe that there were
any jobs available. However, because of the degree of detail collected about current labour market status, it is possible to
explore significant subcategories within the unemployed in a
manner that is not usually possible. Gallie and Vogler, in
Chapter 4, show that there were indeed important differences
among subgroups of the unemployed; in particular, those
claimants of benefit who had not actively sought work in the previous four weeks had a very different attitudinal profile from the
rest of the unemployed.

3. CAUSES OF UNEMPLOYMENT

The upward surge in unemployment rates in the OECD countries
in the 1970s and 1980s makes it very hard to believe that personal characteristics of the unemployed provide the underlying

dynamic; we would have to believe that something approaching a mass epidemic of idleness had struck the labour forces of all industrialized countries. However, a debate has continued about the extent to which supply-side or demand-side features of the labour market have led to the undeniable deviations that have occurred from this basic international trend. Characteristics of the supply-side at which the finger of blame has been pointed include the real wage levels of those in work, institutional features pertaining both to tax and social security systems and to trade union arrangements, and the correlated effect of these on the beliefs and attitudes of the unemployed themselves. On the other hand, the low level of aggregate demand, particularly in the countries of the European Community, has also contributed substantially to the problem (Bean *et al.* 1986).

One persistent danger with using data derived from a survey of employees is that there will be a bias towards testing supply-side explanations of unemployment. It would, for example, be very hard to investigate the effect of aggregate demand in a cross-sectional single-country study. With this caveat, however, some interesting light can be cast on some of the debates about the effects of institutional and attudinal factors in the prevalence and duration of unemployment.

Two chapters in this volume address these issues directly. Gallie and Vogler, in a wide-ranging chapter examining in great detail the respondents' behavioural and attitudinal commitment to work, document several findings highly germane to this debate. First, they show that intrinsic work commitment (measured as a stated desire to go on working even if there were no financial necessity so to do) was in fact highest among those currently unemployed. It was not substantially different between men and women, and was also highest among those whose partners were not in work.

The picture they paint suggests that substantial minorities of the unemployed were prepared to retrain completely or to move to a different area to get work. Among certain categories of the unemployed, majorities demonstrated this sort of 'flexibility'. Only among claimants who were not looking for work was the pattern of attitudes substantially different and less flexible; non-claimants who were seeking work were usually indistinguishable from claimants seeking work. Furthermore, in contrast to economists' assumptions that the unemployed look for work with a 'reservation wage' in their mind that is set with reference to the income they could obtain through social security payments, Gallie and Vogler present evidence about the expectations of the unemployed while job-searching. It is striking that over half the unemployed said they were prepared to take 'anything that's going'. Furthermore, the pay expectations of the unemployed were relatively modest, with only 12 per cent aspiring to more than the average pay for their previous job.

A major debate has developed about the disincentive effects of social security benefits paid to the unemployed. It has been argued that such payments undermine the commitment to find work and therefore have an important effect on the duration of unemployment. The higher the benefits received in relation to potential or past earnings, the stronger the disincentive. The empirical evidence for such a 'benefits effect' is very mixed (Atkinson and Micklewright 1985). The trend analysis of General Household Survey data suggests a positive relationship between the level of benefits and duration of unemployment (e.g. Lancaster and Nickell 1980). The security of these results has, however, been disputed by Atkinson (1989, ch. 9), who entered actual benefits received rather than hypothetical marginal amounts receivable by a standard family into the equation predicting unemployment duration: the effects of benefits on unemployment duration disappears when this is done. Nickell *et al.* (1989) detected a benefits effect for the unemployed studied in the 1978 DHSS Cohort sample. But apart from the rather dated nature of the original study, it must be remembered that the sample was confined to the registered male unemployed. Moreover, the benefits' effect only emerges consistently in their analyses for the younger, teenage, categories.

Those who have argued that the benefits system acts as a disincentive to the unemployed to look for work have not usually had recourse to empirical data on the causes of work commitment; they have preferred to argue about the likely course of action adopted by rational economic actors in the market-place as the benefit/earnings ratio increases and the reservation wage correspondingly increases (e.g. Minford 1983). The analysis which Gallie and Vogler present in Chapter 4 shows that, while unemployment does indeed cause a great deal of financial distress, those who suffered greater financial hardship were not induced by this into greater preparedness to take lower-paid jobs or to move house.

It is still possible, however, that cross-sectional associations such as these hide important selection effects among the unemployed. The punch line to Gallie and Vogler's argument comes when they present some evidence from the follow-up survey conducted nine months later, in 1987, of 377 of those who were originally unemployed in 1986. If work attitudes were a crucial causal factor determining who gets and who fails to get another job, this should have shown up in whether and when different groups of unemployed respondents had found work. None of the work attitudes which they studied acted as generally good predictors of re-employment. Nor did they find that the degree of financial pressure on the unemployed generally affected the speed with which they found a job.

However, another chapter in this volume suggests that there are aspects of the benefits system that make it rational for some people to leave the labour market altogether. Even if the general argument is unreliable, there may be a 'benefits effect' with respect to married women. It seems that a disincentive to remaining in employment may exist under benefit rules which took away any income earned by the wives of the unemployed men on benefit, on a pound for pound basis, beyond a low threshold. The lower-paid can face effective marginal 'taxation' rates of over 90 per cent when they work, through loss of various entitlements to benefits either for themselves or for other household members. Married women's pay may not be sufficiently great to make it worth their while working if their husbands are unemployed and the family can claim a sum equivalent or near to this in social security benefit. Once again, cross-sectional data have a hard time sorting out the paths of causal effect, as husbands and wives tend to be similar in all sorts of ways, not least in facing similar labour market conditions, even if not competing directly for the same jobs. When we find, as we do, that families in which the husband is unemployed are very much more likely also to contain a wife without employment, how can we be sure that this is not just because the local factors that make one partner likely to lose their job also make the other likely to lose theirs or discourage them from seeking work? Indeed, there are a host of other possible non-causal explanations to do with selection effects.

A very elegant solution is presented in Chapter 5 by Davies, Elias, and Penn. They make use of the timing of the sequences of episodes of employment and unemployment that are available from the work history section of the questionnaire. They essentially look at the likelihood of wives leaving their jobs after the husband has become unemployed. They employ some path-breaking techniques in the analysis of this type of event history data, which allow them to control for individual preferences in variables, both measured and unmeasured, in their analysis. And they conclude that there is a significant, if modest, negative effect of husband's unemployment on wife's employment: when he loses his job, she is (moderately) likely to give up work. The really convincing part of the story that they tell comes in the timing: they pinpoint the period one year from the onset of the husband's unemployment spell as the time when the wife is most likely to quit the labour force. This is precisely what one would predict from knowledge of the benefits system, since after one year the husband would transfer from insurance-based unemployment benefit to means-tested benefit, where the wife's effective 'taxation' rate would become extraordinarily high.

Chapters 4 and 5 enable us, then, to specify more carefully the likely nature of the benefits effect. It should be noted that there is a difference in the dependent variable: in Chapter 5 Davies *et al.* consider influences upon withdrawal from employment, whereas in Chapter 4 Gallie and Vogler are predicting transitions specifically from unemployment into employment. There is no reason to believe that these two processes should be the inverse of each other; it would seem that financial pressures do not speed up job-finding among those who are looking for work, while at the same time financial considerations do eventually weigh with women in work when their husband transfers from unemployment benefit to income support. Davies *et al.*'s results were based solely on women and were only very clear-cut in the higher unemployment labour markets. Thus a benefits effect may exist in areas where people suspect that a husband's unemployment spell could last for a long time, but in all it had little effect on general unemployment durations. The overall effect of the benefits system on encouraging unemployment is unlikely to be large if the effects on this relatively small subgroup are so modest.

So what does predict who becomes unemployed and how long they remain unemployed? The sheer variability of the unemployment level by locality of course tells us that demand-side factors are of considerable explanatory importance. The SCELI work history data also allows us to make some important generalizations about the typical pattern of an unemployment career. Gallie and Vogler, in Chapter 4, discussed above, which suggested that high commitment to work was a distinguishing feature of the unemployed rather than of those who were successfully employed, dismiss employment instability *per se* as a casual factor in the process of long-term unemployment: the unemployed had not experienced significantly more jobs or shorter average tenure in their longest jobs.

But there are nevertheless some important distinguishing features of the unemployment 'career'. One does not need to subscribe to a condemnatory 'culture of poverty' thesis, or to believe that cycles of disadvantage are some people's genetic inheritance, to believe that unemployment at time t might in and of itself increase the likelihood of unemployment at time $t + 1$. Gershuny and Marsh suggest that labour market fate is best viewed as a process of 'recursive determination', in which current state is the product of both a set of initial characteristics which are fixed throughout adult life, and a set of lagged effects in which labour market status some time prior to the present has an effect on the present state. Through repeated multivariate analysis of predictors of unemployment across increasing years of individuals' participation in the labour market, they show that the most important predictor of unemployment in any one year is the unemployment record of that individual in the immediate past. However, the effect of a bout of unemployment does not last for ever, and although a small effect of an unemployment bout at the beginning of someone's work history can be discerned, in general it is proximate effects which count.

This is an important finding. It has more content than the traditional economists' assertion that the present depends on the past, since it is based on microdata, on the analysis of individuals' experiences, and not on labour market aggregates, where variables tend to move up and down together and coefficients of determination over 0.98 are not unknown. It is arrived at holding the effect of educational qualifications, occupational entry points, and, more importantly, age, period, and the level of unemployment in the national economy constant.

There have been, Gershuny and Marsh suggest, important changes in the processes of employment and occupational attainment during the period covered by the SCELI work history data (mid-1940s to mid-1980s). As unemployment has risen, so has it fallen more heavily on those already in lower social status, manual occupations, although that relationship has been much stronger for men than women. The recession of the 1970s and 1980s had the greatest impact on the younger age-groups, but not because the younger groups are always the most susceptible to changes in labour market conditions: analysis of previous cohorts suggests that this was not always the case.

4. THE SOCIAL CONSEQUENCES OF UNEMPLOYMENT

The literature on the experiences of the unemployed in the great recession of the 1930s left a graphic picture of the disruption and suffering caused by unemployment. There was, moreover, a remarkable similarity in the accounts provided from research in different countries. Unemployment was reported to lead to psychological distress and to a loss of self-esteem, to increased tension within families, to social withdrawal and the isolation of the unemployed from others in the community, and to a sense of powerlessness and resignation that coloured people's broader attitudes to politics and society. A number of factors, however, suggested that conditions in the 1980s were very different from those in the inter-war years. In particular, improvements in the welfare system had removed much of the risk of total economic destitution, even if people were still likely to see a sharp reduction in their standard of living. It was possible, too, that the reduction in normal work hours and the greater value attached to the home and to leisure activities made it easier for people to adapt to life without employment. A central question of recent research, has been whether the experience of unemployment in the 1980s has been markedly different from that in the 1930s.

4.1. The Psychological Consequences of Unemployment

There was a notable revival of interest in the social consequences of unemployment from the 1970s, in the context of the sharp deterioration of the labour market following the oil shock of 1973–4. Particularly influential was Dennis Marsden's (1975) in-depth study of the lives of unemployed men at the prime of their working lives. It strongly suggested that, even in the post-war era, unemployment remained a devastating experience. If the very first days of unemployment were sometimes experienced as a relief from the constraints of the rat race, this soon gave way to a sharp decline in morale. Anxiety about finding a new job and coping with financial worries made it difficult to concentrate upon, let alone enjoy, alternative activities. The unemployed were beset by difficulties in sleeping, by tiredness during the day, and by loss of appetite. As the length of unemployment increased, they lost a sense of meaning in their lives and even their sense of identity.

For all the richness of the insight it provided, it was difficult to know from such a study how typical these experiences were among the unemployed. In the 1980s, however, a major programme of research into the psychological consequences of unemployment was launched by the Social and Applied Psychology Unit at Sheffield, under the direction of Peter Warr. Using the General Health Questionnaire (GHQ) as the main measure of psychological well-being, these studies showed that unemployment led consistently to higher levels of psychological distress among men. Since many of these studies were cross-sectional, it might be objected that it was difficult to disentangle cause and effect. However, a longitudinal study (Warr and Jackson 1985) showed that once people returned to employment, there was a marked improvement in their psychological well-being, indicating that unemployment was the real causal factor.

There has been much less research evidence about the psychological consequences of unemployment for women. A number of reasons have been advanced why women's experiences of unemployment may be rather different from those of men (see e.g. Marshall 1984; Kelvin and Jarrett 1985). Since they are typically in less-skilled and less well-paid work, with fewer opportunities for career promotion, women's experience of employment may be less enriching and its loss correspondingly less traumatic. Further, given that women often shoulder the double burden of paid employment and domestic work, the loss of employment may ease a very demanding work-load. Finally, women's domestic role may offer an alternative identity and set of activities that may shield them from some of the severest effects of unemployment. Marshall suggests that women's reaction to unemployment is likely to vary considerably depending on the nature of household and family structure.

The research reported in this volume certainly confirms the general association between unemployment and psychological distress. For instance, Chapter 10, by Gallie and Vogler, shows that the currently unemployed had a lower level of psychological well-being than any labour market group other than currently non-active people who had been previously unemployed or who had an unemployed partner. It was notable, however, that there was no evidence that unemployment was any less harsh in its effects on unemployed women than on unemployed men.

While the evidence suggests that unemployment in the 1980s continued to have a marked effect on psychological well-being, there is less agreement about the mechanisms that lead to this. What are the most important aspects of the experience of unemployment that generate psychological distress? Perhaps the most influential account of the processes by which unemployment undercuts people's psychological stability has been provided by Marie Jahoda (1982). Jahoda suggested that employment, whatever its hardships, fulfils a number of vital latent functions. It provides an enforced pattern of activity and gives people a clear time-structure to the day, it is a source of social contacts outside the household, it gives people a sense of participating in a wider collective purpose, and it is a source of social status and identity. In essence, then, Jahoda's explanation focuses on the need for life-structure and for ties with the community. In the conditions of advanced capitalist societies, she suggested, it is only through employment that such categories of experience can be adequately met.

There has been a sustained debate in the literature about the adequacy of Jahoda's account. Peter Warr (1987) has suggested that many of the effects of Jahoda's categories of experience may be curvilinear, rather than linear, with people suffering from both relatively high and relatively low exposure to them. Fraser (1981) has argued that Jahoda has heavily underestimated the significance of sheer financial deprivation. Kelvin and Jarrett (1985) have placed the major explanatory emphasis on the way in which unemployment affects identity, leading to increased self-consciousness, the undermining of people's self-concept, and the return to a state of psychological dependence on others (with its implication of enhanced vulnerability). It is clear too that Jahoda's thesis does not address adequately the issue of whether or not there is a difference between men's and women's experiences or the argument that roles outside employment may provide benefits that compensate for the loss of employment-based experiences.

Despite the wealth of theoretical critique, there has been a remarkable dearth of systematic empirical examination of different explanatory approaches. Some small-scale research (Miles 1983) has provided some evidence in support of Jahoda's position. Although very valuable as an exploratory study, it focused only on men in one particular locality (Brighton), the sample was not randomly selected, and there was only a very small control group of employed people.

The analyses reported here, therefore, are concerned particularly with the nature of the causal connections between unemployment and psychological distress. Chapter 7, by Jonathan Gershuny, focuses directly on Jahoda's argument, looking at the relationship between unemployment and the categories of experience. It shows that unemployment clearly reduces access to the types of experiences that Jahoda has highlighted. It also examines the extent to which the out-of-work activities of the unemployed may compensate for the psychological effects of employment loss. When unemployed people were compared in terms of levels of leisure activity and sociability with people outside the household, it clearly was the case that the more active and the more sociable had greater access to the categories of experience. However, the highest-scoring group of the unemployed were still lower than the lowest-scoring group of the employed. In short, while activities outside employment can provide to some degree experiences of the type that Jahoda has seen as vital for psychological health, they would not appear to be a satisfactory substitute for employment itself.

Is Jahoda correct, however, that it is the degree of access to these experiences that is crucial in explaining psychological health? Our evidence certainly reveals a relationship in the direction that Jahoda anticipated. Moreover, it remains significant even when income effects are controlled for. It is, however, a relatively weak relationship and can provide at best only a limited part of any overall explanation of the psychological effects of unemployment. Further, its effects are clearest for men and very marginal for women.

Chapter 6, by Brendan Burchell, suggests a rather different explanatory approach. Rather than emphasizing life-structure, links to the community, or low income, it points to the importance of insecurity in generating psychological stress. Labour market insecurity covers a much broader range of situations than that of unemployment, although unemployment is likely to constitute an extreme form. Jobs may be short-term and inherently precarious, or people in hitherto stable jobs may know in anticipation that there is a real threat to their future security. If insecurity is a major factor, people in such jobs should reveal characteristics rather similar to those of the unemployed, even though (since they are employed) they still have access to the various categories of experience that are decisive for Jahoda's argument.

Burchell compares the psychological well-being of the unemployed with that of a group of employed people that are characterized by past downward mobility, past unemployment, and low current job security. Using the GHQ score as a measure of psychological stress, he finds that there was no significant difference between the level of stress among the unemployed and among this highly insecure category of the employed. Further, by following a subsample across time, he is able to demonstrate that for men the connection between insecurity and ill health is a causal one. Unemployed people who moved into a secure job showed a significant improvement in psychological well-being, whereas those who moved into insecure jobs showed only a very slight improvement. Moreover, the difference could not be explained in terms of pay levels. The pattern that emerged for women, however, was rather different. It was the fact of getting a job, rather than the security of the job, that made a major difference. This suggests that the heightened sense of insecurity generated by job instability may be mediated by expectations and by household gender roles. It is notable that very similar conclusions to Burchell's emerge from Chapter 10, although the category of the insecure is operationalized in a rather different way. Gallie and Vogler find that the insecure employed have markedly worse psychological health than those in secure employment, although this effect is largely attributable to the insecure male employees.

A major mechanism generating psychological ill health would appear, then, to be insecurity. Unemployment, in this context, can be best understood as an extreme case of a more general phenomenon of labour market insecurity. It will be seen later that the same conclusion emerges from two other papers in the volume, focusing on the relationship between unemployment and marital dissolution and on the consequences of unemployment for social and political attitudes.

4.2. Unemployment and the Household

There are two aspects of the consequences of unemployment for household relations that have been of central concern. The first is the way in which unemployment affects household organization, in particular gender roles with respect to financial decision-making and domestic work. The second is the effect of unemployment on the degree of tension in social relations within the household and on the stability of the marital relationship.

Several of the inter-war studies noted that male unemployment was associated with a shift towards female management of household budgeting. This could be explained in terms of the need for unified control when resources were very scarce and by the fact that expenditure was now predominantly in the area of women's traditional domestic responsibility—namely, food and other basic necessities. Small-scale post-war studies also noted the tendency for the whole wage system of financial management in the household, in which the man handed over his pay or benefits to the women, to be associated with low income and unemployment (Morris 1988: 392). It was difficult to know the representativeness of such studies, however, and the causal relationship between unemployment and the adoption of specific household financial arrangements had not been established.

With respect to the domestic division of labour, earlier

research has tended to point to the strength of traditional gender roles and the lack of any significant change in the way in which household work is organized when the male becomes unemployed. Pahl (1984), for instance, in a study carried out on the Isle of Sheppey in South-east England, concluded that unemployment, if anything, reinforced traditional patterns of domestic work. Other research (Morris 1985; Harris 1987), focusing on workers that had been made redundant from the Port Talbot steelworks in South Wales, also emphasized the rarity and limited nature of change.

Earlier research has tended, then, to link unemployment to a shift in household roles with respect to financial decision-making, but to lack of change in the domestic division of labour. The data provided by the SCELI surveys have made possible a more systematic investigation of these issues. With respect to both financial management and the organization of domestic work, the conclusions differ significantly from those predominant in previous research. Chapter 8, by Gallie, Gershuny, and Vogler, shows that there is no evidence of a specific effect of unemployment on household financial management systems. There was no significant difference between the employed and the unemployed in the extent of women having sole responsibility for managing household finances. Further, when unemployed people were asked directly about change in financial arrangements since becoming unemployed, it was found that such change was extremely rare. Household methods of financial management were clearly related to much longer-term factors, such as educational qualifications, class position, and the practices that people had experienced as children in their parental families.

In contrast, using a variety of approaches, there was consistent evidence that unemployment did have an effect on the way in which domestic work was organized in the household. In households where the male partner was unemployed, men took a greater share of the domestic work. In the majority of cases, this shift was a modest one, still very far from an equal sharing of domestic work. The pattern was heavily mediated by the employment status of the woman. Where the woman was without employment, it tended to be more traditional; where the woman was in employment it tended to be more egalitarian. However, the difference between the unemployed and the employed did appear to be directly related to the experience of unemployment, rather than merely reflecting other background factors. A substantial proportion of people reported that there had been a change in the way in which domestic work was organized since the onset of the current spell of unemployment, and change was in the direction of greater male involvement in household tasks.

A second major area of concern has been with the impact of unemployment on the level of stress in marital relations. There appears to be a high level of consensus that unemployment places severe strain on the family. An intensive study by McKee and Bell (1985, 1986), for instance, drew a vivid picture of the way in which it could increase family divisiveness. In particular, money was a key source of conflict. In an intensive study of twenty-two households, Fagin and Little (1984) pointed to the tensions that could develop between partners about the responsibilities for repeated failures to get a job. The nature of other sources of tension, they suggest, varies considerably depending upon the particular 'developmental stage' that the family has reached. For recently married couples, for instance, the major problems revolve around decisions such as whether or not to delay starting a family. For couples with adolescent children, in contrast, the key difficulties revolve around the maintenance of paternal authority.

While previous work has highlighted the types of friction that unemployment may generate, it has not been in a position to determine whether this is of an intensity that is likely to significantly increase the probabilities of a marriage breaking up. It is this issue that Richard Lampard addresses in Chapter 9. He draws on the detailed life and work history data provided by the SCELI surveys both to establish the chronology of spells of unemployment and marital dissolution and to develop sophisticated statistical models of the relationship between them that control for a wide range of background factors. His evidence points firmly to the conclusion that unemployment does directly increase the risk of marriages breaking up. Indeed, his estimates suggest that the chances of the marriage of an unemployed person ending in the following year were 70 per cent higher than those of a person that had never been unemployed.

Further, Lampard finds that not only unemployment, but also job insecurity, has a marked effect on the chances of marital dissolution. It was seen earlier that those in insecure employment had levels of psychological distress that were close to those of the unemployed, suggesting that unemployment should be understood as an extreme point along a more general dimension of labour market insecurity that had profound implications for people's well-being. Lampard's conclusions are entirely compatible with this and, indeed, they suggest that the stress generated by job insecurity is sufficiently intense to destabilize relations in the family and to precipitate the break-up of people's marriages.

Finally, using a case-study control approach, he also finds some evidence that the causal process may also work in the reverse direction, with the break-up of marriage increasing people's chances of becoming unemployed. Even more than five years after the date of separation, the risk of unemployment is still higher for individuals whose marriages have dissolved than for individuals in surviving marriages. Part of this, however, may be explicable in terms of longer-term personality or environmental characteristics that increase the chances both of marital dissolution and of unemployment.

4.3. Leisure Activities and Social Networks of the Unemployed

The most graphic account of the impact of unemployment on social relations in the community was provided by M. Jahoda *et al.* (1972) in their study of Marienthal in the inter-war period. Unemployment brought about the virtual disintegration of what hitherto had been an active community life. No effort was made to keep up the public park, people lost interest in participating in the once popular theatre club, and loans of library books dropped dramatically (1972: 36 ff.). The unemployed retreated into a passive and primarily home-based life, in which, at least among the men, the lack of structured activity began to dissolve the very sense of time.

There is some indication from post-war research that the ability of the unemployed to make use of their time is something that may have changed. Such studies as have been carried out (and there are relatively few) still point to a reduction in the activity levels and the sociability of the unemployed, but they do not support a picture of a level of withdrawal into the household that implies the collapse of involvement in the local community (Veal 1986; Trew and Kilpatrick 1983).

There is less agreement about the impact of unemployment on patterns of sociability. McKee and Bell (1985), for instance, provide a picture of the social isolation of the household that is not far removed from that of Marienthal. The impact of the lack of financial resources on social contacts was aggravated by the fear of being denounced for illegal activity. Further, unemployment affected the social lives not only of the unemployed men themselves, but also those of their families. 'We found evidence of a *double isolation* with the contacts and social ties of women being dramatically curtailed in response to husband's job loss' (McKee and Bell 1986: 143). This reflected the discouragement by husbands of wives' outside links and the withdrawal of contact by friends, either out of respect for marital privacy or as a result of 'perceptions of the husband's mastery of his home'.

Other studies, however, point to a greater resilience of patterns of sociability. In their study of unemployed male manual workers, Warr and Payne (1983) found that people were more likely to report an increase than a decrease in the amount of time that they spent with friends and neighbours since becoming unemployed. Martin and Wallace (1984) found that unemployed women reported similar amounts of interpersonal contact before and after job loss. These various studies are based on different subgroups of the unemployed, and the conflicting patterns may reflect the influence of differences in class position, age, or household situation. Moreover, most studies had the methodological limitation of focusing uniquely on the unemployed, which made it impossible to disentangle the impact of unemployment from that of other factors such as low income.

Gallie, Gershuny, and Vogler's Chapter 8 provides a broader-based and more systematic investigation of the differences between the employed and the unemployed in their patterns of activity and sociability. To begin with, it is clear that there is no general tendency for the unemployed to withdraw into inactivity. Indeed, the frequency with which they engage in leisure activities is not significantly different from that of the employed. There is evidence that there has been a shift in the nature of activities, in particular towards less expensive types of leisure. Unemployed people, for instance, go out less to the pub and to clubs, but they more frequently make social visits to other people's homes. However, although such a shift in types of activity may well have been experienced as a form of deprivation, it did not constitute the type of retreat into passivity that was highlighted by the inter-war literature.

The maintenance of previous levels of leisure activity was of course compatible with an increase in the amount of dead time that the unemployed experienced, since there were many more hours of the day to fill. The overall pattern of time use was examined using detailed weekly time budget data. Compared with the employed, the unemployed certainly spend more time on passive leisure activities, but there is still no sign of the degree of inactivity and the lack of structure that characterized the unemployed people of Marienthal. The unemployed also spent substantially more time on domestic work and on home-based leisure activities, such as hobbies. In short our evidence supports the view that activity patterns have remained much more resilient than would appear to have been the case in the inter-war period.

There was more support for the view that unemployment undercuts sociability. The unemployed were notably less likely than the employed to engage in leisure activities with other people outside their own household. This decline in sociability varies considerably depending on the characteristics of the unemployed person. It is most striking among single people, and least marked among women in partnerships. However, there must be some doubt about whether differences in the level of sociability reflect the impact of unemployment *per se*, as distinct from other background characteristics. Although a majority of the unemployed reported that they had changed the frequency with which they saw people since becoming unemployed, those reporting a change were equally divided between those saying that there had been an increase and those saying that there had been a decrease in their sociability.

The major impact of unemployment was on the nature rather than on the extensiveness of networks. The data indicate a remarkably high level of segregation between the social networks of the employed and the unemployed. Whereas the networks of the majority of those in employment consisted primarily of other people in work, this was the case for only a minority of the unemployed. This segregation of the unemployed into networks consisting largely of other unemployed people was particularly marked for men. Moreover, the nature of people's networks was related to important differences in the effective support that they could call upon when they needed help. The unemployed were less likely than the employed to have somebody that they could rely upon if they felt depressed, or if they needed financial assistance, or if they wanted help in finding another job. Such support was particularly problematic where both partners were unemployed. But it was also notable that the higher the proportion of a person's friends that were unemployed, the less likely they were to have a strong network. The segregation of the social networks of the unemployed, then, increased their vulnerability and helped to lock the unemployed into a position of labour market disadvantage.

4.4. The Political Attitudes of the Unemployed

For the researchers studying Marienthal in the inter-war period, the breakdown of community relations with unemployment was integrally related to the disintegration of forms of political activity. The decline of cultural life, reflected by the sharp fall in the borrowing of library books and in newspaper reading, was parallelled by a loss of interest in politics. Across the spectrum, political organizations lost their membership, despite reducing membership fees to a nominal level.

Post-war studies have also emphasized the fact that, despite the sharp deprivation it produces, unemployment does not generate more radical attitudes to the prevailing social order. The most systematic study was carried out in the United States by Schlozman and Verba (1979). The American unemployed of the mid-1970s were certainly much less satisfied with their income and indeed with their lives more generally than people in employment. However, discontent with material deprivation did not lead to more radical political and social ideologies. The key to understanding this non-politicization of deprivation lay, the authors suggest, in people's assimilation of the ideology of the 'American dream', with its emphasis on individual opportunity and the importance of hard work for success in life. To an important extent, the unemployed regarded themselves as responsible for finding work and for coping financially, and this deflected resentment away from the political élites and from the nature of the wider social structure.

Research in Britain (Marshall *et al.* 1988) largely confirmed Schlozman and Verba's conclusions about the lack of impact of unemployment on political ideologies, but questioned the adequacy of the explanation that had been provided. This lack of political radicalism could not be attributed to commitment to an ideology of individual achievement. As was the case with British manual workers more generally, the unemployed had a class rather than an individualistic understanding of the sources of social inequality and the majority did not regard the existing distributional order as just. Marshall *et al.* suggest that the lack of political radicalism among the unemployed has to be explained, not in terms of commitment to an individualistic ideology, but in terms of an awareness of the effective constraints on action.

There appears then to be a substantial consensus that the experience of unemployment does not lead to major ideological change or to any desire for a revolutionary overthrow of the current structure of society. It remains, however, possible that unemployment radicalizes in a more modest way by increasing the importance that people attach to collectivist as against individualist principles of social organization. It is this that is the focus of Chapter 10, by Gallie and Vogler. Collectivism is defined as an attachment to the objective of redistributive state spending and taxation—very much the issues that have lain at the heart of the programmes of reformist left movements for social change. The unemployed are compared with a number of other labour market groups. Among the employed a distinction has been made between those that are low-paid and those that are higher-paid, and both of these categories have been divided into a secure and insecure component on the basis of whether or not they had experienced unemployment in the previous five years. A similar distinction was made among the non-employed.

The analysis showed that the unemployed were clearly more collectivist in their social attitudes than any other labour market group and this result persisted when a wide range of other controls were introduced, for instance with respect to previous class position, age, and education. Although people's political allegiances and early political socialization were important for their attachment to collectivism, the effect of unemployment was still evident when these had been taken into account. It was notable, however, that there appeared to be a pervasive effect of labour market insecurity. All of the groups that had experienced insecurity were more collectivist than those that had not, irrespective of income. This reinforces a conclusion that has emerged with respect with other themes in the volume. A critical factor in the experience of unemployment and in its implications of other areas of people's lives would appear to be the insecurity it generates. This implies that it is best thought of as an extreme point along a more general dimension of labour market insecurity.

Finally, it was possible to examine the argument that the growth of unemployment is leading to a new type of social polarization that cuts across the traditional solidarities of the manual working class. Unemployment, it has been suggested, is generating an increasing divide between the social values and political preferences of those with employment and those without. In particular, these differences in labour market situation create diverging interests with respect to the welfare state. Those in employment, influenced by the fact that they are taxpayers, are seen as resentful of the cost of welfare provision and, therefore, as increasingly sympathetic to political programmes that wish to cut back on the welfare state. In contrast, the unemployed, faced with cumulative and growing economic disadvantage, are increasingly favourable to an extension of welfare provision.

The evidence in Gallie and Vogler's Chapter 10 certainly reveals a very sharp difference between the life chances of those in secure employment and the unemployed. There can be little doubt that the unemployed do suffer from a process of cumulative disadvantage and that their weak labour market position is accompanied not only by much greater financial difficulty, but by disadvantage in both health and housing. Moreover, it has already been seen that the experience of unemployment leads to a stronger attachment to collectivist principles. But the central question with respect to the issue of polarization is whether the differences in the social values of the employed and the unemployed are growing greater. Our analysis of the pattern of change over time suggests that this is not the case. Collectivism had increased in importance among both the employed and the unemployed. Indeed, it had increased most strongly among the employed, leading to an overall decline in value differences between the employed and the unemployed. It seemed probable that this reflected the importance of political influences in

moulding people's attitudes towards social policies and in mediating the relationship between labour market position and wider
social values. Unemployment, then, leads to social polarization at
the level of economic and social experiences, and it heightens
political radicalism.

5. CONCLUSION

What can we say in summary about the unemployed as a group?
One question which has recurred in the literature on unemployment is whether those who pay the costs of society's economic
difficulties are the same group of people across time, and whether
they are sufficiently distinctive a group to be deemed a 'social
class' or, more specifically, an 'underclass' beneath the ranks of
the working class. Such ideas attracted a great deal of controversy, in both Europe and the USA. Some of this controversy
has been somewhat confused, failing to distinguish between two
elements of the underclass thesis. The first research is merely
descriptive: it says that there exists a distinctive group of people
who suffer the burden of society's unemployment. Although
there is much movement into and out of unemployment, it is the
same people—an underclass—who are affected over and over
again, and they come to be a quite identifiable group.

The second element of the underclass thesis is stronger, involving a causal claim about why this group stays at the bottom.
There are different accounts within this version, but all have at
the heart of the argument the idea that members of the underclass remain in that position because of their own inadequacies.
There have been many historical versions of this idea, from
nineteenth- and early twentieth-century ideas that genetic weakness was the central characteristic of this group to ideas of a
recurrent and self-perpetuating culture of poverty and disadvantage in which parents pass on an entire alienated way of life to
their children. The modern version of this thesis invokes the welfare state as an important dynamic of this process: because
people are allowed to survive on welfare, they lose their employability, skill, and eventually their will to work (e.g. Mead 1985).

This volume presents some evidence in favour of the first part
of the thesis. Gershuny and Marsh show how powerfully one

experience of unemployment increased the chance of a subsequent bout, although it is important to note that the effect was short-term rather than affecting people's entire careers (Chapter 3). Further, the unemployed faced cumulative disadvantage: as well as being deprived of work they were disadvantaged in health and housing (Chapter 10). They became involved in local social networks consisting primarily of other people without work and were sharply segregated from the social networks of those in employment (Chapter 8). This ensured that they had lower levels of social support and tended to lock them into a position of labour market disadvantage. There was also evidence in different chapters of the attitudinal distinctiveness of the unemployed. In terms of attitudes towards work, they felt greatly deprived and placed a high premium on working; along with other insecure groups in the labour market, their deprivation bordered on psychological depression. They were also more inclined to support collectivist economic measures designed to improve labour market security and focused on extension of the welfare state to protect the victims of economic difficulty.

But to what extent can the unemployed be seen as responsible for their own disadvantages? The general claim that the attitudes to work of the unemployed underlay their inability to find work were not borne out. Most of the claimant unemployed were actively seeing work; a minority were not seeking work and were substantially less flexible and concerned about unemployment, but the majority were not so alienated that they had given up trying. Moreover, when claimants who were seeking work were compared to non-claimants who were seeking work, these two groups were indistinguishable in their work attitudes; this suggests that the claiming of benefits *per se* is not generally implicated in the unemployment cycle. The third way in which the underclass thesis is flawed is that work attitudes did not form an important predictor of who did and who did not get re-employed.

In general, the evidence marshalled in this volume suggests that the unemployed form a distinctive group at the bottom of the social heap, who experience recurrent difficulties. However, it would be a cruel step to move from this descriptive statement to the conclusion that they were in this condition through some fault of their own or as a result of the operation of the system of welfare. Rather the results of this volume suggest that people may be caught in a spiral of disadvantage in which small events may have large repercussions. Through an initial accident of job loss, a person may get trapped in a cycle of further unemployment. Unemployment frequently leads to depression, family break-up, and social isolation, which in turn makes the next job more difficult to find. After the event we may identify a group with a distinct life-style at the bottom of the heap, but they were not destined to be there, and under different labour market conditions, as the work history analysis shows us, they would not have been there.

2

Economic Convergence: A Tale of Six Cities

CATHERINE MARSH AND CAROLYN VOGLER

1. INTRODUCTION

This chapter draws mainly on sources of data outside the Social
Change and Economic Life Initiative (SCELI), in order to provide a profile of the history of the occupational structure in the
six labour markets. In the first half, a thumbnail sketch is given
of the employment traditions in the six areas from their first
industrialization up to 1971, showing how the areas industrialized
in very different periods and in very different ways. The second
half presents the more recent industrial histories of these locations, drawing on data from the Census of Employment in 1971
and 1981, as well as information about unemployment compiled
by local Department of Employment Jobcentres.

2. HISTORICAL TRADITIONS OF THE SIX LOCALITIES
UP TO THE EARLY 1970s

The six SCELI towns entered the recession which began in
1973–4 and which accelerated dramatically at the end of the
1970s with the stamps of their histories still clearly marked upon
them. In this section we shall present something of the histories
of the six areas, two of which were in Scotland—Aberdeen and
Kirkcaldy—and the other four of which—Coventry, Rochdale,
Northampton, and Swindon—were in England.

The Industrial Revolution began, as every school child knows,
in Britain; indeed, it was the location for several decades of

* This chapter draws on material presented by Carolyn Vogler and Colin
Mills to the Sixth Urban Change and Conflict Conference at the University of
Kent at Canterbury in September 1987.

virtually the whole world's industrial production and modern financial accounting. Three great transitions were involved: from sparse to dense population, from peasant and handicraft to industrial and capitalist modes of production, and from rural to urban society.

The transition from urban to rural society was well under way at the end of the eighteenth century, and by the middle of the nineteenth century more people lived in the town than in the country. In this respect, Britain was almost one century advanced on most of mainland Europe. Economists, social historians, and politicians have devoted a great deal of effort to deciding how important being first in the field was for Britain's subsequent development: having had such a head start, having been able to industrialize on the basis of relatively inexpensive capital equipment without fear of competition, gave Britain an unrepeatable advantage, but the corollary was that, in relative and competitive terms, the only path away from this position was downwards.

Industrialism brought with it unemployment in its modern sense. Surplus labour certainly existed in peasant societies, although the burden was probably spread more evenly across a wider range of producers. But, unlike in subsistence economies, making goods for a mass market separated the process of production from that of consumption and thus opened up the possibility of plans, both speculative and sober, going very badly wrong if the hoped-for sales failed to materialize. It is only relatively recently that modern production techniques, involving computerized stock control, have enabled some manufacturers once again to wait to begin production until there was an order on the books.

By the end of the eighteenth century Britain stood poised for industrial take-off. The population was large enough and its agriculture productive enough to sustain a labour force which could be drawn into new industries. The domestic economy was already market-oriented and had a large and growing manufacturing sector. Transport costs were not overwhelming and reduced as new canals were cut. And Britain was well placed politically, with a commercially oriented aristocracy and with good colonial links both westwards and eastwards to be able to profit from the expansion that was to take place.

2.1. Cotton and Rochdale

'Whoever says industrial revolution says cotton' (Hobsbawm 1968: 56). And cotton meant Lancashire, with its damp climate, its abundance of water power, and its proximity to the great colonial and slave-trading port of Liverpool. Between 1780 and 1840 the construction of cotton factories in Manchester, Salford, and their satellite towns in the Pennines, such as Rochdale, transformed the face of the countryside. Chimneys were added as the factories adopted mechanical steam power, and their illumination by gaslight permitted a seemingly unnatural extension of the working day. Trade in cotton had opened up as international commercial and colonial links first with India, but then, more importantly, with the southern slave states of the USA, expanded. International markets supplied not only the raw materials but also the markets for this new textile, which decimated the linen industry whenever the two were brought into competition. During its heyday, which lasted only a few decades, Lancashire dominated the world production of cotton goods. Simple technological improvements, predominantly in spinning, combined with revolutionary changes in social relations to improve productivity by hitherto unimaginable amounts, allowed capital accumulation, which soon acquired a dynamic of its own.

The first employees to be drawn into the new cotton factories were women, and although legislation soon put severe controls over the times and conditions of women's work in factories, the tradition of female full-time employment in cotton manufacturing remained. Thus in Rochdale the tradition of female employment was much higher than in our other areas: 53 per cent in 1931, for example.

Before long, cotton also revealed a feature which was to turn out to be endemic to industrial capitalism, namely, structural unemployment. During the eighteenth century the development of the flying shuttle had enabled weavers to keep pace with developments which by the end of the eighteenth century took spinning into factories. Although the power loom had been invented earlier, it was not widely used until after the Napoleonic wars, when it was introduced into factories and operated in a highly gendered division of labour by women and children, while their menfolk literally starved outside. The plight of the handloom weaver was recorded by official investigations of the time and vividly described by Marx and Engels as they sought to understand the dynamic of the changes they were witnessing. Destitute weavers formed the core of the demonstrators in Manchester at the end of the Napoleonic wars, calling on the government for reforms and the relief of distress. These protests gave rise to one of the rare occasions in Britain when civil discontent led to blood being shed—the Peterloo massacre of 1817. Soon, the cotton industry in general, and Rochdale in particular, developed forms of organization which proved stronger and produced more results than these pre-industrial forms of protest behaviour.

For much of the nineteenth century Rochdale rode on Britain's pre-eminence in textile manufacture and export, and there was little incentive to update its relatively simple technological base. After the First World War, however, British cotton exports increasingly lost out in competition to Egyptian and Indian cotton, especially since the drive to preserve sterling's gold standard made British exports very expensive. After the Second World War the collapse of the British cotton industry proceeded much faster, suffering under pressure of Asian competition in the home market, and the government was forced to intervene with the 1960 Cotton Industry Act, which aimed to reduce the size of the industry and to modernize its capital equipment.

Despite the fact that cotton was in serious decline, the industry still faced severe problems in recruiting and retaining workers: working conditions were often unchanged from the nineteenth century, pay was low, and the general mood of the industry bleak. Moreover, the installation of more expensive capital equipment led to the establishment of continuous shift-working, and many white workers quit for jobs elsewhere. Cotton thus became increasingly dependent on immigrants from the New Commonwealth and Pakistan, who were drawn into the country in large quantities. Rochdale experienced an influx of Asians, principally from the Punjab, during this period (Anwar 1979), who took the worst-paid, dirtiest jobs in Rochdale's textile factories, often on permanent night shifts, effectively segregated from white workers. Indeed, the availability of relatively cheap immigrant labour in the 1960s propped up an industry whose decline might otherwise have occurred earlier[1] (UMS 1977).

Rochdale, however, never suffered quite the levels of distress of the other Pennine cotton towns for two reasons. First, it had specialized in heavy textiles for industrial uses and the finishing trade, and these were not hit so badly by foreign competition during the twentieth century (Penn and Scattergood 1989). In fact, in all the censuses prior to 1981 Rochdale's first industry remained textiles, employing a stable 30 per cent of the labour force in the town. Even at the end of the twentieth century the physical landscape is still dominated by the great cotton mills of the nineteenth century. Secondly, during the second half of the nineteenth century Rochdale also acquired an important engineering industry, which set it apart from other Pennine textile towns. While it was dominated by one industry, it was never a sole-industry town.

2.2. Railway Engineering and Swindon

While textiles were the core industry of the first phase of capital accumulation in the Industrial Revolution, the railways can be argued to form the key to a second, more enduring and transformative phase. Railways responded to the transport demands of the emerging industrial economy to convey raw materials and goods from point of production to point of consumption. But the development of the steam-engine and of the railway in turn provided an outlet for the investment of capital accumulating in other sectors. Indeed, investing in the building of different designs of locomotive and in constructing new rail links appealed to the imaginations of the newly rich industrialists, who supported many frankly unviable schemes in the railway mania of the mid-nineteenth century. (In many cases it took nationalization of the industry to cut these down to size during the 1960s.)

This new investment had two important consequences. It gave a tremendous push to the spiralling expansion of output, especially by giving a critical spur to the key coal and iron industries; the take-off in engineering and capital goods later in the nineteenth century would not have been possible without the expansion of iron first demanded by the railways. But it also encouraged the development of joint-stock companies, whereby shareholders uninvolved in production put up finance for large ventures of this kind. By the end of the nineteenth century financial capitalism had developed a dynamic of its own, and monetary services increasingly came to dominate the structure of British capitalism.

While Swindon cannot claim to lie in the cradle of this development in the way that Rochdale can with cotton (credit for that must go to the North-east), its birth as a railway town dates back to 1935, when the Great Western Railway (GWR) established what was to remain until the 1980s one of the world's largest locomotive and wagon workshops. Britain was not only the first country with a complete domestic railway system, it was soon providing the world, especially the vast land masses of colonial Africa and India, with railway systems which could not be provided by their indigenous economies. Swindon was the hub of that production, and during the nineteenth and early twentieth centuries labour was drafted in from Ireland and other depressed regions of Britain such as Scotland and East Anglia to work in the massive complex which may have been the largest industrial undertaking in Europe (Eversley 1959: 215). In numerical terms, the heyday of GWR was the period immediately before the First World War, when around 70 per cent of the economically active inhabitants of Swindon were employed in the works. It was a prototypical case of a traditional proletarian occupational community (Lockwood 1966), based on skilled male manual employment in a single industry. Swindon historically had a very low female participation rate: 25 per cent in 1931.

GWR was a model paternalistic nineteenth-century employer, pioneering company housing; in 1900 the town had the highest proportion of owner occupation in the UK (60 per cent). The company also provided its staff with some of the earliest recreational and insurance facilities, building hospitals, baths, and laundries, encouraging insurance schemes and friendly societies. Employees of GWR had reason to believe that a job with the company made them secure for life.

The railway industry was, however, particularly prone to the slumps and recessions that international trade and the growth of financial capital were encouraging. Large-scale unemployment became an endemic feature of life at the turn of the century, fuelled by cyclical crises of demand which grew in frequency before the outbreak of the First World War and in severity after it. On top of the general world recession of the 1920s, the competition posed by the motor industry contributed to an inter-war picture of falling orders and rising costs.

During the 1930s, initially in response to world recession, employment at the works began to decline. The tide had turned for rail as the dominant mode of transport. But decline was not as precipitate as, say, for shipbuilding, and the existing railway infrastructure still continued to need repair and maintenance. Although employment at the works, which had been at its height at around 15,000 before the First World War, slipped gradually to around 12,000 by the early 1930s, and to around 10,500 by the outbreak of the Second World War, the local unemployment rate remained well below the national average (5.2 per cent in 1931 compared with 11.5 per cent nationally). What made the recession of the 1930s so different from that of the 1980s was that some sectors of manufacturing were still growing strongly; Swindon was well placed for redundant workshop employees to be able to find work in the expanding car factory at Cowley, thirty miles away.

After the war, the local council was faced with two problems. The first was how to expand and whether to diversify the industrial base to avoid a return to the depression of the 1930s. Some aircraft and electronic industry had been attracted to the town during the Second World War, and, despite those who thought that Swindon should continue to concentrate on what it did best, the council tried to encourage industrial diversification. The government, however, refused to grant the necessary development certificates, trying to concentrate new growth on the depressed areas. Secondly, the council also identified the need to renovate the physical structure of the town: Swindon was the original object of John Betjeman's ringing description: it 'contained very little architecture and a great deal of building' (quoted in Harloe 1975: 43). However, without the income from industry, little physical reconstruction could be contemplated.

During the Second World War, a Ministry of Town and Country Planning had been established, and its planning powers were consolidated in the Town and Country Planning Act of 1947. A plan emerged to expand existing country towns to allow for growth in industry and population which were currently located in the conurbations. Swindon Council lobbied hard, and in 1952 Swindon was designated one of the first New Towns. This achieved what the council had been unable to achieve on its own, bringing modern industrial development and a mass of good-quality cheap housing. People, especially young families from Greater London, followed; Swindon's population, which had been slightly declining in the 1930s, grew at six times the national rate in the 1950s (Harloe 1975: 66).

The hard core of industrial diversification was based on three firms, two of which had originally moved some operations to Swindon during the war: Pressed Steel, who moved into Swindon to open a car body plant; Plesseys, who brought high-technology telecommunications manufacturing; and Vickers, who expanded their aircraft industry. In short then, while the railways suffered severe job losses (4,000 jobs) and continued to decline when the Beeching Plan to rationalize the railways was introduced in 1963–4, there were still jobs in vehicles and electrical engineering available in the town.

Part of Swindon's success as a new town was due to its strategic geographical placement. The town had long served as an important railway junction, with stations on the Midland and South-western as well as the Great Western Railway. As rail gave way to road, Swindon's location on the main thoroughfare from London to the south-west of England increased its importance as a communications centre, since it came to form part of a successful post-war corridor of development. The M4 corridor has been the centre of the development of the sunrise telecommunication and other high-technology industries, and Swindon benefited greatly from this.

2.3. Footwear and Northampton

The borough of Northampton is a town of great antiquity, and had long served as the local cattle market, supporting a tanning and leather trade and its obvious corollary—a boot- and shoe-making industry. The craft skills of the Northampton boot- and shoemakers were a matter of repute as early as the seventeenth century, and even before the industrial revolution the industry expanded continually on an out-work basis.

Rural Northamptonshire with its productive farmland was the focus of a particularly fierce movement at the end of the eighteenth century which enclosed over half of its land, creating a large and hungry class of wage labourers. (They were not referred to as 'unemployed'; that term grew with the recognition of the social causation of joblessness and with systems of social insurance against it (Williams 1976).) But despite this abundant surplus labour, modern industrial methods of production were introduced only slowly into the boot and shoe industry, where methods of production were not mechanized until the second half of the nineteenth century. Part of the spur was technological invention: factory boot- and shoemaking was introduced in the 1860s, as machines, particularly the hinged last, were developed to cut and stitch leather.

But changes in demand were as important as changes in techniques of production. From the middle of the nineteenth century, working-class wages in the country as a whole began to rise significantly. By the 1870s shops selling a wide range of already manufactured merchandise had made their arrival, and factory production slowly geared itself to the mass of the working and lower-middle classes. Dressmakers, tailors, and shoemakers gave way to factories mass-producing these items and to shops which displayed and sold them. The shoe industry led the way in this new market (Jefferys 1954).

Northampton as a town benefited greatly from the expansion of the footwear trade. The county borough of Northampton was created in 1888, and it developed into the local centre providing all kinds of professional services for the surrounding county. Northampton was one of the six towns studied by Bowley (1911) in his pioneering *Livelihood and Poverty*; at the time of the survey of Northampton in 1911 Northampton was a prosperous town, paying good wages to both men and women, with only 8 per cent of the households falling beneath the poverty line drawn by Rowntree on the basis of his York studies.

Footwear is a good example of an industry in which, since the Second World War, British technology and expertise has been unable to compete with foreign manufacture, and Northampton has witnessed this decline in the form of unemployment in its traditional industry. As late as 1950 footwear manufacture accounted for 22 per cent of Northampton's total employment and 42 per cent of its manufacturing employment. It was still strongly characterized by female employment: 43 per cent of the industry was female, compared to 30 per cent of other manufacturing employment in the area. Despite the post-war decline, footwear was still the dominant industry in Northampton up until 1971.

The problems of the footwear industry were clear to the local council throughout the post-war period. Like Swindon, the council found it hard to attract new industry in competition with other areas which could offer assistance with development, so they lobbied to become incorporated as a New Town. They were finally successful, and in 1968 Northampton became one of the last towns to be granted Provincial New Town status.

2.4. Vehicles and Coventry

The Midlands of Great Britain as a whole escaped the early Industrial Revolution; small workshops and independent producers continued much later. Coventry had a small traditional woollen textiles industry, and was noted for its dyeing and ribbon manufacture. It remained almost totally unindustrialized until the 1880s, when its dyeing industry expanded and carpet manufacture was mechanized. But it was the local watchmaking craft which provided the skills base which initially attracted a profitable sewing-machine business and later a new bicycle industry to the town. Because of its late start in industrial production, Coventry had no problems of technical obsolescence to overcome, and adapted quickly to new industries such as the manufacture of vehicles, machine tools, and synthetic fibres, achieving economies of scale from the start.

The bicycle industry was the pivotal development in Coventry's modern history; Riley, Singer, Starley, Rover, Humber, Hillman, and, above all, Triumph, were all originally bicycle manufacturers in the city. In 1907 Rudge-Whitworth Cycle, the largest industrial unit in Coventry, was already employing 1,800 people, a vast number by the standards of the time. Large-volume cycle production grew dynamically, and soon involved the addition of motor power. The Triumph motor cycle in particular became very popular during the First World War. It was a short step from motor cycles to cars.

Historians of Coventry like Richardson and Harris (1972) write proudly of the early years of the car industry, in which many small firms experimented enthusiastically with new styles, designing sports models in small workshops which they raced against each other. But the availability of large factory space was probably the main reason why Coventry was so attractive to the cycle and car manufacturers, few of whom were natives of the city; factory space was specifically cited as a reason attracting Daimler to Coventry at the turn of the century, for example (Lancaster and Mason 1987: 19). Although it was home to many exclusive, small-volume quality cars such as Daimler and Jaguar, Coventry also pioneered economies of scale and a detailed division of labour in the bicycle industry even before Henry Ford had applied them to car manufacture in the USA. Morris Motors soon applied the formula of mass production and cheap cars to Britain; the engines were made in Coventry and the cars assembled at Cowley.

Vehicle construction attracted a wide range of metal-manufacturing jobs. Coventry soon had firms making steel components and ball-bearings and, most significantly, machine tools. Britain's largest machine tool company, Alfred Herbert, was based in Coventry. The manufacture of magnetos also gradually drew GEC into Coventry and into more general telecommunications, making radios and telephones. But Coventry also attracted other new, non-metal-working industries. An important man-made fibre industry arose from the ashes of ribbon-making; during the 1920s Courtaulds began making artificial silk in Coventry.

As observed in the discussion of Swindon, there were parts of Britain which continued to expand during the depression of the 1930s. There were over a million cars on British roads by 1930 (Marwick 1970), and a high proportion of them were built in Coventry. The slow but gradual growth during the 1930s changed into boom employment during the Second World War as the various components of the vehicle industry were converted into a vital arsenal for the war effort. As long as there was demand for labour, people moved in. Throughout the inter-war years Coventry was the country's fastest-growing industrial centre, attracting migrants from depressed regions of South Wales, Scotland, and Ireland. The embourgeoisement of the working class which many claimed to discern in the post-war epoch was visible in Coventry in the 1930s, with both men and women being paid good wages by the standards of the time.

Coventry was savagely bombed during the Second World War, and was as devastated as many German cities. After the war, however, its car industry failed to attract anything like the same levels of investment as the German car industry, but despite its ageing capital equipment, Coventry's car industry continued to be profitable in the long post-war boom, and immigrants from the New Commonwealth and Pakistan exercised their rights as British citizens (which began to be eroded after 1962) to enter the country to look for work. As in Rochdale, they ended up taking jobs that others did not want, especially those with high labour turnover such as steel-forging and the nastier jobs in the car industry.

Towards the end of the 1960s major problems began to emerge with Coventry's vehicles economy as the town's share of the British market slipped in line with Britain's share of the world market. Profitability and investment were too low to enable the firms mass-producing cars to achieve sufficient economies of scale. Rootes was eventually bought out by the North American giant Chrysler to achieve such economies. Coventry's aircraft industry was in an even worse state; changes in defence policy in the 1960s hit Coventry particularly hard. Nevertheless, even as late as 1971, 28 per cent of Coventry's labour force were still employed in vehicle production, with many others employed in related industries such as mechanical engineering.

2.5. Coal and Kirkcaldy

Fuel was an essential ingredient for the Industrial Revolution: it had to be cheap and plentiful enough to sustain the tremendous demand that rising manufacture made for energy, and of high enough quality to permit the manufacture of high-quality iron ore and steel which could be made into precision tools.

Since the Middle Ages coal had been used for domestic purposes, and in the north of England around Newcastle and in areas of Scotland such as Fifeshire (Kirkcaldy's county home) it lay close enough to the surface and was sufficiently transportable by water to be mined extensively in open-cast mines and shipped by sea to London and overseas. As woodland was stripped in the sixteenth and seventeenth centuries, coal came to replace timber as a source of domestic fuel, and early experiments were made to use it instead of charcoal in the smelting of iron ore.

For many, the coal miner has come to symbolize the essence of the proletarian worker, and in many countries miners' organizations have played a central role in the labour movement. In the early and middle twentieth century, for example, the miners of the Fifeshire coalfield played a leading part in working-class politics. Yet there is an irony in this. The drive to revolutionize production methods (to divide tasks and to power production mechanically) which was characteristic of manufacturing was never applied to coal. Mining remained extremely primitive, often unmechanized, with production methods that had changed little since they had been introduced into Britain by the Romans. Its rate of expansion was determined primarily by the ease with which the coal could be transported from the mine. It was not until nationalization after the Second World War that new technical developments were introduced. Kirkcaldy may have been the birthplace of Adam Smith, but coal did not provide a model of the capitalist mode of production.

Similarly, the social relations under which coal was extracted also remained more feudal than capitalist; indeed miners in Scotland were legally treated as serfs right up until 1799. Mining communities, whether in Fifeshire, South Yorkshire, Nottinghamshire, or even Kent, remained essentially village communities. Despite a massive increase in coal production in the second half of the nineteenth century, the coal industry did not experience the concentration and merger which were typical of manufacturing industries. Coal-mines were still owned by Britain's old landed aristocracy such as the Duke of Bridgewater.

In some respects Kirkcaldy bears the social stamp of coal communities everywhere. Solidarism and community spirit have been an enduring feature of coal villages (Dennis *et al.* 1956; Samuel 1977). In other respects, however, Kirkcaldy differed from other coal communities. Of the six towns studied in the initiative, Kirkcaldy was least dependent on one single and all-dominant industry. Traditionally, Kirkcaldy's second industry was its production of linen and canvas, an industry where women had traditionally been centrally involved. When cotton production became widespread in the mid-nineteenth century, the competition it offered to linen production hit Kirkcaldy quite hard, although not as badly as elsewhere, and a moderate quantity of linen production continued in Scotland long after the industry had been wiped out south of the border. The linen industry gave Kirkcaldy a feature most uncharacteristic of mining communities elsewhere: a long tradition of women's employment.

The town's third important industry was the manufacture of linoleum. Oilcloth and 'lino' were actually invented in Kirkcaldy by a nineteenth-century inventor, Michael Nairn, and the Nairn family business and a few satellite businesses continued to provide a substantial number of jobs in the town up until the Second World War. Lino is typical of the low-cost export industry which was buoyant in Scotland in the nineteenth and early twentieth century. It began to falter during the inter-war depression before being decimated after the Second World War by vinyl floorings.

Kirkcaldy, however, was never a wealthy town, and a broader industrial base never developed, hampered by two features characteristic of Scottish capitalism: poverty and lack of capital. In turn these often led to a greater reliance on imports and a low-wage economy. Housing was poor and overcrowding common. In the 1921 census 12 per cent of the inhabitants of Kirkcaldy district lived at more than four to a room, and even by 1951 many parts of the area registered more than 10 per cent living more than two to a room. Unemployment in Kirkcaldy was traditionally much higher than elsewhere in Great Britain.

During the post-war years, the town's economy suffered badly, particularly in comparison with the other study areas. An accelerating programme of pit closures led to a steady and large loss of mining jobs, as coal-mining was gradually rationalized around two working mines along the shores of the Firth of Forth, and the linoleum industry was almost completely devastated.

In an attempt to bring new employment to the town, Glenrothes New Town was established as one of the earliest New Towns. Glenrothes is geographically distinct from Kirkcaldy town, although the physical gap between the two has gradually become built up. The town planners set about their task of diversification with vigour, and were successful in attracting new light industry, particularly in electronics and telecommunications, into the town.

2.6. *Aberdeen before Oil*

Aberdeen was the last of the six localities to be drawn into the Industrial Revolution. Agriculture in north-east Scotland resembled Scottish lowland farming more than highland crofting, but the land was poorer, the range of holdings of different sizes more diverse, and the pace of development of capitalist methods of agriculture slower (Carter 1979). Resident farm servants, working for board and clothing and often too poor to marry, were still numerous at the end of the nineteenth century, but, as capitalist agriculture took hold, they gradually gave way to a class of rural wage labourers. The establishment of a trading route by steamship from the South which brought cattle feed was an important stimulus, and the famous north-east breeds such as Aberdeen Angus were developed.

Aberdeen itself was relatively prosperous compared to the surrounding areas. Like Northampton in the eighteenth and nineteenth centuries, Aberdeen in the nineteenth and twentieth centuries functioned as a county town and service centre, providing lawyers, doctors, tailors, and cobblers, who serviced the wealthier members of the surrounding countryside.

At the end of the nineteenth century, industrialization spread to the country town of Aberdeen. It centred on expansion and rationalization of the native fishing and farming industries. Geography and its consequent transport costs seemed to rule out the production of goods for export too far outside the area, so local industrialization was based on the processing of local textiles, timber, and food for local consumption. Development was slow and piecemeal, and there was no build-up of one major industry. Industrial diversity, however, meant that, while poor, Aberdeen never suffered the terrible slumps characteristic of our other localities in the nineteenth and twentieth centuries.

Wage levels in Scotland have always been low, and those in Aberdeen were among the lowest in Scotland. Men tended to migrate out of Aberdeen to seek work (Bonney 1985), and during the 1960s unemployment was second highest of the areas studied.

By 1979 Aberdeen's occupational structure contained a higher proportion of services than the other five areas (as it also did in the 1931 and the 1951 censuses). But this can be seen as an index of the relative underdevelopment in other sectors; services formed a higher proportion of the total mix of employment because primary and manufacturing industries were so weak; the service industries formed a low-wage sector, which, apart from those working in the retail side of the food-processing industry, provided services only for the immediate locality.

2.7. Summary of the Six Localities by 1971

Thus by 1971 each of the study towns had a very different and distinctive employment profile. In five of the six towns, the industry which had provided the engine of the town's growth still dominated the employment picture; in the sixth the single most important industry in its history (oil in Aberdeen) had not yet developed. The areas had coasted on the post-war boom, which represented the longest wave of growth and development that capitalism had ever seen. The structural problems of capital and product development had not yet fully emerged.

3. RESTRUCTURING OF EMPLOYMENT IN THE SIX LOCALITIES BETWEEN 1971 AND 1986

Nationally during the 1970s the gradual rise in employment, which had broadly matched the gradual rise in the size of the labour force, came to a halt and after 1978 turned into a net loss of jobs. As we shall see in the next section, this had a devastating impact on newcomers to the labour market, and thus on unemployment rates. First, however, we shall consider what happened to employment in the six areas in the recessionary years between 1971 and 1986, drawing on data from the 1971 and 1981 Censuses of Employment.

The discussion focuses on change in the major sectors of industrial activity: primary and extractive industries, manufacturing and the service sector, with construction considered separately. For each, we show how the typical level of activity in that sector changed over the intercensal decade 1971–81. We shall also consider the extent to which the profile of industries within that sector grew more or less like the profile for Great Britain as a whole.

This latter question is pursued by constructing an index of dissimilarity, calculated as follows. The percentage working in each industry in each locality was expressed as a ratio of the percentage working in that industry nationally at the same time (often called the 'location quotient'). The result was then logged to ensure that an industry employing double the national average contributed as much to the index of dissimilarity as one which employed one half the national average. The only problem arose with zeros (no employees in a particular industry), which technically cannot be logged; they were arbitrarily set to -2. The absolute values of the logged ratios for each industry were summed and their mean value found. The result is an index which pays as much attention to an area having fewer than would be expected employed in a particular industry as well as to an area having more than would be expected. (Full details of the data which form the base of this measure are given in Table 2.A1.)

3.1. Primary Sector

The primary sector comprises agriculture, mining, quarrying, and fishing. The historic decline of agriculture as a large-scale employer of labour and its extraordinary growth in productivity is well known. But the proportion of the population working in other primary sector occupations—fishing and mining—has also declined dramatically during the twentieth century.

The experience of the six localities with regard to primary industries is shown in Figure 2.1. Let us consider first panel *a*, showing the level of activity in this sector. The figure for Great Britain shows that the long-run decline continued during the 1970s, and contributed to the unemployment problem. The same pattern is reflected in five of the six localities, with Kirkcaldy in particular continuing to see a major erosion of employment in its coal-mining industry.

The largest change in panel *a* of Figure 2.1, however, was for Aberdeen, as this was the decade of Aberdeen's oil bonanza. At the beginning of the 1970s the world's need for fossil fuels had fundamentally altered the global balance of power. The oil-producing countries formed a powerful cartel (OPEC), which restricted production and kept the price of oil high. The resulting sudden rise in prices gave the industrialized world a shock which

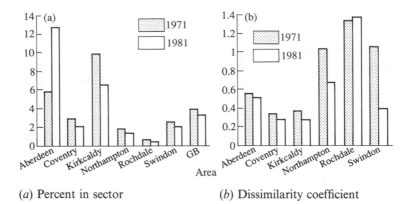

(a) Percent in sector   (b) Dissimilarity coefficient

FIG. 2.1. Change in primary sector industries, 1971–1981, in six areas.
Source: data in Table 2.A1

put an end to the long post-war boom and heralded the recession. When the second oil shock came at the end of the 1970s many industrialized countries, Britain included, were hit extremely hard. Unemployment soared as governments attempted to curb inflation by means of traditional deflationary policies.

It was during this period, however, that Britain also became not just an oil producer but a net oil exporter. Huge finds of oil and gas under the North Sea bought time for the ailing industrial economy, and the income generated by exporting oil made it possible to support people made redundant in other sectors of the economy on social security benefit. Were it not for oil, unemployment could well have been much higher than the 3 million peak in the early 1980s.

As a result of these huge finds of workable oil and gas, Aberdeen experienced a very sharp rate of increase in employment in the 1970s—one of the fastest of any labour market in Britain during the 1970s—and the growth was almost entirely due to oil and oil-related industries. Wages and house prices soared in the surrounding area. However, growth came to a halt in the mid-1980s, around the time of the SCELI study, as the world economy slowed and the price of oil slumped.

Panel *b* of Figure 2.1 shows large variations in the size of the primary sector in the six localities—not surprisingly, given that primary industries are heavily dependent on the physical terrain. If the dissimilarity coefficients in panel *b* of each of Figures

2.1–2.4 are compared, it is clear that primary-sector industries are more variable than any other sector. Panel *b* of Figure 2.1, however, also shows that the locational dissimilarity of the primary sector declined in the ten-year period. The only area that stands out as widely different from the national average is Rochdale, principally because of its *lack* of any primary, agricultural, and extractive industries.

3.2. Manufacturing

For the past 200 years, the mainstay of Britain's wealth has been derived from manufacturing goods and trading them with other countries. As we saw in the previous section, despite the entry of other countries into world markets, a process which gained ground especially after the Second World War, the period of peace and growth was long enough and sustained enough for manufacturing to survive even on a relatively outmoded and uncompetitive base. With the advent of the recession in the 1970s all this changed, and British manufacturing industry suffered a tremendous jolt. Indeed, between 1980 and 1983 alone one-quarter of Britain's manufacturing disappeared.

As can be seen in panel *a* of Figure 2.2, between 1971 and 1981 all the six study areas registered a net loss of jobs in manufacturing. For five of the six areas (all except Aberdeen), this involved reductions in the staple industry of the town. These were smallest in Swindon, but only because the decline of the railway workshops had occurred substantially earlier, and to a great extent even before the Second World War. Rochdale's textile industry was all but dismantled: between 1971 and 1981 the proportion of the labour force employed in textiles fell from 30 per cent to 13 per cent (Table 2A1). The sharpest falls were at the turn of the decade: between 1978 and 1982 some 43 per cent of the industry's employees were made redundant. Because of the high number of women working in textiles, the result was as devastating for women as it was for men.

In terms of absolute job loss from the dominant industry, the sharpest fall of all was in Coventry, where vehicle manufacture declined from employing 28 per cent of the work-force to employing 11 per cent of the work-force (Table 2.A1). Between 1974 and 1983 employment in Coventry's manufacturing

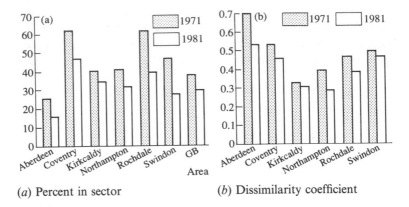

(*a*) Percent in sector   (*b*) Dissimilarity coefficient

Fig. 2.2. Change in manufacturing sector industries, 1971–1981, in six areas. *Source*: data in Table 2.A1

sector fell by half, most of the decisions being taken by large multinational companies in which top decision-making was located outside the area. Because manufacturing industry was predominantly male in Coventry, male unemployment rose dramatically, as we shall see in the next section.

In relative terms, Northampton's once dominant industry suffered the worst, experiencing near annihilation. By 1981 Northampton's boot and shoe industry declined to a mere 4 per cent of all employees compared with 22 per cent in 1950. Finally, in Kirkcaldy, on top of the job losses in mining discussed above, the finishing touches were also put to the end of the linoleum industry.

However, the six areas had different degrees of success in finding substitutes for their declining traditional industries. Kirkcaldy and Northampton were much more successful than the other towns in attracting expanding industries to compensate for losses in their declining industries. A range of light industries such as food, drink, and tobacco were brought in to both towns, and a significant light engineering and electronics industry was established in Kirkcaldy. Both had been established as New Towns under the Act mentioned earlier, and it is tempting to account for their relative success in this way. Swindon, however, serves to keep such explanations in check; also incorporated as a New Town, Swindon in the recession of the 1970s and 1980s, never really solved its inter-war problems of lack of diversity.

In summary then, during the decade between 1971 and 1981 the six study areas lost much of their manufacturing distinctiveness and grew much more like the national average. The implications of this change will be discussed further below.

3.3. The Service Sector

Before considering the changes in the service sector which occurred in the period after 1971, it is important to consider what we mean by services. We can distinguish service industries from service occupations and service functions. Banking is a service industry (and banks may employ engineers to service their equipment). Accountants perform a service occupation which can be done in any industry. Having orderly accounts is a service function that can be filled either by employing an accountant or by buying a microcomputer and self-servicing. As societies get richer, service functions appear to increase as a proportion of total human needs. But there is no inevitable law saying that societies will increasingly fulfil these functions by employing people in service occupations or in service industries; indeed, given the slow rate of productivity growth in many service occupations, there are good grounds for expecting a rise in self-provisioning using capital goods (Gershuny 1983).

During the period between 1971 and 1986 the service sector was the only area in the British economy in which new jobs were being created. Between 1971 and 1981 service industries in Great Britain as a whole grew from 54 per cent to 63 per cent of total employment, the most successful service sector industries being professional and financial services. The national pattern of growth of this sector was echoed in each of the six study areas, as Figure 2.3 shows. Areas with the lowest original proportion of service sector employment grew fastest; Rochdale took the lead with a 55 per cent growth in its service sector, followed by Coventry (43 per cent) and Swindon (38 per cent). The result was that between 1971 and 1981 variations in service sector employment among five of the six localities declined sharply. Kirkcaldy was an exception, which actually moved away from the average in Great Britain during the decade.

Greater insight is gained by considering the kinds of new service sector jobs which grew in each area (full details in Table

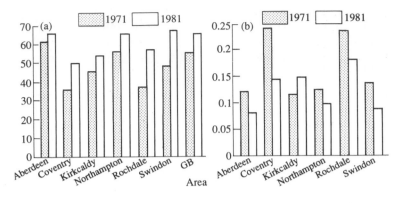

(*a*) Percent in sector   (*b*) Dissimilarity coefficient

FIG. 2.3. Change in service sector industries, 1971–1981, in six areas.
Source: data in Table 2.A1

2A1). There was a general expansion of public sector services, creating extra jobs for teachers, nurses, home helps, and so on. Since these services are distributed out of the public purse on a per capita basis, it is not surprising that employment growth in these sectors led to a greater similarity of employment structure. Rochdale's higher rate of service growth may have resulted from the fact that national growth in service occupations had a greater effect on the composition of the labour force in Rochdale, where manufacturing industries had declined so fast. Kirkcaldy's exceptional rise in dissimilarity compared to Great Britain over the period resulted from its failure to match national employment growth in the utilities and in transport. Northampton and Swindon in particular, however, also made successful transitions to private service sector employment, the most rapid growth being in financial and business services.

3.4. Construction

Finally, to complete the picture we should consider construction. As one would expect, the percentage of jobs in construction was relatively stable over the decade, with the smallest amount of differentiation between areas. This is the sector in which all six areas resemble Great Britain as a whole most closely (panel *b* of Figure 2.4, compared to panel *b* of Figures 2.1–2.3). The four

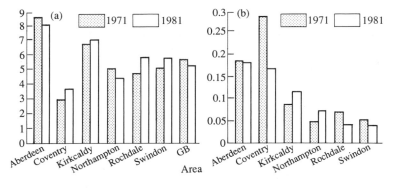

(*a*) Percent in sector   (*b*) Dissimilarity coefficient

FIG. 2.4. Change in construction, 1971–1981, in six areas. *Source*: data
in Table 2.A1

sectors (primary, manufacturing, services, and transport) seem to
be ordered on a continuum in terms of geographical specialization. We shall postpone summarizing these occupational changes
until we have considered changes in unemployment rates in the
six areas.

4. UNEMPLOYMENT IN THE SIX AREAS

Changes in employment do not automatically translate into
changes in the rate of unemployment, because the size of the
labour force may also change. The 1980s recession was so acutely
painful because it coincided with the largest ever cohort of new
entrants to the labour market. Moreover, women's rising participation in the formal economy also continued its secular increase,
seemingly little-affected by the economic difficulties being experienced. It is therefore important to trace the history of unemployment separately from the history of employment.

4.1. Geographical Distribution of Unemployment

Figure 2.5 shows the trajectory of unemployment in the six study
areas over a period of nearly thirty years between 1960 and 1988.
The trends look broadly similar to the national trajectory shown

in Chapter 1. The similarity of the patterns suggests that similar structural, macrolevel forces were at work affecting the overall level of economic activity. Unemployment seemed to act as an external force, operating in a similar manner on very different local labour markets.

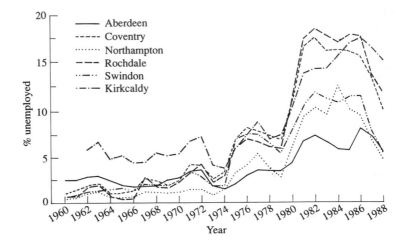

FIG. 2.5. Level of unemployment in the six localities, 1960–1988. *Source*: *Department of Employment Gazette* (Sept. each year)

Figure 2.5 also shows a pattern which was clearly evident in the depression of the 1930s: higher levels of unemployment in the old industrial areas in the north of England and Scotland. While the absolute differences between the areas increased as unemployment rose, closer inspection reveals that the relative ratios between the unemployment rates in the different areas actually closed up. Other commentators have described the change in relative unemployment rates during the recession of the 1970s and early 1980s as the moving of the North–South divide in a southerly direction (Massey 1984). What is less commonly recognized is that this aspect of the North–South divide actually closed up during this period. Kirkcaldy, for example, had a distinctively higher unemployment level in the 1960s, but by 1980 other areas, notably Rochdale and Coventry, had caught it up. Indeed, Coventry, the huge inter-war success story, became a symbol of the new unemployment; by the 1980s its male unemployment rate placed it near the bottom of the league table of all British labour markets. Aberdeen's rank order changed as a result of the oil boom discussed above.

We get the same result if we drop down a level within these labour markets and ask how different neighbourhoods were affected. Proponents of polarization would predict that neighbourhoods would become more socially distinctive as unemployment rose, concentrating the problems of economic difficulty into ghettoes within towns. However, an examination of census tracts (areas averaging 200 households) of the counties containing the four English labour markets—the West Midlands, Greater Manchester, Northamptonshire, and Wiltshire—suggests that this was not the case.

Certainly, unemployment was highly concentrated within neighbourhoods. While almost all the neighbourhoods in the four counties had some significant experience of unemployment in 1981, the spread was very great (interquartile range from 7.6 per cent to 21.4 per cent), and in the top 1 per cent, at least 44 per cent of the work-force in the neighbourhood was unemployed. Yet when we focus on changes in the rate of growth over time (by plotting the logged unemployment rate and differences between 1971 and 1981 in the logged rate), it becomes clear that unemployment grew disproportionately in areas where it had previously been low. Geographically, unemployment became much more dispersed; the correlation between change in (log) unemployment and (log) level in 1971 is –0.51; areas with an unemployment rate of around 1 per cent in 1971 on average grew by 5.7 per cent, whereas those which already had a rate of 10 per cent in 1971 only grew by 2.1 per cent.

4.2. Social Distribution of Unemployment

Although unemployment was spread more widely geographically by the mid-1980s than it once had been, it still affected certain groups of people disprotionately. In Britain, as elsewhere in Europe, the young, as new entrants to the labour market, were hit particularly hard. However, the risk of unemployment was also differentiated by sex. Unlike the rest of Europe, women in

Britain had a *lower* risk of unemployment. Whereas for men the risk of unemployment was broadly U-shaped, falling in middle age and rising again towards retirement, the risk for women fell away consistently with age: older women of course were not more likely to be in work, but were much more likely than men to declare themselves as economically inactive (see Figure 2.6).

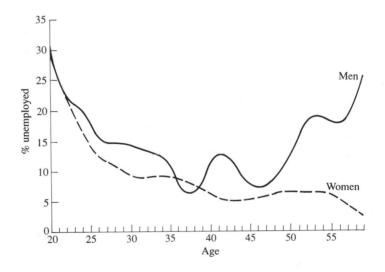

FIG. 2.6. Risk of unemployment (smoothed)* by age. (*Resistant median smoothing algorithm in *Minitab* package.) *Source*: The Work Attitudes/Histories Survey 1986

The lower rate of unemployment among women in Britain has traditionally been explained in terms of aggregate demand-side factors: women are disproportionately concentrated in service sector jobs, which have been growing. The higher risk of young ages is explained as representing the difficulties of newcomers to a crowded scene, while the rising risk for older men, on the other hand, is thought to stem from the difficulties they face in becoming re-employed once they have been made redundant. This suggests a selection process which might be termed 'discriminatory'.

As can be seen in Table 2.1, the risk of unemployment was also much higher among ethnic minority members than it was among whites. While the numbers are small, they confirm data from the Labour Force Survey (Department of Employment 1988). The contrast was most marked for men: West Indian men had double the risk of unemployment and Asian men three times the risk of white men. Among women, Asians seem to resemble whites in their risk of unemployment, but this conceals a much lower participation rate among Asian women. The number of cases is not sufficient to separate the effects of being black from working in industries with high propensity to unemployment, but the suspicion must remain that some process of discrimination in hiring practices may partly explain this differential risk of unemployment.

TABLE 2.1. *Unemployment rate by ethnic group*

Ethnic status	Men		Women	
	Unemployment rate		Unemployment rate	
	(%)	No.	(%)	No.
White	13	2,963	10	2,936
Asian	37	84	9	80
West Indian	24	12	20	13
Other	18	6	4	10

Source: The Work Attitudes/Histories Survey 1986.

Table 2.2 shows that unemployment also varied with educational background, although the relationship was very slightly U-shaped owing to a higher risk of unemployment among those with university degrees. To check that this was not just the spurious result of an association with age, the table was run for those aged 30 and under; this showed an even higher unemployment rate among those with degrees and thus an even greater departure from a monotonic relationship with education.

Relatively high concentrations of unemployment among people with low educational qualifications can be explained in two radically different ways. On the one hand, it may provide evidence of a skills mismatch: the jobs which are available in the economy require a higher (or at least different) level of skill to that possessed by the unemployed. Alternatively, viewing

TABLE 2.2. *Risk of unemployment in different educational categories*

Educational category	Men		Women	
	Unemployment rate (%)	No.	Unemployment rate (%)	No.
Degree	8.8	259	11.7	136
Other higher education	5.9	371	7.0	412
A level	16.8	374	7.7	198
O level	10.1	935	10.1	764
CSE	15.9	231	13.9	369
Other/none	21.8	901	10.7	1,162

Source: The Work Attitudes/Histories Survey 1986.

qualifications merely as credentials, the association could result from a bumping-up process as unemployment grows: jobs which previously demanded A levels now demand degrees, jobs which previously demanded O levels now demand A levels, and so on.

One final aspect of the social distribution of unemployment concerns its concentration within households. As Lampard shows in Chapter 9, unemployment is clearly associated with marital status: the unemployed are much less likely to be married and much more likely to be single or divorced. Furthermore, as Davies, Elias, and Penn argue in Chapter 5, the benefits system, which in 1986 penalized an unemployed person pound for pound for all earnings above a very low threshold, also acted to encourage a concentration of unemployed people in households where no one worked. Overall, as Table 2.3 shows, unemployed respondents were much more likely to be single-person householders or single parents, and when they live with other adults, these others were likely not to be in work.

In summary then, while unemployment became geographically more dispersed during the 1980s, it was still socially concentrated among particular groups of the population. The extent to which this social distribution represented a change from what had gone before is the topic of several of the following chapters.

TABLE 2.3. *Household composition by employment status of respondent (%)*

Structure of respondent's household	Employment status of respondent		
	Working	Unemployed	Non-employed
No adults, no children	6	12	6
No adults, children	2	8	6
Other adults not working	17	34	21
Other adults working	75	45	67

Source: The Work Attitudes/Histories Survey 1986.

5. HOW DID THESE SIX LOCALITIES RESEMBLE GREAT BRITAIN AS A WHOLE IN 1985?

In the first part of this chapter we concentrated on the differences between the towns, in an attempt to give the reader a flavour of their very different histories, both past and recent. Many of these differences, however, declined overtime. In fact, it is reassuring to note that when the areas are put together, their diversity adds up to a picture which on average looks not unlike Great Britain taken as a whole.

This is supported by Table 2.4, which examines the performance of the six study areas on a widely used measure of economic success. The index, developed by the Centre for Urban and Regional Development Studies at the University of Newcastle (CURDS), is based on five indicators: population change, past employment change, more recent employment change, unemployment rate, and the percentage of households with two or more cars (Champion and Green 1985).

We can therefore feel fairly confident in pooling the interviews from all six areas, as is done in most of the chapters of this book. When this is not done (as in the discussion of the psychological effects of job insecurity in Burchell's chapter), this is because relevant data was only available for one study area.

Furthermore, there is an important reason why it is not only sensible but actually desirable to treat all the areas together. The work history data used in most of the chapters of this book was collected from the *current* inhabitants of the town. In fact, only

TABLE 2.4. *Six study areas compared with national pattern on indicators of economic health*

Area	Population change 1971–81 (%)	Employment change 1971–8 (%)	Employment change 1978–81 (%)	Unemployment May 85 (%)	Households with 2 cars (%)	CURDS index
Aberdeen	8.9	25.4	11.5	7.3	15.8	0.634
Northampton	18.0	25.0	−2.3	10.9	17.7	0.570
Swindon	9.7	10.9	−1.2	10.6	19.6	0.537
Coventry	−3.3	−3.4	−14.4	15.0	14.2	0.336
Kirkcaldy	−2.3	16.7	−9.8	15.6	10.2	0.367
Rochdale	6.0	−4.9	−4.5	17.9	12.3	0.328
Average of 6 areas[a]	4.8	11.6	−3.4	12.9	15.0	0.462
National average[b]	6.2	8.1	−3.7	13.4	16.1	0.454

Source: Champion and Green 1985.
  [a] Averages of the six study areas are unweighted means of all six areas.
  [b] National averages are medians of all local labour markets.

half of the SCELI respondents had lived in the town since they were 14 years old, as Table 2.5 shows. Furthermore, the towns have had different experiences of in- and out-migration.

The sampling bias created by out-migration cannot be resolved for every town taken on its own, but by treating the localities together the worst biases cancel out, as the areas with net out-migration are balanced by those with net in-migration.

TABLE 2.5. *Migration experience of adults in six study areas (%)*

Area	Lived in town since age 14	Lived in town for last 10 yrs	Moved to town in last 10 yrs
Northampton	41	28	31
Swindon	44	32	24
Aberdeen	53	24	23
Rochdale	50	31	20
Kirkcaldy	54	30	16
Coventry	57	29	14

6. CONCLUSION: CONVERGENCE NOT POLARIZATION

Growing divergence and polarization of economic experience has become a widely repeated theme of economic sociology. Doeringer and Piore (1971) were among the first to propose a theory of segmented labour markets, with a secure primary sector and an increasingly insecure secondary component. More recently, Atkinson and Meager (1986) have suggested that firms increasingly seek flexibility by offering security only to those at the core, leaving the periphery to respond more to the slings and arrows of demand in the market-place. R. E. Pahl (1984) describes the growing polarization of employed and unemployed households, arguing ironically that only the former have access to the informal economy. Geographically, Fothergill and Gudgin (1982), Massey (1984), and Champion *et al.* (1987) all argue that Britain has reversed the trend of the 1960s towards regional convergence of economic structure, since new jobs were being disproportionately concentrated in areas which already had the highest levels of employment.

Close examination of the history of the SCELI areas tells a somewhat different story. The six study towns, which ended the long post-war boom looking strikingly different and bearing the birthmarks of their very different economic histories, emerged from the recession in the 1980s looking much more similar in economic terms. Moreover, when added together the six SCELI areas also provide a very similar economic profile to that of Britain as a whole.

Census of Employment data show that economic convergence was based on three processes. First, the growing homogeneity of the structure of the manufacturing sector in each area. This may reflect a basic process of industrialization, with areas taking off on the basis of success in one particular industry but then gradually diversifying. On the other hand, more ominously, it could suggest the decline of specialist expertise, which could pose long-term problems for a nation reliant on a positive balance of trade. The second process underlying convergence was increasing similarity in the size and composition of the service sectors in the six areas. The third process was a similar rise in the unemployment rates in all areas, whatever their historical experience of economic success. The argument is not that all six areas had converged: in fact they remained strikingly different in many respects in 1986. But the trend of development was towards greater similarity.

Not all economic sociology focuses on processes of polarization. Lash and Urry (1987), for example, argue that the era of organized capitalism (characterized by centralization, technical efficiency, rationalization, and the specialization of industrial locations) may be over. It is being replaced, they suggest, with disorganized capitalism as firms are coming to operate in a global market-place, independently of political control. This is thought to be associated with a decline in both the manufacturing sector and the industrial working class, which in turn accounts for the decline of specialist regional economies. This is supported by the evidence in this chapter. The six study areas looked significantly more like each other at the end of the 1980s than they had done fifteen years previously, let alone fifty years previously. The corollary of the decline of manufacturing has been the rise of the service sector with a much more uniform structure. This is not to suggest, however, that the history of occupational change is an inevitable march from primary through to service sectors, as was argued earlier. Aberdeen, for example, had a large proportion of its labour force in the service sector as long ago as 1931: a reflection of the low level of industrialization and capitalization in Aberdeen at the time.

The remaining chapters in this volume explore the implications of these changes in labour market structure for the suppliers of labour. One problem, of course, is that the manual, often craft, skills which many of the individuals had acquired for particular jobs were no longer required when those jobs disappeared. But the importance of this can be exaggerated. The normal operation of a labour market involves continuous job-changing by employees and job-redefining by employers. The experience of Aberdeen shows how, where necessary, new skills can be instilled through training or by importing them from other areas. While skill level may determine the pecking-order in which people are made redundant, and therefore predict unemployment, several studies of vacancies at the end of the 1980s came to the conclusion that the skill requirements of jobs that were available matched very closely the skills possessed by the unemployed at the time (Meadows *et al.* 1988; IFF Research Limited 1988; Marsh 1990).

The chapters following this will show in various ways how the experiences of the suppliers of labour are formed by these structural features of labour markets rather than by any predispositions of the individuals involved. Indeed, the different job opportunities in the six localities make it abundantly clear how limited a role supply-side factors such as preferences and pre-existing skills are able to play in labour market behaviour.

NOTE

1. Sir Keith Joseph claimed, in an argument reminiscent of Marxist analysis of the effect of low wages among the handloom weavers of the early 19th century, that the influx of immigrants into Britain's obsolete industries in the 1950s and 1960s may have actually contributed to the industry's failure to retool with new more capital intensive production methods (House of Commons 1980; *Guardian*, 24 Jan. 80).

TABLE 2.A1. *Detailed industrial change in the study localities, 1971–1981: percentage of people in employment in each locality employed in different industries*

Industry	1971						
	Aberdeen	Coventry	Kirkcaldy	Northampton	Rochdale	Swindon	GB
Primary	6	3	10	2	*	2	4
Agric., forestry, fishing	5	*	3	2	*	2	2
Mining and quarrying	*	2	7	*	*	*	2
Manufacturing	25	60	39	39	59	46	36
Food, drink, and tobacco	9	1	4	3	1	3	3
Coal, oil, and chemicals	*	*	1	2	1	1	2
Metal manufacture	*	1	1	*	2	2	2
Mechanical instrument engineering	2	8	7	9	11	5	6
Electrical engineering	*	7	6	4	2	13	4
Shipbuilding and marine engineering	2	*	*	*	*	*	1
Vehicles	*	28	*	4	*	15	4
Other metal goods	*	3	1	1	3	1	3
Textiles	2	6	4	*	30	*	3
Clothing, shoes, leather	*	2	2	10	3	2	2
Timber, furniture	2	1	2	1	1	2	1
Paper, printing, publishing	5	1	5	2	2	1	3
Other manufacturing	*	*	5	2	1	1	1
Construction	9	3	7	5	5	5	6
Services	60	34	44	54	35	47	54
Gas, water, electricty	1	1	2	2	1	1	2
Transport	7	3	6	5	3	4	7
Distributive trades	14	8	11	13	9	13	12
Financial and business	3	2	2	5	1	1	4
Professional and scientific	19	10	11	10	11	13	13
Miscellaneous services	12	7	8	7	5	8	9
Public administration, defence	5	3	5	11	4	6	7

1981

Primary	13	2	6	1	*	2	3
Agric., forestry, fishing	3	*	1	1	*	2	2
Mining and quarrying	10	1	5	*	*	*	2
Manufacturing	16	46	34	31	38	27	28
Food, drink, and tobacco	3	1	5	4	*	2	3
Coal, oil, and chemicals	1	*	1	3	2	2	2
Metal manufacture	*	1	2	*	2	*	1
Mechanical instrument engineering	2	8	3	6	8	4	4
Electrical engineering	1	7	8	3	3	5	3
Shipbuilding and marine engineering	2	1	1	*	*	*	1
Vehicles	*	11	*	1	1	8	3
Other metal goods	1	3	1	1	2	1	2
Textiles	1	5	1	*	13	*	1
Clothing, shoes, leather	*	2	1	6	2	1	1
Timber, furniture	1	1	2	1	2	1	1
Paper, printing, publishing	2	1	4	2	2	1	2
Other manufacturing	*	1	3	3	2	1	1
Construction	8	4	7	4	6	6	5
Services	63	49	52	63	55	65	63
Gas, water, electricty	1	1	1	1	*	1	2
Transport	7	3	4	6	6	7	7
Distributive trades	13	10	12	15	13	18	13
Financial and business	4	4	3	8	2	7	6
Professional and scientific	18	12	14	18	18	16	17
Miscellaneous services	14	10	13	10	9	11	12
Public administration, defence	6	8	6	4	5	4	7

Source: Census of Employment, 1971 and 1981.
* ≤ 0.5%.

3

Unemployment in Work Histories

JONATHAN GERSHUNY AND CATHERINE MARSH

1. INTRODUCTION

The Stratification of Unemployment

There are two possible views of the social distribution of unemployment. In the first there is an unemployment 'underclass', made up of those who experience repeated periods of unemployment, starting from their first entry to the work-force, and spanning the whole of their working lives. The Social Change and Economic Life Initiative (SCELI) surveys do not suggest the existence of a substantial group of people who fall into this category. (The nature of our sampling frame, however, excludes the homeless and destitute.) In the second view, there is not an unemployment 'class', but simply a differential proneness to unemployment across the adult population. Unemployment, in this second view, is just one aspect of a broader process of stratification, systematically related to other aspects of people's economic positions—the higher the status in the occupational hierarchy, the less the susceptibility to unemployment. In our data we find strong evidence of this sort of stratification, at least for the historical period covered by our survey. We find, indeed, a substantial growth in the social stratification of unemployment.

The process of stratification works through a pair of linked mechanisms: the effect of the economic characteristics of the individuals' household of origin on the subsequent trajectory of economic positions, and the effect that economic position in turn has on proneness to unemployment. We see that people whose parents' jobs are relatively low in status and badly paid, and who have low levels of education, themselves take relatively low-prestige jobs; and those in low-prestige jobs in turn are very much more likely to become unemployed than those in high-prestige jobs. This is in itself not very surprising. What seems to emerge from our data, however, quite contrary to the optimistic interpretation of British post-war social history, is that both links in this chain of ill fortune seem to have become stronger over the period we study. It appears that, in the UK over the period from the 1950s to the 1980s, the connection between origin and attainment became rather stronger, and rates of unemployment for people at various levels of occupational attainment became more sharply differentiated.

1.1. *Cross-sectional versus Longitudinal Data*

Any random sample survey will provide evidence of the demographic, social, and economic characteristics of the unemployed. By variously cross-tabulating and breaking down standard 'face sheet' variables, we may discover (as we saw in Chapter 2) that the unemployed are disproportionately male, young, or old, but not middle-aged, and less well educated. They also have parents from outside the service class, and their previous jobs tend to be relatively low in pay and status.

These are all 'cross-sectional' characteristics, attributes of a particular group at one particular point in time. But are the associations between these particular characteristics and the circumstances of being unemployed at the date of the survey evidence of the causal process through which the unemployment has come about? For example, is the relatively high rate of unemployment of the young people in the SCELI data simply a consequence of their being young people—or does it result from the historical fact that this particular group of young people entered the labour force in a period when jobs were hard to find?

The one directly observable characteristic of any causal process is its historical sequence. If *A* is causally prior to *B* it must in principle also be temporally prior to *B*. Yet the essential characteristic of standard questionnaire data is precisely its simultaneity. To make adequate causal inferences about historical processes, we need historical data, we need evidence of sequences of events.

We should say immediately that for many purposes cross-sectional data are quite adequate. That a disproportionate number of unemployed people are young and poorly educated may provide quite adequate and proper grounds for the introduction of work-related training programmes as an alternative to unemployment (at least for younger workers), irrespective of whether unemployment is a randomly distributed transient phenomenon or one with long-lasting consequences for individuals' subsequent careers.

But for other purposes cross-sectional evidence may be insufficient. Our particular concern in this chapter is with careers, and specifically with the influence of prior experience in the labour market on subsequent unemployment. We have some cross-sectional evidence that individuals' occupations influence their susceptibility to unemployment, which means that the determinants of occupational status are also in part the determinants of proneness to unemployment; so we make a brief diversion to consider the outlines of a model of occupational careers. But our central interest in this chapter is in unemployment careers. What part does unemployment play in the determination of current unemployment? How does an individual's unemployment history interact with other aspects of personal history and with general (economic) historical events?

A more fundamental understanding of the processes of becoming, remaining, or ceasing to be unemployed can only derive from longitudinal data; it requires the gathering of evidence on individuals' sequences of work experience. This chapter will use the work and life history data collected in 1986 to understand the social processes within which unemployment is embedded.

We adopt what might be described as a 'recursive determination' model. Individuals' current employment position has a number of different characteristics, including employment status (i.e. whether they are currently non-employed, unemployed, or employed, and, if employed, whether employed full- or part-time), sectoral location (the nature of the industry and firm that employs them), and job or occupational level (occupational prestige, relative pay rates, or level of supervisory responsibility). These current characteristics are subject to two classes of determinant: the individuals' initial characteristics (including class of origin and education attainments); and those characteristics that they have accumulated through their previous employment positions. At each point in time, particular aspects of people's current employment positions cohere so as to modify their position in the socio-economic structure; positions in the social structure in turn determine the possibility of future changes in employment position. What we do now becomes what we are; and what we are in part determines what we do next.

The recursive determination model suggests, as we shall see, at least one way in which the rich and complex store of information in the work history narratives may throw light on people's unemployment circumstances. The problem that we start to tackle, in this paper, is that of moving from the level of theoretical assertion to effective and parsimonious (or at least non-wasteful) exploitation of the empirical material.

1.2. Handling Narrative Sequence Data: A 'Symmetrical File' Approach

The technical literature on the analysis of event histories describes a number of rather sophisticated statistical techniques (most notably proportional hazard modelling), combined with quite straightforward data handling processes (Allison 1984; Blosfeld *et al*. 1989). It deals typically with attempts to explain single states or events, classified as binary variables, by a set of prior circumstances. We have, by contrast, attempted to use rather simpler and more familiar statistical techniques (analysis of variance) to consider rather more complex data structures. We take as our dependent variables, not the occurrence of simple binary events to individuals, but the multiple sequences of complex states that constitute an individual's personal history.

The work history data consist of sequential accounts of the respondents' employment 'events' since the age of 14. Each change of employment status (i.e. change into or out of employment, change of employer, or change of job description whilst remaining with the same employer) was counted as a distinct 'event'. And each such event is described in terms of a number of different characteristics (its starting month and year, a precise occupational title, the nature of the employer's business, whether or not the respondents had any supervisory responsibilities, how pay compared with the immediately previous job, hours of work, and so on). Each respondent's work history therefore consists of an irregular number of data fields, each data field referring to a period with a varying duration. And for each respondent, in addition to the work history, there is a life history account, organized in a fixed grid of years detailing housing, educational qualifications, and family circumstances.

The structure of the data is clearly not the simple, symmetrical, constant-numbers-of-variables-per-case format assumed in standard social science data analysis packages. It is, however, possible to distribute this data into a symmetrical 'rectangular' data file. We have constructed an SPSS-X system file (SPSS Inc. 1988), which takes the individual respondent as the case, and contains details of various employment and family attributes for each year the respondent has been in the labour force. Since we know the respondents' ages and years of first entry to the labour force, we can control this data straightforwardly by the historical year of entry to the labour force.

2. MODELLING RECURSIVE DETERMINATION: OCCUPATIONAL STATUS THROUGH THE LIFE-COURSE

2.1. Recursive Models

A recursive model is one in which the causal linkage between any pair of variables goes in one direction only: for any variables A and B in a recursive model, A has consequences for B, B does not have consequences for A. A non-recursive model by contrast is one which includes one or more reciprocal causal paths. Recursive models can be straightforwardly estimated using standard regression techniques. Non-recursive models are in general more difficult to estimate and in some circumstances (specifically, for our purposes, in the case of 'under-identification') cannot be estimated at all.

The distinction between these two classes of model is the statistical principle that underlies the advantages of longitudinal over cross-sectional data. In a cross-sectional data set we may have multiple simultaneous indicators of a range of variables (such as employment and occupation status) without sufficient information to allow us to establish causal hierarchies among them: What proportion of the correlation between the two variables reflects the influence of people's occupational attainment on their risk of unemployment, and what proportion reflects the reciprocal influence of unemployment proneness on occupational attainment? But with longitudinal data we can look for lagged associations among such variables (i.e. between employment status at time $t-1$ and occupational attainment at time t, and between occupational attainment at time $t-1$ and employment status at time t) which (since causality cannot flow backwards in time) are causally unambiguous. Asher (1984: 27) tells us, though with some reservations, that 'one way to handle feedback loops and reciprocal linkages within a recursive model is . . . to collect observations on our variables at repeated points of time'. Longitudinal data are superior to cross-sectional, in part because they provide the necessary statistical basis for causal inferences.

The recursive structure of the models of occupational careers which follow also has clear similarities with the 'causal chain' approach proposed by Blau and Duncan (1967: 177–88) in their classic study of the American occupational structure. They suggested the use of path estimation techniques to compare the relative causal influences of family background, education, and previous occupational attainment on current occupational status at successive points in the life-course. These authors, however, had access only to cross-sectional evidence, and proposed their 'causal chain' as a speculative suggestion of how longitudinal data might be used were it to become available. Their speculation was pursued during the 1970s using longitudinal data originally collected for other purposes (e.g. Featherman 1971; Kelley 1973, using evidence from the Princeton Fertility Study). But their suggestion has not (as far as we can discover) been employed in the analysis of the new 1980s generation of purpose-collected work history data.

2.2. Human Capital

The theoretical orientation described briefly in the first section of this chapter is somewhat akin to the human capital approach (e.g. Bourdieu 1986). 'Capital', used in the context of 'human capital', is of course no more than a metaphor. Indeed, in two somewhat connected ways it is a rather inappropriate metaphor. Capital in the non-metaphoric sense depreciates in use: the act of production itself and of necessity depletes the productive equipment that is employed. Central to the recursive determination approach, however, is the proposition that human 'capital' is on the contrary enhanced by use. Developing skills in production adds to them. And capital is by nature inherently a positive (or at the very least neutral) characteristic; the sorts of acquired characteristics accumulated through the life-course that concern us, however, may as well disqualify as qualify the individual for employment. So we use 'human capital' here as a sort of short-hand for 'the accumulation or achievement of characteristics relevant to employment'.

The initial state characteristics that we have in mind are pretty much the same as those identified by human capital theorists. There are the economically relevant cultural characteristics (the work habits and orientations, the attitudes to risk and mutual responsibility) that the child acquires through the mere fact of membership of the household of origin. There is the network of personal acquaintance and the knowledge of informal procedures for access to advantageous positions (otherwise 'social capital') similarly derived. And there is educational attainment.

This last may be quite directly indicated by the respondents' years of full-time education. But the initial economic culture is more difficult to treat empirically from the data; we can only use parents' occupational status or social class as a rather inadequate proxy. The more strictly social advantages derived from the household of origin are difficult (and in some cases by definition impossible) to identify through a questionnaire. But the outcomes of these special initial advantages (i.e. results of 'string-pulling' and the use of special knowledge of advantageous positions in the economy) might perhaps be manifested in minute variations in the industrial or occupational location of the very first job in the individual's work history. (The location of the first job may also serve as a proxy for the effects of the other characteristics of the household origin.) So, in what follows, the first job characteristics are sometimes used together with, and in one case as a substitute for, variables indicating the individual's initial state.

We might consider the individual's position in the labour market as classified on a multiplicity of dimensions. At any historical point an individual will have a particular employment status (i.e. be full-time, part-time, or non-employed), and in a majority of cases will have a particular occupation, with an associated rate of pay, which is viewed by other members of the society as prestigious or otherwise, and which has certain intrinsic characteristics (tightly controlled or autonomous, with or without supervisory responsibilities, interesting, varied or monotonous). Given our particular concern with unemployment, we take just two of these dimensions: employment status, and occupational prestige (which is, as we shall see, an important predictor of unemployment; we use as the indicator for the latter the respondent's Hope–Goldthorpe occupational prestige score, chosen on the grounds that it correlates reasonably well both with wages and with the intrinsic characteristics).

The current position in the labour market has consequences for the individual's personal characteristics. Each week in employment adds a week to the individual's employment record, a week of unemployment adds to his or her unemployment record; tenure of a job at a particular prestige or pay level for a period similarly adds to the individual's accumulated or achieved characteristics, as does a particular trajectory between different pay or prestige levels over a period.

The achieved or accumulated employment-related characteristics themselves contribute to future employment opportunities. They do so in three ways: (1) individuals' past work experiences directly affect their abilities to perform their current jobs; (2) potential employers (or promotion boards or their functional equivalents) use the accumulated experiences to judge the suitability of candidates for jobs; and (3) occupying particular employment positions may give access to special information about the availability or advantage of future employment opportunities (this also might alternatively be interpreted as an addition to initial social or cultural capital).

The accumulated characteristics may have either positive or negative effects. Just as, in the eyes of potential employers, past achievements may appear to qualify individuals for particular jobs, apparent failures may appear to disqualify them. (These judgements may not necessarily be fair or even rational; to choose a particularly pertinent example, a record of unemployment may be interpreted by potential employers as a 'failure to hold down a job', irrespective of the actual circumstances, and, as such, be used as reason for not appointing that individual.) However, just as successful tenure of a job may improve the individual's technical skills, unemployment may actually erode skills, or unaccustom the individual to workplace disciplines. And a period outside the work-force certainly does remove people from the circuits of information exchange which provide those currently in jobs with privileged access to new and better jobs.

Figure 3.1 illustrates a simple example of a recursive determination model. The three initial state characteristics remain constant through the life-course, having an impact, year by year, on both employment status and occupational level. In year 2, status and employment depend entirely on the initial position, but in

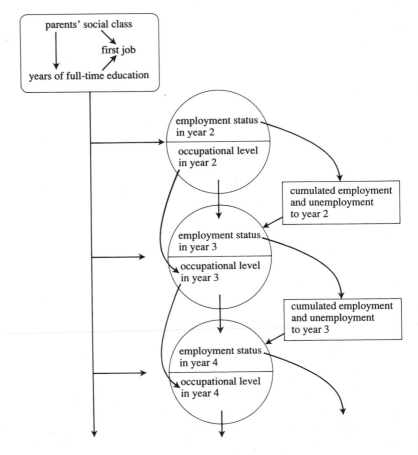

FIG. 3.1. A recursive determination model

year 3 and subsequently, employment level and status are determined through the combined influences of the initial state variables, the cumulated totals of employment and unemployment
experience, and the occupational level in the previous year. Other
versions of such a model which we have experimented with use
occupational trajectories (i.e. the extent of change in occupational
levels through previous periods) and less straightforward cumula-
tions of employment (e.g. total months' unemployment experienced between two and seven years previously as predictors of
the current employment position). The essence of the model is,
however, simply that the current employment circumstances are
determined by the combined influences of the initial conditions
and the previous operations of the model.

2.3. A Life-Course Model of Occupational Attainment

Understanding occupational attainment is not the central purpose of this chapter. It is, however, introduced here because of
the importance of occupation in determining the risk of unemployment. We have used, to summarize occupational position,
the detailed Hope–Goldthorpe occupational prestige score (here-
after 'H–G score'—see Goldthorpe and Hope 1974), which has
the advantage of being a 'continuous' variable, with a roughly
normal distribution, with the very lowest-ranking occupations
scoring in the range of 10 20, and the highest, around 80–90 In
this section we consider the pattern of determination of occupational level through the life-course; in subsequent sections we
consider the effect of occupational level (among other factors) on
the risk of unemployment.

Table 3.1 sets out the results of a hierarchical analysis of variance for men, with H–G score as dependent, carried out for the
age cohort that entered the work-force during the 1960s. The
0.12 value in the year 2 column indicates that 12 per cent of the
variation in the respondents' H–G score may be explained by
their parents' social class. The 0.21 in the 'years of school' row
indicates that 21 per cent of the total year 2 variation in the H–G
score may be explained by respondents' total years of full-time
education. (Note that, while the dependent variable is the continuous H–G prestige scale, we nevertheless use the truncated 7-
category version of the Goldthorpe class scheme—taking the

TABLE 3.1. *Factors accounting for current occupational status level, Hope–Goldthorpe score, men, entry cohort 1961–1971*

	Proportion of variance explained, by year since entry													
	2	3	4	5	6	7	8	9	10	11	12	13	14	15
Initial state variables														
Parents' Goldthorpe class	0.12	0.15	0.13	0.16	0.15	0.16	0.17	0.17	0.16	0.15	0.15	0.14	0.15	0.16
Years of school	0.21	0.20	0.22	0.22	0.21	0.20	0.18	0.20	0.20	0.21	0.21	0.20	0.19	0.21
First job: industry	0.03	0.03	0.03	0.02	0.03	0.02	0.03	0.03	0.03	0.03	0.02	0.03	0.03	0.04
First job: H–G score	0.44	0.32	0.22	0.12	0.09	0.08	0.06	0.06	0.05	0.06	0.07	0.06	0.06	0.06
Current state variables														
Life cycle stage	0.00	0.00	0.00	0.00	0.00	0.00	0.00	0.00	0.00	0.01	0.01	0.01	0.00	0.01
Age of youngest child	0.00	0.00	0.01	0.00	0.01	0.00	0.01	0.00	0.01	0.01	0.01	0.00	0.00	0.01
Unemployed cumulative months		0.00	0.00	0.00	0.00	0.00	0.00	0.00	0.01	0.01	0.01	0.01	0.02	0.02
Non-employed cumulative months		0.00	0.00	0.00	0.00	0.00	0.00	0.00	0.00	0.00	0.00	0.00	0.00	0.01
H–G score last year		0.10	0.16	0.24	0.32	0.36	0.39	0.39	0.37	0.38	0.40	0.43	0.43	0.40
Total variance explained	0.80	0.80	0.77	0.77	0.81	0.83	0.84	0.85	0.84	0.86	0.87	0.88	0.89	0.91

fathers' social class but substituting the mothers' where fathers' class is missing—as an independent variable. The parents' Goldthorpe class is employed as no more than a rough indicator of the 'inherited' human capital—we could alternatively have taken the parents' H–G score, but the use of a categorical variable was marginally more convenient for the hierarchical procedure.)

The variables were entered in the order in which they appear in the table; by choosing this particular hierarchical order among the variates and covariates, we are also asserting a causal sequence. In Table 3.1 we enter class of origin ahead of education, on the assumption that this best reflects the causal priority (if education had been put ahead of class it would have served to explain 30 per cent of the variation while class would have explained less than 5 per cent). Class and education are held jointly to influence the characteristics of the first job. Class, education, and first job are taken together to represent the respondents' initial state; these variables remain unchanged throughout the subsequent life-course. (We will return to life cycle stage and age of youngest child shortly.)

The remaining independent variables change on a year-by-year basis. Again we have good reason to place these at the bottom of the hierarchy of variance explanation. If we were to enter the previous year's H–G score first, it would explain virtually the whole of the variance in this year's H–G score (if for no other reason than that most people do not change their jobs every year). But part of the explanatory power of last year's H–G score may come from the influence of the initial conditions, which are embodied in previous years' H–G scores in just the same way that they influence this year's score. The hierarchical procedure ensures that we see the influence of last year's achieved characteristics, excluding the influence of the initial characteristics which they embody.

Consider the influence of the previous year's H–G score through the first fifteen years in employment. It is not, of course, surprising that last year's score should explain so much of the variance in this year's, nor that the influence increases through the life-course. Quite apart from our recursive determination-based expectation that last year's score provides an indicator of accumulated skills and abilities, we know that job changes are less frequent in later life, so that the growing level of explanation through the life-course reflects in part increasing job stability.

What is noteworthy, however, is the continuing effect of the initial variables. Class of origin explains a more or less constant 15 per cent of the variation in H–G score throughout the life-course, education around 20 per cent, and, after the first few years in which their influence is more a matter of tautology than causality, the first job characteristics explain a regular 10 per cent of the variance. In total, the initial state variables explain a remarkably constant 45 per cent of the variation in occupational prestige through to year 15 (which, since this is the 1960s entry cohort, corresponds to the early to mid-1980s).

Figure 3.2 presents a graphical comparison between these results for the 1966–75 entry cohort and the 1946–55 cohort. Exactly the same pattern of influence is repeated, though the absolute levels of influence of the initial variables are much lower for the earlier cohort. (Presumably this indicates a much higher level of social and occupational mobility through the economi-

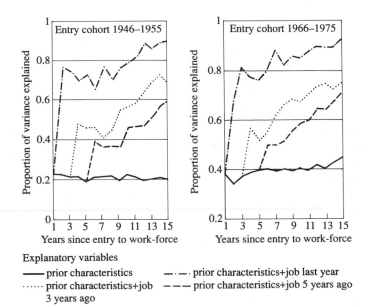

F IG. 3.2. Proportion of variance in Hope–Goldthorpe scale explained by prior characteristics and subsequent experiences, men

cally expanding 1950s and 1960s than in the relatively depressed 1970s and 1980s.) For the two cohorts there is the same pattern of approximately constant effects of the initial state variables, and rising influence of the recursively accumulated or achieved characteristics.

In these calculations we have also included, in addition to the influence of last year's occupational locations, the influence of those of earlier years (three and five years previously), placing these hierarchically ahead of last year's H–G score in the analysis. The earlier years show (though, as we would expect, to a reduced degree) the same pattern of influence rising through the life-course; and in these cases the influence of the accumulated characteristics certainly cannot be entirely explained away as a result of more job stability.

Table 3.2 reproduces the analysis of Table 3.1 for women: again the pattern is repeated. But the effects of class background and education are considerably less marked than in the case of men. We might explain the lesser importance of the initial state variables for women as resulting from their generally intermittent presence in full-time work. Interruptions to employment during the life-course mean that the recursive chain which links the advantages from the household of origin to present advantages is broken. If we step off the career ladder for whatever reason, we must subsequently step on to a lower rung of it. Interestingly, life cycle stage (i.e. family status—single/married/parent) and age of youngest child have no more influence on women's H–G score than they do on men's; perhaps all of the variance associated with these has already been mopped up by class and education, with which they are also correlated. Or perhaps these variables only have their effect on the decision whether to work or not, rather than on what to do once the decision to work has been taken.

3. A PRELIMINARY LIFE-COURSE MODEL OF UNEMPLOYMENT

3.1. A Contingency Approach

It would be convenient if we could simply repeat the same pattern of analysis, substituting months of unemployment in each

TABLE 3.2. Factors accounting for current occupational status level, Hope-Goldthorpe score, women, entry cohort 1961–1971

	Proportion of variance explained, by year since entry													
	2	3	4	5	6	7	8	9	10	11	12	13	14	15
Initial state variables														
Parents' Goldthorpe class	0.10	0.09	0.10	0.09	0.09	0.09	0.10	0.10	0.11	0.10	0.11	0.09	0.09	0.09
Years of school	0.25	0.21	0.20	0.18	0.15	0.16	0.15	0.12	0.12	0.12	0.13	0.13	0.11	0.12
First job: industry	0.03	0.04	0.04	0.04	0.03	0.04	0.04	0.04	0.03	0.03	0.03	0.04	0.04	0.04
First job: H–G score	0.39	0.27	0.22	0.16	0.13	0.12	0.10	0.08	0.07	0.09	0.08	0.06	0.06	0.06
Current state variables														
Life cycle stage	0.00	0.00	0.00	0.01	0.01	0.01	0.01	0.01	0.01	0.01	0.01	0.01	0.01	0.02
Age of youngest child	0.00	0.00	0.00	0.00	0.00	0.01	0.01	0.01	0.02	0.01	0.02	0.01	0.00	0.01
Unemployed cumulative months		0.00	0.00	0.00	0.00	0.00	0.00	0.00	0.00	0.00	0.00	0.00	0.00	0.00
Non-employed cumulative months		0.00	0.00	0.00	0.00	0.00	0.00	0.00	0.00	0.00	0.00	0.00	0.00	0.01
H–G score last year		0.14	0.24	0.29	0.41	0.41	0.43	0.64	0.47	0.48	0.49	0.54	0.50	0.50
Total variance explained	0.77	0.76	0.81	0.77	0.83	0.83	0.83	0.99	0.83	0.85	0.87	0.88	0.83	0.84

year for the H–G score. But unfortunately this is not a very tractable dependent variable for a variance decomposition, since its distribution is very skewed, with the great majority of all SCELI respondents in any one year having no unemployment. We must therefore proceed cautiously, and investigate a conservative transformation of the unemployment variable: truncating it to a dichotomy, taking the value 0 if there is no unemployment in the particular year, and 1 if there is some unemployment.

We could use a multivariate approach to modelling the process of determination of this variable. But, since we shall return to the analysis of variance and the full 'months of unemployment' variable once we have shown the basic structure of the relationship between life experiences and the dichotomous unemployment variable, we shall instead use a much simpler procedure, an independent variable that combines information about the individual's educational level, the occupational level of the first job, and the level of the most recent job. For each year the value of this variable is set to 0 if the respondent's first job had an H–G score below 30, and to 1 if 30 and above; furthermore, if the H–G score of the job held in the immediately previous year was above 40, the derived variable was set to 2; and for all those respondents with some higher education the derived variable was set to 3.

Let us start once more with the men in the 1960s entry cohort. The first part of Table 3.3 shows what happens when the constructed variable is cross-tabulated against a binary variable indicating whether the respondent was unemployed during the relevant year. Consider, for example, year 15, the final column. Of those who entered at a low occupational level and remained there, 24 per cent had an episode of unemployment during the year; of those who entered at a higher level but who subsequently did not rise above an H–G score of 40, 13 per cent were unemployed during the year; of those without higher education who achieved an H–G score above 40 by year 15, 5 per cent were unemployed at some time during this year; and of those with higher education only 1 per cent were unemployed during this year.

This composite constructed 'human capital' variable was put together on a pragmatic basis, dichotomizing each of the component variables at the level that served best to predict unemployment. Nevertheless, the resulting predictors correspond to the

TABLE 3.3. *Risk of unemployment by work history characteristics, men, entry cohort 1961–1971*

	Proportion unemployed, by year since entry														
	1	2	3	4	5	6	7	8	9	10	11	12	13	14	15
Model 1: entry and achieved occupational characteristics (H–G scores)															
Low entry, still < 40	0.07	0.10	0.09	0.05	0.07	0.09	0.08	0.11	0.11	0.13	0.16	0.13	0.23	0.30	0.24
Entered > 40	0.03	0.01	0.03	0.03	0.03	0.05	0.06	0.06	0.06	0.06	0.08	0.07	0.08	0.13	0.13
Low entry, now > 40		0.01	0.01	0.02	0.04	0.04	0.05	0.03	0.03	0.04	0.03	0.04	0.04	0.05	0.05
Some higher education	0.03	0.02	0.01	0.01	0.03	0.02	0.01	0.02	0.01	0.03	0.01	0.03	0.03	0.01	0.01
Mean unemployment	0.03	0.02	0.02	0.02	0.03	0.05	0.04	0.05	0.04	0.05	0.05	0.05	0.07	0.08	0.08
Uncertainty reduction	0.01	0.12	0.08	0.02	0.02	0.02	0.04	0.04	0.05	0.03	0.08	0.03	0.08	0.12	0.10
Significance (chi-squared)	0.21	0.00	0.00	0.41	0.21	0.10	0.04	0.01	0.00	0.01	0.00	0.01	0.00	0.00	0.00
Model 2: entry and achieved occupational characteristics (H–G scores) plus unemployment history															
No unemployment last year															
Low entry, still < 40	0.07	0.07	0.03	0.01	0.04	0.06	0.03	0.05	0.03	0.08	0.06	0.04	0.11	0.13	0.08
Entered > 40	0.03	0.01	0.02	0.02	0.02	0.03	0.02	0.01	0.03	0.03	0.02	0.03	0.02	0.06	0.04
Low entry, now > 40		0.01	0.00	0.02	0.03	0.02	0.03	0.01	0.03	0.02	0.01	0.03	0.03	0.02	0.03
Some higher education	0.03	0.01	0.01	0.01	0.01	0.01	0.00	0.01	0.01	0.02	0.00	0.02	0.01	0.01	0.00
Some unemployment last year															
Low entry, still < 40		0.50	0.63	0.43	0.75	0.43	0.57	0.83	0.63	0.57	0.78	0.60	1.00	0.75	0.58
Entered > 40		0.14	0.67	0.14	0.29	0.57	0.57	0.69	0.57	0.43	0.73	0.53	0.79	0.88	0.75
Low entry, now > 40		0.00	0.50	1.00	0.50	0.67	0.57	0.71	0.17	0.43	0.83	0.63	0.40	0.70	0.50
Some higher education		0.25	0.33	0.50	1.00	0.50	0.33	1.00	0.33	1.00	0.40	0.50	0.75	0.25	1.00
Mean unemployment	0.03	0.02	0.02	0.02	0.03	0.05	0.04	0.05	0.04	0.05	0.05	0.05	0.07	0.08	0.08
Uncertainty reduction	0.01	0.22	0.37	0.20	0.23	0.24	0.34	0.51	0.28	0.23	0.52	0.29	0.43	0.42	0.44
Significance (chi-squared)	0.21	0.00	0.00	0.00	0.00	0.00	0.00	0.00	0.00	0.00	0.00	0.00	0.00	0.00	0.00

principles of advantage in the labour market set out in previous sections. And they do seem to predict successfully. Regularly throughout the first fifteen years of the life-course, those least advantageously placed in terms of their initial characteristics and their subsequent achieved characteristics are reliably the most at risk of unemployment. And the extent of the risk of unemployment of the least well-placed increases remarkably through this period. Admittedly, this was a period of generally rising unemployment: on the basis of this subsample, unemployment (of more than one month's duration) rose from around 2 per cent to 8 per cent over this period. But our least-advantaged group faced a risk of being unemployed, for each of years 9 to 15, around three times as high as the average, while those more advantaged in terms of our predictor variable faced a considerably lower than average risk of unemployment throughout this period.

Variance reduction statistics, as we have suggested, may be inappropriate for a very seriously skewed-distribution binary variable such as the yearly risk of unemployment. But statistics concerning the 'reduction of uncertainty' (i.e. the extent to which the value of the dependent variable may be predicted by knowledge of the independent) are appropriate. The statistics for uncertainty reduction using the composite advantage variables to predict unemployment rates in Table 3.3 are somewhat unstable. But it does seem that towards the end of the period our composite predictor variable reduced uncertainty (i.e. 'explained') about 10 per cent of the occurrence of unemployment.

This leaves quite a lot of the unemployment in our records unexplained. But so far we have not used one of the most promising predictors of unemployment—the respondent's previous history of unemployment. The second part of Table 3.3 shows what happens when we split each of the values of the derived predictor variables by whether or not the respondent was unemployed during the previous year. This new 8-value derived predictor is very much more effective at reducing uncertainty: the coefficient is still unstable, but lies in the range 30–50 per cent. Broken down by previous unemployment in this way, origin and occupational achievement seem to make less difference. Those who entered the work-force in low-status occupations who have not risen far in status terms and who have not had previous experience of unemployment are still more at risk than others who have not previously experienced unemployment—but the margin of difference of risk is now very much smaller.

Or to put it another way, a very large part of what might otherwise appear to be an occupation-related risk of unemployment may alternatively be interpreted as a previous-unemployment-related risk of unemployment. Unemployment is certainly concentrated among those in low-status occupations. But within the low-status occupation groups (as in the other groups), most of those who become unemployed in a given year have also been unemployed in the previous year.

3.2. Some Problems

There are two serious potential problems with the analysis so far. Spells of unemployment often last for more than a year, so what we see here might in principle be no more than a large number of long-term unemployed (just as the power of last year's H–G score for predicting this year's H–G scores must be in part at least related to people staying in the same job). And potentially even more subversive of our argument is the possibility that it is not previous unemployment that determines present unemployment, but some third, so far unidentified, characteristic of the individual that predicts both. We can in fact go some way to resolving both of these issues.

We can cope with the first of them very directly, by excluding the longer-term unemployed. Table 3.4 is constructed by taking, for each year, only those respondents who had some employment during the previous year. Of around 70 unemployed people in this cohort's year 15 in the labour market, 25 are excluded by this procedure. But having extracted all of the cases where the previous year's unemployment continues into the subsequent year, we still find (row 3) a quite considerable reduction in uncertainty about each year as a result of knowing whether or not the respondent was unemployed in the previous year. Part of the result in the previous paragraph reflects no more than the continuity of long-term unemployment; the uncertainty coefficient of 0.22 in year 15 does correspond to a 0.39 coefficient when the longer-term unemployed are included. But more than half the effect remains when they are excluded.

The second objection can only be approached somewhat

TABLE 3.4. *Explanatory power of alternative measures of previous unemployment experience by years since entry to the work-force, men, entry cohort 1961–71 (base excludes cases with continuous unemployment from previous year)*

Experience of unemployment	Uncertainty reduction coefficients, by year since entry								
	7	8	9	10	11	12	13	14	15
1 During previous 5 years	0.17	0.36	0.04	0.10	0.30	0.06	0.19	0.17	0.16
2 Since entry	0.19	0.23	0.04	0.08	0.22	0.04	0.17	0.13	0.13
3 Previous year	0.16	0.41	0.10	0.08	0.35	0.13	0.22	0.16	0.22
Row 1/row 2	0.87	1.55	1.11	1.26	1.36	1.68	1.17	1.31	1.30

indirectly. If indeed there is some such unidentified characteristic, it must presumably inhere in the individual's background or personality, and apply through the life-course. Let us hypothesize that any such hidden characteristic has its effects randomly through the life-course; then, presumably, the more of the previous life we include in a predictor variable for the present state, the better should be our prediction. Compare rows 1 and 2 in Table 3.4. Row 1 uses a binary unemployment experience/no unemployment experience variable calculated from the previous five years as a predictor; row 2 uses a similar variable, but calculated for the whole work history (in both cases excluding, on a yearly basis, those with no employment in the previous year). Contrary to our null hypothesis, the five-year variable performs substantially better than the whole-life variables. (Only in year 7 does the 'whole career' variable perform better than the five-year variable; but the 'whole career' is in this case just six years long.)

We conclude for the moment that part of the explanatory power of recent history of unemployment on current unemployment probably relates more to the unemployment experience itself, or to the circumstances that surrounded it, than to some other prior state of the individual. We presume the existence of some mechanism of disqualification of the sort we have previously outlined. The evidence is not yet conclusive: we need in particular to attach some extra controls to allow for the influence of historical changes in labour demand in the economy.

But though we cannot yet be completely certain of the mechanism, at the level of description, we do certainly have a definite conclusion: men of the 1962–71 entry cohort who have been recently unemployed are greatly more at risk than men of otherwise broadly similar occupational background who have not been recently unemployed. Unemployment is thus concentrated more narrowly than on simple occupational groups. And the result is not restricted to this entry cohort. Table 3.5 estimates the same model over the longer time span available for the 1946–56 entry cohort. Very similar results emerge: it is those who have been unemployed who become unemployed.

3.3. An Aside: Women and the Family Cycle

We had expected to find very different results for women's unemployment. After all, in our recall data we have only people's own descriptions of their employment status. Very few men of working age ever describe themselves as non-employed, presumably because of the very strong normative pressures towards employment. Women, by contrast, are subject to, at the least, conflicting cross-pressures towards paid jobs and family care. We had assumed that periods outside employment would be retrospectively classified, in women's accounts, largely into periods of non- rather than unemployment. Indeed non-employment does figure much more strongly in women's accounts than in men's.

We can nevertheless reproduce something very similar to the men's unemployment model from the women's data. The effect of occupational location is less marked (this may well turn out to be connected with the previously noted relative disjunction between women's initial state variables and current occupational location). But the effect of past unemployment follows a very similar pattern to that of men (Table 3.6).

We can impose the male model, but this may not be appropriate. Precisely because women may choose not to define themselves as unemployed, precisely because there is an alternative definition available for a period outside paid employment, so unemployment must have a different meaning for women. Rather than looking at unemployment in its conventional sense, it may be more sensible to consider male unemployment in parallel with female non-employment.

Just as men's employment status reflects achieved characteristics, so does women's. The most relevant characteristics for men are occupational; for women, occupational characteristics may be less important, but family responsibilities may be more so. Table 3.7 has the same structure as Tables 3.3 and 3.5, but replaces occupational position as predictor with the age of the youngest co-resident child as a proxy for the stage in the family cycle.

The results produced are by no means unfamiliar. Women with no children have jobs, women with children are less likely to have them. The high rate of non-employment of women with co-resident children in their first year in the work-force probably relates to younger siblings in the household of origin. The apparently relatively high rate of employment of women with children under one year old may reflect employment before birth (we have no information on the dates of children's births).

But otherwise the pattern is just what we expect: full-time

TABLE 3.5. *Risk of unemployment by work history characteristics, men, entry cohort 1946–1956*

	Unemployment rate by years since entry														
	1	2	3	4	5	6	7	8	9	10	11	12	13	14	15
Model 1: entry and achieved occupational characteristics (H–G scores)															
Low entry, still < 40	0.04	0.04	0.08	0.03	0.05	0.04	0.06	0.04	0.04	0	0	0.02	0.04	0.04	0.02
Entered > 40	0.02	0.02	0.01	0.01	0.00	0.02	0.01	0.03	0.00	0.03	0.03	0.03	0.03	0.02	0.03
Low entry, now > 40	0.01	0.01	0	0.02	0.02	0.01	0.01	0.01	0.01	0.01	0.01	0.00	0.01	0.02	0.01
Some higher education	0.05	0.02	0.03	0.03	0.03	0.02	0.02	0	0	0	0	0.03	0	0.02	0.02
Grand mean	2.6	2.2	2	1.8	1.8	1.6	1.6	2	0.8	1.6	1.4	1.8	1.8	2	1.8
Significance (chi-squared)	0.21	0.48	0.00	0.52	0.05	0.49	0.09	0.42	0.08	0.22	0.31	0.30	0.22	0.68	0.57
Uncertainty reduction	0.02	0.02	0.13	0.02	0.08	0.03	0.05	0.04	0.10	0.07	0.07	0.05	0.06	0.01	0.02
Model 2: entry and achieved occupational characteristics (H–G scores) plus unemployment history															
No unemployment last year															
Low entry, still < 40	0.04	0.00	0.03	0.00	0.02	0.00	0.06	0.00	0.00	0.00	0.00	0.02	0.02	0.00	0.00
Entered > 40	0.02	0.00	0.00	0.00	0.00	0.02	0.01	0.02	0.00	0.02	0.02	0.01	0.01	0.00	0.02
Low entry, now > 40	0.00	0.00	0.00	0.01	0.01	0.00	0.01	0.00	0.00	0.01	0.01	0.00	0.00	0.01	0.00
Some higher education	0.05	0.00	0.03	0.02	0.04	0.02	0.02	0.00	0.00	0.00	0.00	0.03	0.00	0.02	0.02
Some unemployment last year															
Low entry, still < 40	1	1	1	0.50	1	0.67	0.00	0.67	0.67	0.00	0.00	0.60	1	1	0.33
Entered > 40	1	1	0.43	0.67	0.50	0.00	0.00	1	0.00	1	0.33	0.50	0.60	0.50	0.33
Low entry, now > 40	1	1		1	0.67	0.50	0.50	1	0.33	0.50	1		1	1	0.67
Some higher education	0.33	0.33	0	0.50	0.00	0.00	0.00	0.00				0.00	0.00		0.00
Grand mean	2.6	2.2	2	1.8	1.8	1.6	1.6	2	0.0	1.6	1.4	1.8	1.8	2	1.8
Significance (chi-squared)	0.21	0	0	0	0	0	0	0	0	0	0	0	0	0	0

	16	17	18	19	20	21	22	23	24	25	26	27	28	29	30
Model 1: entry and achieved occupational characteristics (H–G scores)															
Low entry, still < 40	0.03	0	0.03	0.03	0.03	0	0	0.01	0.04	0.03	0.04	0.04	0.03	0.08	0.09
Entered > 40	0.00	0.02	0.02	0.02	0.01	0.03	0.03	0.03	0.03	0.03	0.02	0.04	0.04	0.04	0.08
Low entry, now > 40	0.00	0.00	0.01	0.00	0.01	0.01	0.01	0.01	0.02	0.01	0.01	0.03	0.02	0.01	0.03
Some higher education	0	0	0	0.02	0	0	0.03	0.02	0.02	0.02	0	0.03	0.05	0.03	0.03
Grand mean	1.2	1	1.4	1.4	1.2	1.4	2	1.8	2.6	2.6	2.2	4.2	4.0	4.7	6.5
Significance (chi-squared)	0.11	0.21	0.47	0.42	0.46	0.21	0.20	0.63	0.75	0.84	0.44	0.99	0.91	0.54	0.40
Uncertainty reduction	0.10	0.09	0.04	0.04	0.04	0.08	0.06	0.02	0.01	0.01	0.04	0.00	0.00	0.01	0.01
Model 2: entry and achieved occupational characteristics (H–G scores) plus unemployment history															
No unemployment last year															
Low entry, still < 40	0.00	0.00	0.02	0.02	0.01	0.00	0.00	0.01	0.03	0.00	0.00	0.01	0.01	0.05	0.05
Entered > 40	0.01	0.01	0.01	0.01	0.01	0.02	0.02	0.02	0.00	0.02	0.01	0.03	0.01	0.02	0.05
Low entry, now > 40	0.00	0.00	0.01	0.00	0.01	0.01	0.01	0.01	0.02	0.01	0.01	0.03	0.02	0.01	0.03
Some higher education	0.00	0.00	0.00	0.02	0.00	0.00	0.03	0.00	0.00	0.02	0.00	0.03	0.02	0.00	0.02
Some unemployment last year															
Low entry, still < 40	0.00	1	1	0.50	1	0.00	0.60	0.33	1	0.67	0.75	0.67	0.25	1	0.50
Entered > 40	0.80	0.40	0.25	0.67	0.00	0.50			1	0.40	0.33	0.50	0.75	0.57	0.75
Low entry, now > 40	0.00	1		0.50	0.50	0.00	0.00	0.50	0.50	0.50	1	0.50	0.71	0.75	0.83
Some higher education	0.00				0.00			0.50	1	0.00	0.00		1	0.67	0.50
Grand mean	1.2	1	1.4	1.4	1.2	1.4	2	1.8	2.6	2.6	2.2	4.2	4	4.7	6.5
Significance (chi-squared)	0	0	0	0	0	0	0	0	0	0	0	0	0	0	0
Uncertainty reduction	0.54	0.49	0.20	0.43	0.27	0.14	0.22	0.26	0.57	0.28	0.47	0.15	0.49	0.41	0.29

TABLE 3.6. *Explanatory power of alternative measures of previous unemployment experience by years since entry to the work-force, women, entry cohort 1961–1971* (base excludes cases with continuous unemployment from previous year)

Experience of unemployment	uncertainty reduction coefficients, by year of entry								
	7	8	9	10	11	12	13	14	15
1 During previous 5 years	0.31	0.16	0.24	0.15	0.27	0.17	0.17	0.13	0.10
2 Since entry	0.28	0.17	0.23	0.14	0.24	0.13	0.13	0.08	0.13
3 Previous year	0.22	0.17	0.35	0.28	0.33	0.22	0.23	0.23	0.16
Row 1/row 2	1.11	0.94	1.07	1.12	1.16	1.29	1.30	1.49	0.76

TABLE 3.7. *Employment rate by family characteristics, women, entry cohort 1961–1971*

	Employment rate, by year of entry														
	1	2	3	4	5	6	7	8	9	10	11	12	13	14	15
Model 1: family characteristics															
No children	0.97	0.96	0.95	0.94	0.94	0.93	0.94	0.94	0.94	0.93	0.94	0.94	0.91	0.88	0.87
Children aged <1	0.69	0.67	0.63	0.53	0.44	0.45	0.32	0.40	0.41	0.34	0.35	0.31	0.34	0.39	0.38
Children aged 1–5	0.80	0.39	0.37	0.41	0.37	0.32	0.33	0.35	0.36	0.34	0.33	0.34	0.37	0.37	0.37
Children aged 5–10	1.00	1.00	1.00	1.00	1.00	1.00	0.92	0.75	0.67	0.71	0.66	0.63	0.65	0.68	0.69
Mean employment	0.96	0.94	0.90	0.84	0.77	0.70	0.65	0.63	0.59	0.55	0.53	0.53	0.55	0.57	0.57
Uncertainty reduction	0.04	0.16	0.25	0.27	0.32	0.33	0.35	0.30	0.25	0.24	0.23	0.20	0.14	0.12	0.11
Significance (chi-squared)	0.00	0.00	0.00	0.00	0.00	0.00	0.00	0.00	0.00	0.00	0.00	0.00	0.00	0.00	0.00
Model 2: family characteristics plus employment history															
No employment last year															
No children		0.12	0.19	0.16	0.16	0.14	0.22	0.16	0.29	0.23	0.38	0.11	0.10	0.33	0.15
Children aged <1		0.00	0.00	0.15	0.05	0.02	0.04	0.07	0.08	0.02	0.04	0.04	0.00	0.07	0.00
Children aged 1–5		0.00	0.22	0.20	0.14	0.11	0.13	0.15	0.12	0.10	0.11	0.14	0.16	0.15	0.14
Children aged 5–10							0.67	0.36	0.20	0.33	0.16	0.16	0.22	0.17	0.24
Some employment last year															
No children		0.99	0.99	0.98	0.98	0.98	0.98	0.99	0.97	0.97	0.99	0.99	0.97	0.96	0.97
Children aged <1		0.75	0.72	0.65	0.62	0.67	0.60	0.72	0.64	0.67	0.63	0.70	0.79	0.62	0.66
Children aged 1–5		0.54	0.45	0.55	0.57	0.57	0.63	0.70	0.74	0.71	0.77	0.73	0.81	0.82	0.82
Children aged 5–10		1.00	1.00	1.00	1.00	1.00	1.00	0.95	0.92	0.97	0.89	0.94	0.93	0.98	0.94
Mean employment		0.94	0.90	0.84	0.77	0.70	0.65	0.63	0.59	0.55	0.53	0.53	0.55	0.57	0.57
Uncertainty reduction		0.55	0.53	0.49	0.54	0.56	0.56	0.53	0.49	0.52	0.52	0.51	0.48	0.52	0.49
Significance (chi-squared)		0.00	0.00	0.00	0.00	0.00	0.00	0.00	0.00	0.00	0.00	0.00	0.00	0.00	0.00

employment until the start of the family cycle, then withdrawal, and gradual re-entry. For the earlier years of the life-course, family responsibilities explain a substantial part of the variation in women's employment. This declines progressively (from year 7 in Table 3.7), while the growth in the uncertainty reduction coefficient for the model that takes last year's employment as a predictor suggests that an increasing proportion of the variation is explained by women's accumulated work experience. Again, a recursive process: those who are in the work-force remain in it, and those outside it are progressively more unlikely to re-enter.

4. A BROADER MODEL OF UNEMPLOYMENT IN THE LIFE-COURSE

4.1. Using More of the Data

We have established in a preliminary manner that unemployment in the immediately previous year considerably increases the likelihood of unemployment in each current year, and that the previous year's unemployment experience is a better predictor of the current year's than either the cumulated unemployment experience since entering the work-force, or unemployment experience at the beginning of the working life. We can now take the argument rather further, and try to apportion responsibility for variation in months of unemployment per year among various antecedent circumstances; we can consider the relative contribution of immediate and more distant unemployment experience, occupational position, and the effect of the external economic condition as reflected in the national unemployment rate. What is the relative importance of immediate as opposed to more distant unemployment experience?

Rather than adopting the full causal modelling path estimation approach, we have again used the rather more straightforward procedure of hierarchical variance decomposition. We know that part of the power that the recent unemployment record has to explain current unemployment derives from the more distant history of unemployment. So if, in our hierarchical model, we first extract all of the variance in current unemployment that derives from the distant history, we will capture both the direct effect of the early unemployment history on current unemployment, and its indirect effect via more recent unemployment history. And the residual association between the recent history of unemployment and the current unemployment will then exclude the effect of the most distant history.

We can use similar arguments for placing other variables within a hierarchical sequence. We expect that occupational status will explain some of the variation in unemployment, and we have already seen that current occupational status is strongly associated with previous educational status, and also the 'initial state' characteristics at entry (education, parents' occupations, etc.). Part of the explanatory power of the unemployment history (recent and more distant) may thus derive ultimately from occupation-related factors. We have seen that unemployment history has very little effect on occupational status. So, by giving hierarchical priority to occupational status over the unemployment history variables, we can estimate the effect of the latter net of the effects of the former.

In a somewhat analogous way, the influence of current economic circumstances should also be given hierarchical precedence over unemployment history in our model. The same economic depression or period of high unemployment may persist over a number of years, so that its effects on unemployment in a given year may be in part embodied within those of the recent unemployment history. To avoid this possibility we extract all the variance associated with economic conditions before we enter unemployment history.

Figures 3.3 and 3.4 summarize the outcomes of a series of analyses of variance, using the work history data summarized on a yearly basis. They show, for each successive year in the labour force throughout the working life, the proportion of the variation in (log) months of unemployment that can be explained by various factors. We have used the 'hierarchical procedure' for each year, first extracting all the variation in unemployment associated with the then current national labour market conditions, as indicated by an estimate of the national unemployment rate (remember that the SCELI respondents might have entered the labour force at any time between the early 1940s and the late 1980s). Then we extract all the variance associated with the respondent's own occupational status in the previous year (which will in turn

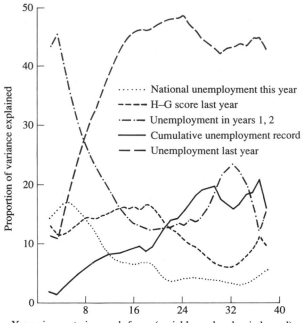

FIG. 3.3. Proportion of variance in (logged) months of unemployment, men, all cohorts

embody part at least of the influence of the 'initial state' conditions and subsequent occupational trajectory). We then extract the variance associated with early unemployment history, and finally that associated with recent employment history. (These and following plots summarize the results of very many variance decompositions—one for each successive year after entry to the work-force. Because of the large size of the sample, all of the R^2 coefficients plotted in Figures 3.3 and 3.4 are significant at the 0.05 level, and the overwhelming majority at the 0.001 level, so we do not report significance levels individually.)

We should treat the pictures with some care. They would seem to provide evidence of clear and dramatic shifts in the balance of influences on unemployment through the life cycle. But in fact the meaning of the pictures is much more obscure than at first

FIG. 3.4. Proportion of variance in (logged) months of unemployment, women, all cohorts

appears. The graphs summarize the influences on susceptibility to unemployment for the whole sample for the whole of their working lives up to the time of the interview. But the members of the sample have lived varying distances through their working lives: some have worked for forty or more years, others for five years or fewer. So the coverage, the evidential basis, for the figure varies systematically from the left-hand side of the graph to the right-hand side. The left-hand side draws on evidence from virtually the whole sample, since all but a few of the respondents have two or more years of work history; but only very few have forty or more years of work, and the right-hand side represents a much diminished minority of the sample.

The size of the sample declines continuously from left to right. And similarly the range of years (and hence the mix of historical

circumstances) from which the evidence is drawn changes systematically from the left-hand side to the right-hand side. The first
part of the life cycle in the figure is estimated from evidence
stemming from dates ranging from the mid-1940s to the mid-
1980s, while the last part of the life cycle is estimated from data
from the mid-1980s alone. And similarly the mix of respondents
differs systematically from the left-hand side to the right-hand
side: the left includes data describing people who entered the
work-force at any time between the 1940s and the 1980s, while
the right includes only data from people who entered the work-
force in the 1940s. So while differences in the pattern of
influences on unemployment between the left and right sides of
Figure 3.3 may reflect life trends, they may just as well reflect differences between the cohorts or generations. For example, if
there are patterns of behaviour specific to 1960s flower children,
these will be represented on the left but not on the right. Or the
apparent life trends may result from the differential representation of historical events; we know, for example, that the estimates for the mid-part of the working life are based on evidence
that combines the booming 1960s, the depressed 1970s, and the
Thatcher 1980s, whereas the evidence for the last part of the
working life is drawn exclusively from the 1980s.

4.2. *Separating the Sample by Cohort*

We must therefore consider the extent to which these pictures do
genuinely represent patterns of influence on unemployment
through the life-course, by separating the sample into cohorts of
entry to the work-force. (We should parenthetically note that
even if we were to look separately at each successive year of
entry, we still would not have an accurate representation of the
working life, since the retrospective nature of the SCELI data
means that we know nothing about entrants to the work-force in
a particular year who did not survive to the time of the survey in
1986.) We use four decade cohorts in what follows: respectively
1946–55 entrants, 1956–65, 1966–75, and 1976–85. (Though, as
we shall see, this last provides information of only rather limited
usefulness since, in all of these plots, the samples are progressively curtailed through the final ten years of the life-course, as
respondents' accounts reach the date of the SCELI interview. It

might perhaps have been preferable to have taken 1940 as our starting-point so as to provide more definition for the final group of labour force entrants. But on balance this consideration was outweighed by a desire to avoid the complications of the labour market in wartime.)

4.3. Current Economic Circumstances

Figure 3.5 is provided as an example of an unsmoothed plot of changing patterns of variance explanation through the working life-course. The first variable entered in the hierarchical analysis is the indicator of current labour market conditions (the year's median unemployment rate). Of course, for any one year, this is a constant. But each decade cohort contains people who entered

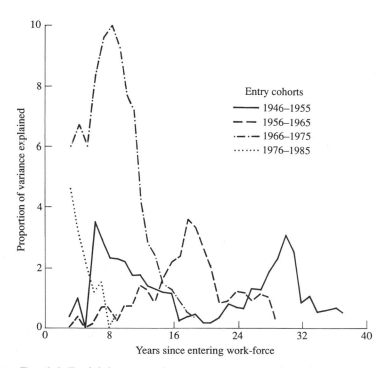

FIG. 3.5. Explaining unemployment, men, proportion of variance explained by national unemployment this year (unsmoothed)

the work-force in any one of ten years, so, at any given year in the working life for any cohort, there will be a range of ten calendar years' unemployment rates. (The range of this variation differs between the various historical periods we are considering, which leads to some minor and, as we shall show, easily resolvable complications of interpretation.) What we see in Figure 3.5 can plausibly be summarized as long-term oscillations through the life-course, together with some short-term instability of estimates, yearly departures from the longer-term oscillations. We argue that the latter are essentially random perturbations resulting from small sample size: this assumption is our justification for smoothing the curves. Figure 3.6 is the smoothed version of the same plot: its essential features are unchanged.

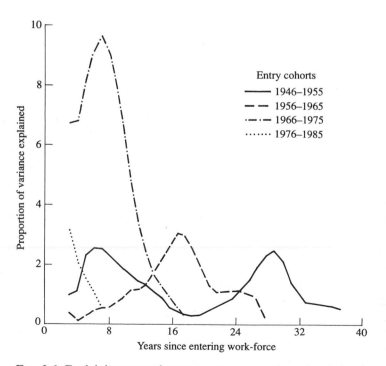

FIG. 3.6. Explaining unemployment, men, proportion of variance by national unemployment this year (smoothed)

What appeared from the general sample plot to be a straight-forwardly declining influence of general economic conditions through the life-course is, once broken down by cohort, revealed to be very much more complex. Clearly this is no longer to be interpreted as a life cycle effect: the changes in the importance of economic conditions come at widely differing life stages. For men in the 1946–55 and the 1966–75 entry cohorts, the importance of national unemployment rate seems to reach a peak after around five years in the labour force. For men in the other two cohorts, there appears to be a trough at exactly the same point in the life-course.

An alternative hypothesis suggests itself: the peaks in Figure 3.6 are approximately ten years apart, and the cohorts are successive decades: perhaps the oscillation reflects historical events. Figure 3.7 is constructed by shifting the previous plots horizontally across the graph. So the *x*-axis now refers to the cohorts' median historical dates rather than years in the work-force, and the graph shows the historically simultaneous experiences for the successive cohorts. Figure 3.8 provides equivalent estimates for the SCELI women.

There are various potential ways of interpreting these sorts of results: perhaps they result from an interaction between age or cohort and historical circumstances. Consider: if, when we plotted the men's curves by historical date, the oscillations had mapped on to each other precisely (i.e. the amplitude of the oscillations for the cohorts had been the same), we would have concluded that there was a simple historical effect—that the economic circumstances at a particular historical juncture have a particularly marked effect on unemployment. Figure 3.7 shows two historical periods, the mid-1950s and the mid-1970s, in which the national unemployment rate seems to have a particularly strong influence on our respondents' unemployment. But plainly the amplitudes of the curves differ: men of different ages (who are also members of different entry cohorts—we cannot of course distinguish between these) are affected to different extents. We can conclude without any qualification that the younger men, from the more recent cohorts, are more affected by historical circumstances than are the older.

For women, the picture is rather different. Successive cohorts seem to have generally increasing sensitivity to the general

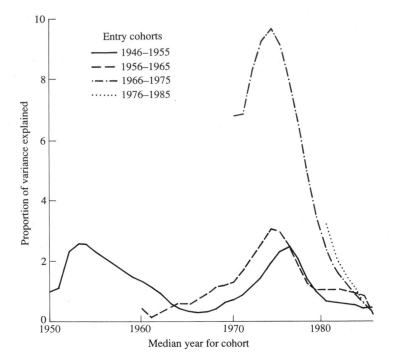

FIG. 3.7. Explaining unemployment, men, proportion of variance
explained by national unemployment this year (smoothed)

unemployment level. This is presumably a consequence of a secular trend of increasing participation in the work-force in the successive cohorts, combined with generally worsening economic
conditions through the 1970s. There is if anything, at least for
the later women's entry cohorts, a declining trend through the
life-course; perhaps women are increasingly willing to categorize
themselves as unemployed rather than non-employed (or the
presence of young children during the earlier part of the working
life may provide an alternative basis for self-definition). Such a
life-course evolution could certainly reduce the apparent effect of
the general economic conditions on variations in unemployment.

The late 1970s peak in the explanatory power of economic circumstances for men's unemployment may be in part at least an
artefact of our estimation procedure as combined with our choice

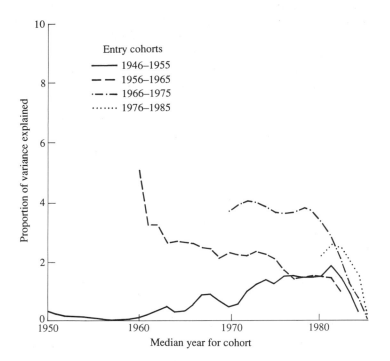

FIG. 3.8. Explaining unemployment, women, proportion of variance explained by national unemployment this year (smoothed)

of decade groups. Each point on figures 3.7 and 3.8 contains data from a spread of ten years. The ten-year spreads during the later 1970s will include a very wide range of national unemployment rates, from around 5 to 13 per cent—a greater range than at any other post-war period. Where an independent variable has more variability, it has (*ceteris paribus*) the potential to explain more of a dependent. So perhaps the late 1970s peak in Figure 3.7 should not be taken too seriously.

But even ignoring the peak, we are still left with two clear conclusions. What looked like a life cycle effect from the plot of the whole sample (in Figure 3.3) is clearly nothing of the sort. And, year by year (that is, for any given level of variation of the national unemployment rate over the relevant ten-year period), people from the more recent entry cohorts are more severely affected by current economic conditions than are those from more distant entries; the younger, the harder hit by unemployment. The apparent life-course diminution of the effect of economic circumstances in the whole-sample plots results from the continuous reduction in the proportional contribution of younger people as we move from the left-hand side of the plot.

This result is not, of course, particularly surprising or unfamiliar. But, having accounted for the effects of current unemployment rates in our hierarchical variance decomposition, we can assume that the effect of the other variables are not reflections of current economic circumstances.

4.4. Occupational Status

The next variable entered in the hierarchical analysis is occupational status (Figures 3.9 and 3.10).

The whole-sample plot (Figure 3.3) suggested that the pattern of influence of occupational status on men's unemployment is irregular, but broadly constant throughout the life-course. Figure 3.9 reveals this again as an artefact. When we separate the cohorts, two clear trends emerge. We see that in each age cohort there is a rising trend, with occupational status increasing its importance as a determinant of unemployment through the life-course. And for the successive cohorts there is a clear upward shift in importance of occupational status. At each stage in the life-course, the current occupation explains an increasing proportion of the variation in unemployment as we move from the older to the more recent entry cohorts. For some of the more recent cohorts, this variable comes to explain 30 or 40 per cent of all variation in months of unemployment per year. (The cohort curves in Figure 3.9 may also be plotted on a historic axis as in Figure 3.7. If we do so we find that the early years of the more recent cohorts map directly on to the later years of the older cohorts; so an alternative interpretation of Figure 3.9 is a simple historical trend, with a continuously rising importance for occupational attainment.)

Table 3.8 gives the estimated mean months of unemployment associated with a range of H–G scores. (These are estimated through the regression-derived MCA procedure, as part of a model including the same variables as in the hierarchical variance

FIG. 3.9. Explaining unemployment, men, proportion of variance
explained by Hope–Goldthorpe score last year

decomposition described in this section.) We see that the effects
of occupational status are effectively linear, or at least monotonic: the higher the occupational status, the less unemployment
per year; within each entry cohort the negative effect of low
occupational status increases regularly with years in the work-
force; and, at any particular age, the absolute difference between
the low and the high occupational attainment grows very substantially through the successive cohorts. So, for example, after
eight years in the work-force, and controlling for the effects of
the other variables in the model, those members of the earliest
cohort (1946–55) whose H–G score in year 7 was below 30, had
on average 0.54 months of unemployment; those whose H–G
score was between 30 and 60 had 0.14 months of unemployment;
and those with an H–G score above 60 had 0.8 months of

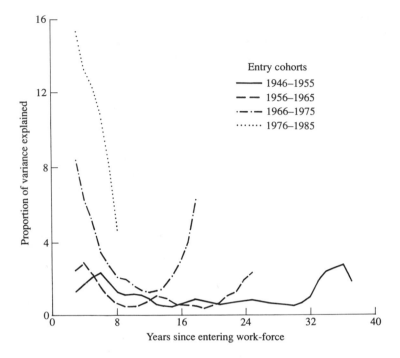

FIG. 3.10. Explaining unemployment, women, proportion of variance
explained by Hope–Goldthorpe score last year

unemployment. For the 1956–65 entry cohort the equivalence
figures were 0.88 months, 0.22 months, and 0.10 months respectively. For the 1966–75 entry we see 2.3 months, 0.58 months,
and 0.34 months respectively; and for the most recent (1976–85),
3.64 months, 1.48 months, and 0.74 months respectively. This
table gives the clearest possible demonstration of the growing
importance of occupational status in the determination of unemployment, through the life-course and over time. In absolute
terms, for the first of the entry cohorts, the difference in mean
yearly time in unemployment between the lowest and the highest
H–G groups could be measured in fractions of a month; for the
last two the difference can be measured in whole months.

The situation for women (Figure 3.10) is as different as could
be imagined. Occupational status is of declining importance in
explaining women's unemployment through the first part of the

TABLE 3.8. *Estimated mean months of unemployment per year by occupational status*

	Months of unemployment, by years since entry to the labour force									
	2	3	4	5	6	7	8	9	10	11
Entry cohort 1946–55										
H–G score										
Below 30	0.20	0.20	0.24	0.36	0.32	0.36	0.54	0.74	0.50	0.48
30 to 60	0.04	0.08	0.08	0.08	0.12	0.14	0.14	0.14	0.18	0.22
Above 60	0.04	0.06	0.04	0.04	0.08	0.08	0.08	0.10	0.16	0.14
Entry cohort 1956–65										
H–G score										
Below 30	0.26	0.38	0.42	0.46	0.58	0.74	0.88	1.26	1.18	1.12
30 to 60	0.06	0.08	0.10	0.12	0.18	0.20	0.22	0.24	0.34	0.38
Above 60	0.06	0.04	0.06	0.06	0.06	0.10	0.10	0.10	0.10	0.18
Entry cohort 1966–75										
H–G score										
Below 30	0.88	1.08	1.30	1.04	1.76	1.94	2.30	2.32	2.60	3.20
30 to 60	0.16	0.22	0.28	0.50	0.48	0.58	0.58	0.74	0.86	0.78
Above 60	0.16	0.22	0.24	0.24	0.24	0.26	0.34	0.38	0.36	0.38
Entry cohort 1976–85										
H–G score										
Below 30	1.68	2.08	2.46	2.80	2.88	3.24	3.64			
30 to 60	0.58	0.72	0.86	1.10	1.34	1.28	1.48			
Above 60	0.46	0.46	0.50	0.56	0.68	0.68	0.74			

life-course, falling to nearly zero. There does, however, seem to be a historical effect; the three oldest cohorts show an increasing importance of occupational status starting from the late 1970s.

The difference between men and women here is dramatic, and all the more surprising since the historical increase in the level of women's attachment to the labour force (as documented by Dex 1988*b*, chapter 1), combined with rapidly increasing level of women's qualifications, might have been expected to lead to a pattern of increase of occupational status faster than that of men. There are various possible reasons for the gender difference: there may be an interaction between expressed orientations to work and occupational status (e.g. women with low occupational status being more willing to define themselves as non- rather than unemployed); or women's characteristically interrupted careers may break the link between occupational status and unemployment; or perhaps the constraints on women's working hours (resulting from their households' division of domestic tasks), which dominate job choices for certain age-groups, have this effect. Here is certainly fertile ground for the cultivating of a very mixed crop of hypotheses.

4.5. *Unemployment History*

Having extracted the variance associated with general circumstances and with the individual's occupational status, we can now turn to the question of unemployment history. Here the whole-sample plot does turn out to provide a not-too-misleading summary.

Figures 3.11 and 3.12 show the effects of a very early experience of unemployment. For women, the successive cohorts show a reasonably regular decline in the importance of early unemployment experience. Of course, in the first years of the working life, the early experience of unemployment is also the recent experience, and perhaps the appropriate summary is that the experience of unemployment in the first two years explains quite a substantial part of the subsequent unemployment experience of the oldest cohort of women, but this proportion falls quite markedly for subsequent cohorts, to the point that it appears likely to explain no more than 5 per cent of the variance of unemployment for the more recent cohorts. The earliest cohort of

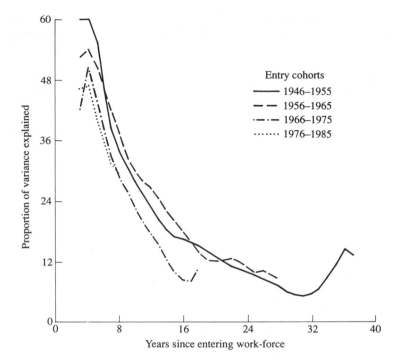

FIG. 3.11. Explaining unemployment, men, proportion of variance
explained by unemployment in years 1 and 2

men shows a rather lower importance for early unemployment
experience through the life-course than does the equivalent group
of women, and the data also show evidence of a decline in the
importance of this variable through the cohorts (though, starting
from a lower level, the decline is less marked for men than for
women). For men overall, the impact of early unemployment
experience is really quite limited, falling to around 10 per cent of
the variance by year 15 in the working life. This effect is small,
but it is still present, and statistically significant, throughout the
life-course. So an alternative interpretation of the evidence might
be that a very small minority are subject to a lifelong impact of
early unemployment.

Figure 3.13 adds the variance associated with the accumulated
months of unemployment up to the previous year to the variance

associated with unemployment in the first two years to provide a broad index of the importance of longer-term unemployment experience. For men it appears that the importance of these factors reduces throughout the working life-course, and has fallen quite remarkably in successive cohorts. The recursive structure of our argument provides a perfectly straightforward potential explanation for these phenomena. We have seen that the importance of occupational status in explaining susceptibility to unemployment is growing both through the life-course and in successive cohorts. There is necessarily an equivalent growth in the importance of occupational status in explaining peoples' unemployment histories. Since, in our hierarchical model, variance associated with H–G scores is extracted before the unem-

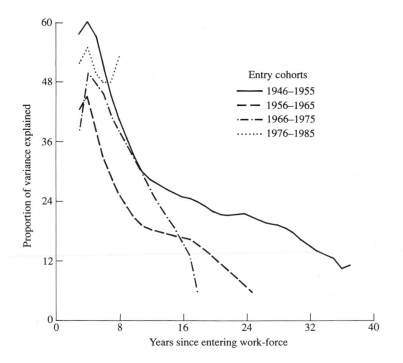

FIG. 3.12. Explaining unemployment, women, proportion of variance explained by unemployment in years 1 and 2

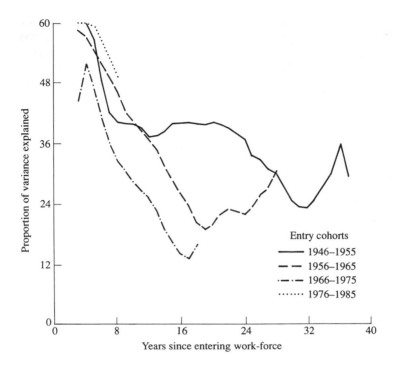

Fɪɢ. 3.13. Explaining unemployment, men, proportion of variance
explained by long-term unemployment history

ployment history variable is entered into the analysis (reflecting
what we consider to be the causal sequence), the importance of
work history would be expected to decline both through the
working life and in successive entry cohorts.

Following this line of argument, the women's pattern (Figure
3.14) is unsurprising. It shows, similarly for each cohort, a slight
fall in the importance of unemployment history through the life-
course as an explanatory factor, from around 45 per cent of the
variance in current unemployment to around 35 per cent (for the
early entry cohort at least). For women occupational status is
much less important in explaining susceptibility to unemployment
than in the men's case; it is not so clearly progressive through the
life-course, and it does not increase so markedly through successive entry cohorts. So the prior introduction to the H–G score in

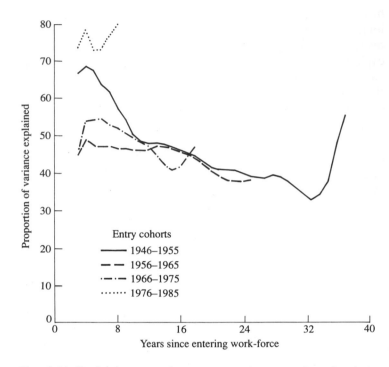

FIG. 3.14. Explaining unemployment, women, proportion of variance explained by long-term unemployment history

the variance decomposition leaves more of women's current unemployment unexplained than in the men's case.

And finally we have the impact of last year's unemployment (Figures 3.15 and 3.16). This variable, entered last in the hierarchical analysis of variance, explains very nearly as much variance as do all the previous variables put together, both for women and for men. It shows some variation between cohorts, apparently decreasing in importance during the early years in the work-force through the successive men's cohorts (perhaps as a reflection of the increasing importance of occupational status in these cohorts). But this feature recurs, for men and women, in all of the alternative analyses we have carried out, and retains its dominating importance in the analysis of variance. The numerical importance of this variable in the decomposition should not, however, mislead us about its causal status. It does not reflect long-term unemployment experience, nor does it relate to the overall economic climate or the individual's accumulated human capital (since all the variance associated with these has been previously extracted). It must therefore reflect something else, something specific to the individual's economic situation, but not systematically related to any of the other factors previously included in the analysis.

It may relate in part to something specific to the individual's own recent personal experiences. But these would have to be of a rather extraordinary nature if they are not already captured by the other variables. So, in most cases, the relevant recent situational characteristics must be those of the local labour market:

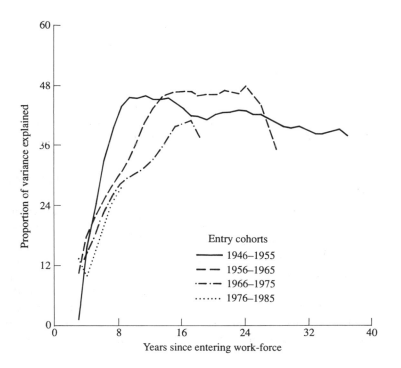

Fig. 3.15. Explaining unemployment, men, proportion of variance explained by whether unemployed last year

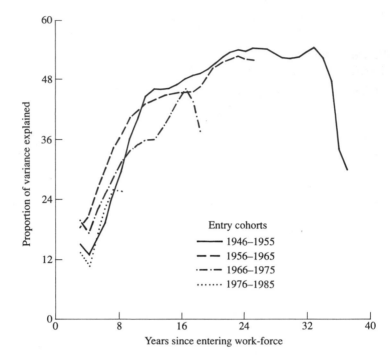

FIG. 3.16. Explaining unemployment, women, proportion of variance
explained by whether unemployed last year

variations in either the conditions of the local economy as a
whole, or in the local state of demand for specific sorts of labour,
result in particular individuals who do not have a longer-term
history of unemployment suffering repeated or lengthy periods
out of work. What is noteworthy in this analysis is that the
larger part of the individual variation in unemployment that can
be explained is not explained in this way. Perhaps, rather than
thinking of this variable as explaining 'nearly as much . . . as all
the other variables put together', we might better summarize the
position as follows: specific local conditions account for less than
half of all the explainable variation in unemployment.

5. CONCLUSIONS

We can summarize the foregoing analysis in terms of a number of general conclusions:

- The link between the characteristics of the individual's household of origin and subsequently achieved occupational status has considerably strengthened over the period covered by our survey.
- Occupational status (as indicated by the individual's position on the H–G scale) explains an increasing proportion of the variation in unemployment through the life-course.
- The relationship between men's occupational status and their susceptibility to unemployment has substantially increased in strength over the period covered by our data.
- Women, by contrast, show no such increasing effect of occupational status on susceptibility to unemployment, either through the life-course, or over successive age cohorts.
- There is evidence of a cohort difference in the impact of the adverse economic circumstances of 1970s and 1980s—they seem to have weighed most heavily on the younger age cohorts.
- The effect of early unemployment does not dominate the subsequent career. There are, however, persistent, small, but still not insignificant, effects of early unemployment throughout the life-course. So a very small minority may have life-long consequences of early unemployment.
- The most important influence on unemployment in any year is the unemployment record of the immediate past. That is to say, unemployment is concentrated among a small group of people (in distinctive geographical or occupational locations).

There is plainly some way to go. We do not have any entirely unshakeable conclusions. We are not yet taking sufficient account of the changing historical context within which our life histories are lived. And we are not yet attempting to model changes in the life-course overall, since we treat each successive year discretely (though it may be that this is in fact the right way to construct the models). But the substantive results are more than suggestive.

We are most of the way to a demonstration that there are unemployment careers. Plainly, unemployment is something that happens to a special subgroup of our sample. A recent history of unemployment is strongly associated with an immediate future of unemployment. Unemployment is not evenly distributed across particular occupational groups; part of this uneven distribution will certainly be attributable to labour demand factors. But an increasing part seems to relate to the acquisition of qualifying or disqualifying characteristics through the life-course.

There is a causal chain linking origin to occupation, and occupation to unemployment. Both links in this chain seem to be getting stronger over time. A degree of cohort–period indeterminacy somewhat weakens our conclusion concerning the second of these links. But it is quite clear that the absolute size of the gap between the unemployment experiences of those in higher- and in lower-status occupations is growing: the lower in the job hierarchy, the harder-hit by unemployment. For the period 1945–85 at least, the social stratification of the experience of unemployment has been increasing.

4

UK

Unemployment and Attitudes to Work

J64

DUNCAN GALLIE AND CAROLYN VOGLER

J28

1. INTRODUCTION

How far must vulnerability to unemployment be accounted for in terms of the personal characteristics and work attitudes of the unemployed themselves, and how far must it be seen as the result of the labour market conditions that the unemployed confront? The argument that the unemployed themselves bear the responsibility for their marginality to the labour market implies that they have qualities that make them difficult to employ. For instance, they may have a degree of behavioural instability that makes it difficult for them to hold any job for long or a low level of commitment to employment, which means that they make little effort to get work once they have lost it. The alternative view is that the unemployed are largely victims of their circumstances: they may have been unlucky enough to have been employed in industries that engaged in large-scale redundancies and find themselves in labour markets where there is little demand for their skills. Finally, there is a set of arguments that emphasize the heterogeneity of the unemployed, suggesting that they should be seen as a set of diverse categories for whom unemployment has a very different significance. For instance, some see a major difference between those that are registered for benefit and those that are not. For others, unemployment is held to have a different significance for men than for women, due to differences in underlying social identities.

This chapter seeks to address this debate in three ways: first, it will examine the work histories of the unemployed and compare

* The authors are very grateful to Martin Range for assistance with programming, and to David Cox for advice on the data analysis.

them with those of people in employment to assess whether there
are systematic signs over time of a lower level of employability;
secondly, it will examine the work attitudes of the unemployed
and their determinants; finally, it will explore the implications of
these attitudes for their success or lack of success in later acquir-
ing a job. The analysis makes use of data from two surveys: the
1986 Work Attitudes Survey and the 1987 Household and
Community Survey. (See the Methodological Appendix at the
end of this book.)

2. CATEGORIES OF THE UNEMPLOYED

One problem from the outset in assessing this debate is that there
is little consensus about who should be included in or excluded
from the ranks of the unemployed. Opinions range from the
'administrative' view that the unemployed consist of those who
are registered for unemployment benefit to the view that the concept of unemployment should be extended to include all those
who want, but do not have, a job. Within these extremes, other
demarcations can be found, depending on the importance
attached to whether or not people are actively seeking work. For
some, the readiness to engage in an active search is the essential
indicator of genuine concern to have a job; for others, it is held
to be of limited significance, given the lack of real opportunities
for work for substantial sections of the unemployed. In the second of these perspectives, the conventional distinction between
unemployment and non-activity is regarded essentially as an
artificial one, masking the processes that lead to progressive
exclusion from the labour market.

The point of departure, then, has been to classify the sample in
terms of categories that would make it possible to examine some
of the assumptions that underlie this debate. The unemployed
have been separated into three groups: the 'claimant seekers',
who were both receiving benefit on grounds of unemployment
and looking for work in the previous four weeks; the 'claimant
non-seekers', who were receiving benefit but had not been looking for work over this period; and, finally, the 'non-registered
seekers', who had been looking for work and had not been
receiving any financial assistance. Those that were neither claim-

ing benefit nor seeking work have been classified in the conventional way as 'non-actives' for the purpose of comparison. The majority of the unemployed in the sample (59 per cent) were claimant seekers, with smaller proportions of claimant non-seekers (22 per cent) and of non-registered seekers (19 per cent).

A first point to note is that these categories were sharply differentiated by gender. While the unemployed as a whole were only slightly more likely to be men than women (58 per cent and 42 per cent respectively), nearly three-quarters of claimant seekers were men, while almost three-quarters of non-registered seekers were women. The claimant non-seekers were split relatively evenly between men and women. There were also significant age differences between the categories. For instance, the male claimant seekers were disproportionately in the youngest age cohort (aged under 30), while the claimant non-seekers had a higher proportion of older workers (55+). Among women, both categories of claimant unemployed drew predominantly from people under 30 (57 per cent of the seekers and 60 per cent of the non-seekers). Finally, there were differences in household circumstances. Whereas only a minority of women that were claimant seekers had children under 15 (43 per cent), the proportion rose to 55 per cent among the claimant non-seekers and to 69 per cent among the non-registered.

Overall, the claimant seekers were predominantly men, with a particularly high proportion of men under 30. The claimant non-seekers were composed of four main groups: women with children under 5 (21 per cent), men over 55 (14 per cent), men under 30 (15 per cent), and single women under 50 with no children (11 per cent). The non-registered seekers were nearly all partnership women, especially women with children under 5 (23 per cent) or with children aged between 5 and 15 (24 per cent). In short, it is clear that the different subgroups of the unemployed have a very different composition in terms of both personal and family characteristics.

Finally, it should be noted that there was a striking difference between categories in the likelihood that people would categorize themselves as unemployed. Whereas 92 per cent of claimant seekers spontaneously described themselves as unemployed, this was the case for only 72 per cent of the claimant non-seekers and 50 per cent of the non-registered. These differences vary substantially by sex. Among men the great majority of all categories considered themselves as unemployed. While the figure remains higher for the claimant seekers (98 per cent), it declines to only 81 per cent among the non-seekers and to 86 per cent among the non-registered. Women, on the other hand, are generally less likely to think of themselves as unemployed and the difference between subcategories is particularly sharp. While a majority of the claimant seekers (75 per cent) and of the non-seekers (63 per cent) say they are unemployed, this is the case for a mere 37 per cent of the non-registered. In contrast, 58 per cent of the non-registered women describe themselves as housewives.

In short, the categories of the unemployed seem to be distinguished in terms of personal and household characteristics, and in terms of people's subjective perceptions of their situation. It is important, then, in assessing the relationship between unemployment and attitudes to work, to consider whether it varies depending upon the particular category of the unemployed that a person belongs to.

3. THE PRIOR WORK HISTORIES OF THE UNEMPLOYED

It should be noted from the start that the great majority of the unemployed had extensive experience of employment behind them. On average, the unemployed had spent 72 per cent of the time in which they had been active in the labour market in employment, and, for those aged over 35, the figure rose to over 80 per cent. But is there any evidence from the prior work histories of the unemployed that they were less stable than the employed in their working patterns? Such instability might be reflected in the frequency with which people changed jobs and in the length of time that they had shown themselves able to stay in any particular job.

Do the unemployed display greater instability in their work careers than the employed in terms of the numbers of jobs that they have had in the past? If the unemployed were inherently less stable, then they might be expected to have changed jobs more frequently than the employed. The evidence suggests that there is in practice very little difference in job mobility between the employed and the unemployed. As can be seen in Table 4.1, the mean number of jobs for the unemployed was the same as for the employed (6). If controls are introduced to standardize the groups in terms of age, qualifications, sex, class, and industry, one particular category of the unemployed—the claimant seekers— emerge as having had more jobs than the employed (Table 4.2). The difference, however, is very small. Claimant seekers were likely to have had only one-twentieth of a job more than comparable employed people. It seems improbable that a difference of this order could reflect any fundamental difference in employability. Much more important in determining the frequency of job changes were age, sex, and industry. By far the strongest effects were simply those of age, with older people having had higher numbers of jobs than younger people. Men had changed jobs more frequently than women, and people employed in the construction industry showed particularly high levels of job mobility.

TABLE 4.1. *Average number of jobs*

Respondents	All employed	All unemployed	Categories of unemployment		
			Claimant seekers	Claimant non-seekers	Non-Claimant seekers
All	6.0	6.0[a]	6.2	5.5	5.7
Men	6.3	6.7[a]	6.6	6.9	7.5
Women	5.7	4.9[b]	5.2	4.2	5.1

Notes: The unweighted no. of unemployed was 908 (477 men, 431 women) and of employed 3,678 (1,835 men and 1,843 women).
[a] Not significant
[b] Significance <0.001.
Source: Drawn from the Work Attitudes/Histories Survey (1986).

Changes of job in the sense used above include both job changes that involve a change of employer and job changes with the same employer. It might be argued that instability is better measured by the frequency of job changes between employers. The great majority of all job changes by people in our sample were in fact external rather than internal moves. If one takes external moves, it is once again the similarity rather than the difference between the unemployed and the employed that is

TABLE 4.2. *Regression of number of jobs involving a change of employer*

Variables in the equation	Beta[a]	T	Significance T
Age <25	−0.40	−25.4	0.0000
Age 25–34	−0.23	−14.3	0.0000
Sex	0.09	6.7	0.0000
Age >55	0.10	6.8	0.0000
Construction	0.08	5.9	0.0000
Energy/water	0.06	4.6	0.0000
Claimant seeker	0.05	3.3	0.0009
Age 45–54	0.05	3.3	0.0008
Distribution hotels catering	0.04	3.1	0.0020
Vocational/O level qualifications	0.04	3.0	0.0027
Class 6	−0.04	−2.6	0.0083
Transport	0.03	2.3	0.0216
(Constant)		56.7	0.0000

Notes: $R^2 = 0.21$. No. of employed and unemployed = 4,537. Non-significant variables were: claimant non-seekers, non-claimant seekers, no qualifications, and the remaining class and industry dummies.

[a] On average a claimant seeker has roughly 5% of a job more than an employed person.

striking. The average number of external moves by the unemployed was 4.9, whereas that for the employed was 4.7—a difference that was not statistically significant. The introduction of controls reveals precisely the same pattern as with the total number of jobs, with age effects dominant and employment status only reaching significance in the case of the claimant seekers (beta 0.05, *t* coefficient 3.5).

A second approach is to look at the duration of the longest job that people have held. If the unemployed were in some sense inherently unstable workers, this might be reflected in a relatively short tenure of their longest job. In practice, while the unemployed were likely to have spent less time in their longest job than the employed, the difference was very small (Table 4.3). The average duration of the longest job of the unemployed was 74 months, while that for the employed was 76 months. If job durations are a good indicator of personal work characteristics, it might be argued that the ability of the average unemployed person to maintain a job for some six years (and only two months less than the

TABLE 4.3. *Duration of longest job: mean number of months*

Age group	People currently in employment	Unemployed				Non-employed			
		Claimant seekers	Claimant non-seekers	Non-claimant seekers	Total	Will return	Will not return	Not known if will return	Total
All[a]	76.0	72.7	75.2	76.6	74.0	60.4	101.5	81.6	81.7
<25	27.2	21.5	20.9	22.9	21.5	27.0	24.1	24.5	26.2
25–34	52.2	53.6	40.6	49.1	50.7	46.7	51.1	56.0	48.2
35–44	76.7	80.3	78.5	77.9	79.3	67.1	60.8	66.0	64.5
45–55	113.2	140.4	120.2	143.3	136.9	112.4	98.2	116.3	102.6
55+	142.4	167.9	176.6	165.8	170.2	180.2	154.2	156.9	156.5
Men[b]	82.5	80.5	101.2	105.8	86.3	122.6	196.8	94.3	163.2
<25	29.4	22.4	18.4	9.5	21.0	16.7	*	*	18.0
25–34	54.8	53.1	44.5	80.7	54.3	64.7	*	*	55.7
35–44	84.6	89.6	89.3	95.5	90.3	102.5	81.1	*	95.9
45–54	126.8	149.7	120.9	192.2	148.6	167.0	169.2	*	162.7
55+	154.3	170.7	178.5	180.6	174.2	187.3	231.5	*	220.8
Women[c]	67.4	52.3	52.0	66.1	56.9	53.5	85.1	79.8	70.1
<25	24.0	19.7	21.9	28.9	22.1	27.9	24.1	25.9	27.0
25–34	48.7	54.6	38.7	42.6	46.6	45.8	52.2	56.0	47.9
35–44	66.7	52.9	68.3	71.1	64.9	64.8	59.4	62.0	62.4
45–54	97.1	108.7	119.3	116.9	114.0	85.4	86.9	121.8	88.8
55+	125.3	*	*	156.3	155.0	169.8	127.1	159.6	130.9

Notes: The number of observations per cell is very variable; cells with fewer than 5 individuals are marked with an asterisk

[a] Significance of age 0.001; significance of whether employed or unemployed 0.001; type of unemployment not significant.

[b] Significance of age 0.001; significance of employed/unemployed 0.05; type of unemployment not significant;

[c] Significance of age 0.001; employed/unemployed not significant; type of unemployment not significant.

currently employed) suggests employability rather than behavioural instability.

It should be noted that the pattern varies substantially by sex and age. Unemployed men actually have longer durations than their employed equivalents, whereas the pattern is inverted for women. It is primarily the younger unemployed that have shorter durations; men over 35 and women over 45 have longer durations than the employed. A common assumption is that claimant seekers have a higher level of employment commitment than those receiving benefits but not looking for work. However, as can be seen in Table 4.3, claimant seekers in fact have shorter durations for their longest job than the non-seekers (an average duration of 72.7 months compared with 75.2).

Overall, the striking feature of the data is the similarity of the work history patterns of the employed and the unemployed, with respect to both job mobility and job tenure. In terms of the number of jobs held in the past, it was only the claimant seekers that emerged as having had a higher number of jobs, and, even for these, the difference was very small. While the unemployed were likely to have spent a little less time in their longest jobs, the average difference (two months) did not suggest any substantial difference in attitudes to work. By a rather different route, this evidence reinforces the conclusions of Chapter 3. Gershuny and Marsh showed that it was recent rather than early or longer-term experiences of unemployment that increased vulnerability to further unemployment. This suggested that people's susceptibility to unemployment was due to changes in local labour market conditions, rather than to any deep-seated personality factors. The evidence in this chapter, which examines the overall pattern of people's work histories, also indicates that the unemployed were not people characterized by a markedly lower level of employability. Rather, in terms of their past job experiences, they showed a level of employment stability that was very close indeed to that of people currently in employment.

4. WORK ATTITUDES AND UNEMPLOYMENT

Evidence about work attitudes drawn from behavioural measures must necessarily remain indeterminate. Differences in job mobility or tenure may reflect the nature of labour market conditions rather than the characteristics of individuals. Further, the past may not be a reliable indicator of people's current attitudes. It is necessary, then, to turn to a more direct examination of the work attitudes of the unemployed.

There are two broad types of argument that could be advanced about the way in which the attitudes of the unemployed might help explain their labour market misfortunes. The first is that they are characterized by a lower level of employment motivation, that they are less likely to regard employment as something to be desired. This might reflect early education and training, the period in the life cycle, gender identities, or individual personality characteristics. The second type of argument would be that the unemployed are distinctive not so much in terms of their commitment to employment *per se* as in their inflexibility about the conditions under which they will take particular jobs. Such inflexibility might relate to their expectations about pay, or to their willingness to change their skills or to accept a job that involves geographical mobility. This section will examine two measures of employment motivation and three indices of job choice flexibility and will then explore the factors that help to account for variations in these.

4.1. Employment Motivation

Is there any evidence that the unemployed, or particular categories of the unemployed, are less interested in long-term participation in the labour market? A well-tested measure of work commitment has been developed by the Social and Applied Psychology Unit (SAPU) at Sheffield (Warr 1982). This asks people whether or not they would wish to continue working (or, in the case of the unemployed and non-actives, work somewhere) if they were to get enough money to live as comfortably as they would like for the rest of their lives.

The relationship between type of unemployment and work commitment was explored further through the construction of an index of employment deprivation. Using a five-point scale, those currently unemployed were asked how strongly they agreed or disagreed with a range of statements about the experience of being without a paid job. The nine statements on which the index was based were:

I find being at home very satisfying.
I get bored being at home.
Not having a paid job doesn't worry me at all.
Not having a paid job makes me feel rather useless.
I don't need to go out to work for the money.
I often get depressed about not having a paid job.
I miss the daily routine of a paid job.
It's easier to make new friends when you haven't got a paid job.
Other people sometimes look down on me because I haven't got a paid job.

Factor analysis of the nine items showed that the first seven were all highly intercorrelated, with one underlying factor explaining 51.3 per cent of the variance. The highest-loading item was that of depression about not having paid work. It should be noted that the item specifically tapping financial need comes only sixth in order of importance, suggesting it is primarily a measure of psychological deprivation with respect to employment. An index of employment deprivation was then constructed from the factor scores of the seven items, producing a scale that varied between +1.6 and –1.7. Positive scores indicated strong and negative scores weak employment deprivation.

The index can be seen as distinct from the previous SAPU measure of employment commitment in that it focuses on the current distress produced by lack of a job rather than longer-term work career preferences. It also takes account of the financial importance of work, whereas the first measure is explicitly one of non-financial commitment. In practice, the two measures are strongly associated. Those committed to employment have an average index score of 0.47, whereas those that were not have a score of –0.12. The employment commitment measure correlates highly with each of the items on the employment deprivation measure, with a range between 0.31 and 0.43.

What do these measures reveal about the importance of employment for the unemployed? A first point to note is that the unemployed as a whole were actually more committed to employment than those in work. Among employees and the self-employed, 66 per cent would wish to continue working if there were no financial necessity. Among the unemployed, the

TABLE 4.4. *Employment commitment by type of unemployment* (%)

Employment commitment	Employed and self-employed	Unemployed				Non-employed	
		Claimant seekers	Claimant non-seekers	Non-claimant seekers	Total	Will return	Total
All							
Work somewhere	66	81	64	82	77	68	67
Remain jobless	34	19	36	19	23	32	33
	100	100	100	100	100	100	100
Significance .001 (no.)	(4,234)	(419)	(149)	(134)	(703)	421	(438)
Gamma 0.2							
Men							
Work somewhere	68	82	66	83	79	87	88
Remain jobless	32	19	34	17	21	13	13
	100	100	100	100	100	100	100
Significance 0.03 (no.)	(2,471)	(300)	(71)	(37)	(48)	(47)	(51)
Gamma 0.05							
Women							
Work somewhere	63	78	61	81	75	66	65
Remain jobless	38	22	39	19	25	34	35
	100	100	100	100	100	100	100
Significance 0.0001 (no.)	(1,764)	(119)	(78)	(97)	(294)	374	(386)
Gamma 0.2							

proportion rises to 77 per cent (Table 4.4). The evidence, then, provides no general support for the view that the unemployed have particularly low levels of work commitment. There is a marked variation, however, between the different categories of the unemployed. Commitment is highest among those who are seeking work, whether claimant seekers (81 per cent) or non-registered seekers (82 per cent), and much lower among the non-seekers (64 per cent).

The pattern revealed by the index of employment deprivation for the different categories of the unemployed is, in broad outline, rather similar to that with respect to employment commitment. The highest level of employment deprivation was experienced by the claimant seekers, with an index score of 0.82, whereas the lowest (0.23) was among the claimant non-seekers (Table 4.5). The main difference is that the index of employment deprivation suggests that the non-registered unemployed suffer less severely than the claimant seekers (0.41), although still considerably more than the claimant non-seekers. Overall, the subjective measures suggest that there are, indeed, important differences in the experience and probable significance of unemployment between the various categories of the unemployed.

Finally, it is possible to compare the unemployed with the non-actives. It is sometimes suggested that the distinction between unemployment and non-activity is an artificial one, in that many women may withdraw from the labour market primarily as a result of the absence of job opportunities. In terms of longer-term employment commitment, the differences between groups are, indeed, not that substantial. Some 67 per cent of the non-actives would wish to have a job irrespective of financial need, compared with 77 per cent of the unemployed. However, when one turns to the more immediate experience of employment deprivation, a sharp difference emerges. Whereas all categories of the employed have a positive score on the index, suggesting that the lack of employment is experienced as a severe problem, the non-actives have a negative score (Table 4.5).

The non-actives can be divided into two roughly equal categories—the 'provisional non-actives', who intend to return to a job at a later period although they are not currently searching, and the 'stable non-actives', who believe that they will remain without employment. As might be expected, the provisional

TABLE 4.5. *Employment deprivation by type of unemployment*

	Unemployed				Non-employed			
	Claimant seekers	Claimant non-seekers	Non-claimant seekers	Total	Will return	Will not return	Not known if return	Total
All	0.82	0.23	0.41	0.61	-0.21	-0.66	-0.54	-0.45
Men	0.88	0.35	0.42	0.74	0.28	0.06	0.54	0.17
Women	0.64	0.10	0.41	0.42	-0.27	-0.79	-0.70	-0.54

non-actives are relatively less satisfied than the stable non-actives, but they are still very much less affected than even the claimant non-seekers. The principal qualification to the pattern is with respect to sex: non-active men do appear to suffer more sharply from lack of employment. However, women non-actives—who constitute the overwhelming majority of non-actives (87 per cent)—appear to be a quite distinct group from the unemployed.

4.2. Labour Market Flexibility

The nature of differences between the various categories of the unemployed can be explored further by looking at how flexible people were prepared to be in the process of job search. In particular, we have focused on three types of flexibility. The first was how demanding people were in their expectations about the pay they would get for the job; the second was their willingness to consider changing their skills; and the third was their openness to geographical mobility.

A measure of pay flexibility was constructed from two questions on people's expectations about future jobs. These questions were asked of those who had been actively seeking work in the past month. People were first asked whether they were looking for a particular kind of work or were prepared to take 'anything going'. Then those looking for a particular kind of work were asked what level of pay they would expect for it. Where people's pay expectations were above the average for the currently employed in their occupational class, they were classified as having 'low flexibility'. In practice, only 12 per cent of the unemployed fell into this category.

The second measure of labour market flexibility was concerned with skill flexibility. This was based on a question asking respondents whether, since becoming unemployed, they had seriously considered retraining in order to get a job. Those that had considered retraining were classified as relatively flexible, those that had not as relatively inflexible. The question was asked of all the unemployed, whether or not they had been seeking work in the previous month. Overall, 45 per cent had seriously considered training and the proportions were very similar for both men and women. Finally, the measure of geographical flexibility was constructed from a question asking people whether they would move if a suitable job became available in another area. This seemed to be the type of flexibility that was least common among the unemployed. Overall, only 40 per cent said that they would be willing to move from the area they were in to obtain a job.

How did the different categories of the unemployed compare with respect to these measures of labour market rigidity? The measure of pay expectations only applied to those that were actively seeking work. There was a small but significant difference between the claimant and non-registered seekers, with the non-registered having slightly higher expectations in comparison to the average earnings of employed people in their class. Among the claimant seekers, 11 per cent were hoping for a higher level of pay than the average for their occupational class; among the non-registered the figure was 16 per cent.

Where the categories of the unemployed differ more substantially is with respect to skill and geographical flexibility. There was a striking difference between the claimant seekers, of whom 52 per cent had seriously considered retraining, and the claimant non-seekers, for whom the proportion fell to 31 per cent. The non-registered seekers were in an intermediary position (46 per cent), but were closer to the claimant seekers than to the claimant non-seekers. The pattern with respect to geographical mobility was rather different. Certainly, the claimant seekers were by far the most likely to be willing to move (48 per cent). However, this time the least flexible were the non-registered (21 per cent). The claimants that had not been actively seeking work in the previous month were in an intermediary position (35 per cent).

The evidence so far has shown that the level of employment commitment of the unemployed is, if anything, higher than with the employed themselves. However, at the same time, the various categories of the unemployed would appear to have rather different attitudes to the labour market. The claimant non-seekers emerged as having particularly low levels of employment motivation, both on the measure of longer-term commitment and on the measure of more immediate employment deprivation. The pattern for flexibility with respect to job search was more complex. The most flexible on all counts were the claimant seekers, with the claimant non-seekers being particularly low on skill flexibility and the non-registered on geographical flexibility. Given the variations described earlier in the social composition of the different groups of the unemployed, it is possible that these attitudinal patterns reflect primarily differences in factors such as sex, age, or household circumstances. The next section, then, will turn to a broader examination of the determinants of work attitudes.

5. THE DETERMINANTS OF WORK ATTITUDES

5.1. Employment Motivation

What factors account for variations in the employment motivation of the unemployed? The results of an analysis of the determinants of non-financial employment commitment are reported in Table 4.6. Since the measure of employment commitment is dichotomous in form, the technique used is that of logistic regression analysis. Four factors contributed significantly to the extent to which people felt that they wanted to continue in employment

TABLE 4.6. *Logistic regression: parameter estimates for the odds of employment commitment*

Variable and level	Multiplicative estimate		
	All	Men	Women
Constant	2.5	1.3	3.7
Type of unemployment			
1 Claimant non-seekers	1.0	1.0	1.0
2 Claimant seekers	2.5	2.2	2.9
3 Non-claimant seekers	3.0	3.9	4.8
Age			
1 <55	1.0	1.0	1.0
2 >55	0.4	0.5	0.2
Partner's employment			
1 Other partnership status	1.0	1.0	1.0
2 Partner unemployed or non-employed	1.8	1.8	1.5
Qualifications			
1 A levels	1.0	n.s.	1.0
2 O levels	0.6		0.5
3 None	0.5		0.3
No.	907	477	430
Minimum significance	0.05	0.05	0.01

Note: n.s. = non-significant. Non-significant variables were: class, sex, number of jobs, duration of longest job, high/low unemployment area, social support, months unemployed, number of times unemployed, decline and stress in financial circumstances, gender traditionalism, age of youngest child.

irrespective of financial need: age, education, the employment status of the partner, and unemployment type.

In general, those that were older were less committed to employment than those that were younger. There is a particularly sharp decline in employment commitment among both men and women over 55. This may have reflected either the increasing health problems of people of this age or some process of anticipatory socialization into retirement. Lower levels of educational qualification also sharply reduced people's longer-term commitment to employment, particularly in the case of women. An important factor that heightened commitment was if the person was living with a partner who was either unemployed or non-employed. This effect was significant both for men and for women, although it was somewhat stronger for men. It casts some doubt on the view that the tendency for exclusion from employment to be concentrated in households is to be explained in terms of the financial motives of the individuals affected (Morris 1990: 169 ff.). Even the wives of the unemployed, who are often depicted as being subject to strong incentives from the benefits systems to leave employment, appear to be particularly convinced of the importance of having a job irrespective of the money. Finally, it should be noted that, even when these other factors have been controlled for, there was a significant difference between claimant non-seekers and seekers (whether or not in receipt of benefit).

The picture that emerges for more immediate employment deprivation is similar in some respects (Table 4.7). Since the measure of employment deprivation is a continuous scale, an ordinary least squares regression analysis has been used. Age, unemployment type, and the employment status of the partner are again important. However, the level of educational qualification was not significant. The most notable new factor to emerge is the impact of the financial difficulty experienced by the household. If one takes either the difficulty that households reported in making ends meet or the extent to which household income was seen to have declined in the past, it is clear that the greater the household's financial difficulties, the more intense the psychological deprivation produced by unemployment. In contrast, the stronger the social support system available to an individual, in terms of people that could be turned to for assistance,

TABLE 4.7. *Regression on index of employment deprivation*

All unemployed respondents (R^2–0.07. No. = 862)			
Variables in equation	Beta	T	Sig T
Claimant non-seekers	–0.16	–4.8	0.0000
>55	–0.14	–4.0	0.0001
Partner unemployed or non-employed	0.12	3.6	0.0003
No qualifications	–0.15	–3.3	0.0009
O levels	–0.11	–2.4	0.0150
(Constant)		25.6	0.0000
Variables not in equation			
<25		0.1	0.9020
25–34		–0.2	0.8631
35–44		0.4	0.7146
Class 3		0.0	0.9680
Class 1 or 2		0.1	0.9302
Class 6		0.1	0.8741
Class 7		–1.1	0.2718
Sex		–0.0	0.9741
No. of jobs		0.4	0.7193
Duration of longest job		0.1	0.9464
Area of high unemployment		0.0	0.9716
Partner in employment		–1.2	0.2373
Social support		–1.5	0.1432
Months unemployed		–0.5	0.6364
No. of times unemployed		–1.0	0.3399
Decline in financial circumstances		1.5	0.1257
Financial stress		0.4	0.6934
Traditional attitudes to gender roles		–0.8	0.4322
Claimant seeker		–1.2	0.2366
Youngest child < 5		0.4	0.6953
Youngest child 5–15		0.3	0.7968
Youngest child > 15		–0.5	0.6461
Men (R^2 = 0.04. No. = 454)			
Partner unemployed or non-employed	0.15	3.2	0.0016
Claimant non-seekers	–0.12	–2.6	0.0101
>55	–0.12	–2.5	0.0112
(Constant)		27.8	0.0000
Women (R^2 = 0.13. No. = 408)			
No qualifications	–0.29	–4.4	0.0000
Claimant non–seeker	–0.30	–4.9	0.0000
>55	–0.18	–3.9	0.0001
O levels	–0.16	–2.4	0.0169
Partner in employment	–0.16	–3.0	0.0030
Claimant seeker	–0.12	–2.1	0.0397
(Constant)		16.0	0.0000

the more people were protected from the impact of being without a job. There is also some evidence that women felt less psychological deprivation from unemployment than men, possibly reflecting a stronger sense of purpose in their non-work lives.

5.2. *Flexibility*

The examination of the determinants of pay, skill, and geographical flexibility suggests that these are different attitudinal dimensions, influenced by rather different personal and structural factors. Taking first pay flexibility, the most significant determinants of whether or not people had relatively high pay expectations were people's level of qualifications, their previous experience of unemployment, their previous employment stability, and their household situation (Table 4.8). Those with lower levels of educational qualification and those that had spent more time unemployed in their work histories were substantially more likely to be flexible. In contrast, where people had spent a relatively long time in their longest job, showing a high level of employment stability, they were less willing to accept relatively low pay. This was not statistically significant for men, but it emerged strongly for women.

Household structure was also important for attitudes to pay in two ways. The first influence was the age of the youngest child. Where the child was under 5, people had relatively high pay expectations; in contrast, where the child was older than 15, people were much more likely to have relatively low pay expectations. One possibility is that this reflects in part the need for women with young children to have earnings that would be high enough to cover the costs of child care. A second aspect of household structure that was related to the attitudes of women (but not of men) was the employment situation of the partner. Where the partner was in employment, women maintained relatively high expectations about pay. In contrast, where the husband was unemployed or non-employed, they were particularly likely to have relatively low expectations. The perception of a reasonable level of household financial security may have made it easier for women to hold out for a relatively good level of payment.

Turning to skill flexibility (Table 4.9), there is, as with employment motivation, a strong effect of age. After people have

TABLE 4.8. *Logistic regression: parameter estimates for the odds of pay flexibility*

Variable and level	Multiplicative Estimates		
	All	Men	Women
(Constant)	4.1	2.8	8.1
Qualifications			
1 A levels	1.0	1.0	1.0
2 O levels	1.7	1.4	1.7
3 None	4.0	3.4	4.4
Months unemployed	4.5	4.2	n.s.
Duration of longest job	0.3	n.s.	0.2
Age of youngest child			
1 No children	1.0	n.s.	n.s.
2 <5	0.6		
3 5–15	1.0		
4 >15	4.4		
Partner's employment status			
1 Single	n.s.	n.s.	1.0
2 Partner in employment			0.4
3 Partner unemployed or non-employed			1.8
No.	606	353	253
Minimum significance	0.02	0.02	0.05

Notes: n.s. = non-significant. Non-significant variables were: age, class, sex, number of jobs, high/low unemployment area, social support, decline and stress in financial circumstances, and type of unemployed. Multiplicative estimates for months unemployed and duration of longest job are estimated for moves across half the ranges of these continuous variables (50 and 215 months respectively).

reached their mid-forties, they become markedly less likely to be willing to consider retraining. This may reflect either lower self-confidence among older workers in their ability to learn new skills or differential willingness to invest effort in training in the light of the probable time left in the labour market. Qualifications were again significant, but the direction of influence was very different from the case of pay. Whereas the least qualified had been the most flexible about pay, they were the least flexible with respect to retraining. Those that were particularly traditional in their attitudes to gender roles in the labour market were also less likely to show interest in retraining.[1] The principal continuity in the influences affecting pay and skill flexibility lay in the impact of people's prior work histories. As with pay, those that had been unemployed for longer were more likely to be willing to retrain, whereas those that had been employed for a longer period in their longest jobs appeared to be particularly fixed in their ways. When all these factors have been controlled for, the unemployed who are seeking work (whether

TABLE 4.9. *Logistic regression: parameter estimates for the odds of skill flexibility*

Variable and level	Multiplicative estimates		
	All	Men	Women
(Constant)	0.4	0.8	0.4
Duration of Longest job	0.6	0.4	0.2
Type of unemployment			
1 Claimant non-seekers	1.0	1.0	1.0
2 Claimant seekers	2.9	3.0	2.6
3 Non-claimant seekers	2.5	2.3	2.5
Traditional attitudes to gener roles	0.7	0.7	n.s.
Qualifications			
1 A level	1.0	n.s.	1.0
2 O level	1.1		1.7
3 None	0.8		
Age			
1 <25	1.0	n.s.	1.0
2 25–34	1.2		1.8
3 35–44	0.9		1.3
4 45–54	0.7		1.0
5 55+	0.4		0.3
Months unemployed	1.3	n.s.	n.s.
No.	907	477	430
Minimum significance	0.05	0.1	0.001

Notes: n.s. = non-significant. Non-significant variables were: class, sex, number of jobs, high/low unemployment area, partner's employment status, social support, number of times unemployed, decline and stress in financial circumstances, age of youngest child.

Multiplicative estimates for duration of longest job and traditionalism are based on half the ranges of these continuous variables (215 months and 6 score points respectively).

claimants or non-registered) still emerge as markedly more flexible than those not seeking work.

Finally, the influences on geographical flexibility were somewhat different again (Table 4.10). To begin with, there emerges for the first time a marked sex effect, with women much less likely to be willing to move than men. This was reinforced by two other factors that point to the particular importance for women's choices of their domestic responsibilities. First, women with partners that were in employment were particularly unlikely to wish to move. Secondly, women with more traditional views about gender roles were more reluctant to move. In contrast, neither of these factors was significant for men. The main influence

TABLE 4.10. *Logistic regression: parameter estimates for the odds of geographical flexibility*

Variable and level	Multiplicative estimates		
	All	Men	Women
(Constant)	1.1	3.4	1.5
Sex			
1 Women	1.0	–	–
2 Men	3.6		
Time in town	0.5	0.5	0.3
Partner's employment status			
1 No partner	1.0	n.s.	1.0
2 Partner in employment	0.3		0.2
3 Partner unemployed or non-employed	0.8		1.3
Qualifications			
1 A levels	1.0	1.0	n.s.
2 O levels	0.5	0.4	
3 None	0.4	0.4	
Traditionalist attitudes to gender roles	n.s.	n.s.	0.5
No.	907	477	430
Minimum significance	0.001	0.001	0.02

Notes: n.s. = non-significant. Non-significant variables were: age, class, number of jobs, duration of longest job, high/low unemployment area, social support, months unemployed, decline and stress in financial circumstances, age of youngest child, and type of unemployed.

Multiplicative estimates for time in town and gender traditionalism are based on half the ranges of these continuous variables (23 years and 6 score points respectively).

on men's attitudes to geographical mobility was their level of qualifications, with those with lower levels of qualification being less likely to consider moving. For both sexes, the length of time that people had spent in the area had a strong effect on their attitudes to moving. The longer the time in the area, the more attached to (or tied to) the locality a person appeared to be. Time in the area is likely to be an indicator of the general level of social integration, in the sense of the strength of social networks and the other community links.

The conclusion that domestic responsibilities, social networks, and community links were of major importance for attitudes to geographical mobility also emerges very clearly from an open question asking why people were reluctant to move. It is notable that the least frequently mentioned response of all was that there were no better jobs in other areas. The most important reasons for staying in an area were largely related to people's social networks and social responsibilities. The most frequent reason given overall was that people did not want to leave their friends or relatives (48 per cent). Further, 29 per cent mentioned constraints deriving from the fact that they were in partnerships and 22 per cent their concern about the implications of a move for their children's education. These social motives were particularly important for women. Seventy per cent of single women mentioned that they did not want to leave friends or relatives, compared with 63 per cent of single men. Moreover, 23 per cent of single women mentioned a concern for their children's education, while there were no such responses among single men. The predominant reason (74 per cent) why partnership women would not move was because their partner was employed in the area, whereas this was given by only 14 per cent of partnership men. Men, on the other hand, were much more likely than women of similar marital status to refer to a general attachment to the area or to their attachment to the house they were living in. Overall, the major factors underlying geographical flexibility appear to be people's household constraints and the extent to which they are socially integrated in their community.

5.3. Determinants: Overview

The preceding analysis has highlighted the central importance of factors such as age, the level of qualifications, and the characteristics of the household in understanding variations in the attitudes to work of the unemployed. With respect to geographical mobility, it has also pointed to the significance of local social networks and to the degree of social integration into the local community. In contrast, it has found little support for the view that financial pressures have any general impact on work attitudes. While the degree of financial difficulty experienced by the household was strongly related to the sharpness of the sense of deprivation caused by unemployment, it was unrelated to any other dimensions of work attitudes.

It should be noted also that, while there are differences between unemployed men and unemployed women, they are rather specific. There is no evidence, for instance, of a difference in longer-term commitment to employment, even though women did appear to suffer somewhat less severely from the immediate experience of unemployment. Women may have had better coping mechanisms when confronted by unemployment, but this did not derive from any lower commitment to the labour market. It is also notable that there was no significant difference between men and women with respect to either pay or skill flexibility. An important difference emerges, however, with respect to geographical mobility, where women's domestic responsibilities and social networks appear to exercise greater constraints.

Finally, despite the introduction of a wide variety of variables, the links between type of unemployment status and employment motivation still emerged very clearly. The claimant non-seekers were particularly unlikely to be committed to employment in the longer-term. Similarly, they experienced lower levels of employment deprivation than either the claimant seekers or the non-registered seekers. It should be noted, however, that the non-registered were just as likely to be committed to employment as the 'officially' unemployed, suggesting that they were in no sense a 'secondary' category of the unemployed. The links between types of unemployment status and flexibility were more severely attenuated once other variables have been taken into account. Indeed, the only association that remains is that with skill flexibility, with the claimant and non-registered seekers more open to the idea of changing their skills than the claimant non-seekers. In general, the picture that emerges is that there is relatively little difference between the work attitudes of the claimant seekers and the non-registered, while there is some evidence of a difference between these two categories and the claimant non-seekers.

6. WORK ATTITUDES AND JOB ACQUISITION

Although there is no evidence that the unemployed in general have lower levels of employment commitment than the employed, it has been shown that there is a substantial diversity in attitudes to work among the unemployed. This raises the issue of whether the nature of such attitudes is of importance in determining the likelihood that people will obtain a job. Are those that show relatively high levels of motivation and flexibility able to escape from unemployment more quickly than those that are less committed to employment and more rigid in their criteria of job choice?

The answer to this question clearly cannot be obtained through cross-sectional data analysis, since this fails to provide the critical information on temporal sequence needed to establish the direction of causality. For part of the sample, however, it is possible to examine their fortunes in the labour market between the period of the initial collection of information on work attitudes in 1986 and the time of a follow-up survey carried out in 1987. Approximately one-third of the original sample was selected for the follow-up survey. Of the total of 1,815 respondents that were reinterviewed, 377 had been unemployed at the time of the first survey. The work histories collected in the first survey were updated, providing detailed information on the timing of any change that had occurred in people's employment status between surveys.

Overall, less than a third (30 per cent) of those unemployed at the time of interview in 1986 obtained a job between the surveys. A proportion (18 per cent) withdrew from the labour market altogether, but by far the largest group remained unemployed. For the purposes of this analysis, the sample has been divided into those that obtained paid employment on the one hand and those that did not obtain it on the other.

In order to examine the relative importance of determinants of labour market outcomes for those unemployed at the time of the first interview, proportional hazard models have been estimated of the instantaneous probabilities of obtaining a job for individuals that differed in their patterns of work attitude and in a range of individual and household characteristics. The durations of the period until job acquisition (or until the time of second interview for those that remained without work) were calculated both from the start of the period of unemployment and from the time of the first interview, and separate models were estimated for both durations. The results for the overall period until job acquisition and for the between-survey duration were very similar, however, and we shall focus on the model for the former.

What factors affected the probabilities of job acquisition and how important were attitudinal factors among them? The first and most notable conclusion to emerge from Table 4.11 is that for the overall sample neither longer-term employment commitment nor the severity of the more immediate experience of employment deprivation were significant determinants of the likelihood of getting a job. As can be seen in Tables 4.12 and 4.13, these general conclusions about the unimportance of employment motivation hold for both men and women.

Nor does the evidence suggest that the flexibility of people in their approach to job search was of much importance in helping them to obtain work more rapidly. Geographical flexibility had no significant effect, while a willingness to consider retraining to acquire a different type of skill was associated with a longer duration of unemployment. In the separate breakdowns by sex, this negative association is significant for men, but not for women (although the estimated effect was in the same direction). Presumably those that were seriously considering retraining were people confronted by a particularly bleak labour market situation, in which there were very few jobs for people with the skills they possessed.

The measure of pay flexibility applies only to those that were actively seeking work. However, as can be seen in Table 4.14, a separate analysis of these categories of the unemployed shows that those that were more demanding about the pay they expected had very similar chances of obtaining a job to those that were less demanding. Overall, the data point to the conclusion that neither employment motivation nor flexibility in attitudes to work have any general significance in improving people's employment chances.

TABLE 4.11. *Determinants of job acquisition, all unemployed*

Log likelihood = −737.4155.
Global chi-squared = 104.62.
Degrees of freedom = 20.
P value = 0.0000.

	Parameter estimates	Parameter estimates/standard error	Exp (coefficient)
Work attitudes			
Employment commitment	0.2172	0.88	1.24
Employment deprivation	−0.1961	−1.37	0.72
Occupational flexibility	−0.4615	−2.52	0.63
Geographical flexibility	0.2756	1.35	1.32
Gender traditionalism	−0.0463	−1.64	0.76
Class and labour market characteristics			
Manual	0.6542	3.12	1.92
Unemployed once before[a]	0.5593	2.31	1.75
Unemployed twice before[a]	0.7943	2.75	2.21
Individual characteristics			
Age <25	−0.5651	−1.98	0.57
Age 25–34	−0.2447	−0.95	0.78
Age 45+	−0.2881	−1.00	0.75
No qualifications	−0.6531	−2.13	0.52
Vocational or O level qualifications	0.2075	0.78	1.23
Sex	−0.0296	−0.14	0.97
Type of unemployment			
Claimant seeker	0.8960	2.84	2.45
Non-registered	1.5657	4.66	4.79
Type of Locality			
High unemployment	0.0596	0.33	1.06
Household characteristics			
Partner full-time or part-time	0.5652	2.40	1.76
Partner unemployed or non-employed	−0.1691	−0.70	0.84
Financial stress	−0.1865	−0.90	0.83

Note: Exponentiated coefficients are measures of the risk associated with each category, relative to the base category. At any particular point in time an unemployed manual worker, for example, is 92% more likely to get a job than an otherwise comparable unemployed non-manual worker.
[a] In the last five years.

Source: Unemployed respondents in the Work Attitudes Survey who were reinterviewed in the Household and Community Survey (no. = 377).

TABLE 4.12. *Determinants of job acquisition, male unemployed*

Log likelihood = −301.8966.
Global chi-squared = 58.33.
Degrees of freedom = 19.
P value = 0.000.

	Parameter estimates	Parameter estimates/standard error	Exp (coefficient)
Work attitudes			
Employment commitment	0.4371	1.17	1.55
Employment deprivation	−0.3163	−1.35	0.60
Occupational flexibility	−0.7608	−2.82	0.47
Geographical flexibility	0.4360	1.60	1.55
Gender traditionalism	−0.0599	1.43	0.70
Class and labour market characteristics			
Manual	0.8071	2.28	2.24
Unemployed once before[a]	0.9021	2.59	2.46
Unemployed twice before[a]	0.7413	1.98	2.10
Individual characteristics			
Age < 25	−0.5415	−1.19	0.58
Age 25–34	−0.5844	−1.49	0.56
Age 45+	−0.6565	−1.48	0.52
No qualifications	−0.8930	−1.97	0.41
Vocational or O level qualifications	0.3932	0.99	1.48
Type of unemployment			
Claimant seeker	0.9121	1.86	2.49
Non-registered	0.8393	1.28	2.31
Type of locality			
High unemployment	−0.2318	−0.85	0.79
Household characteristics			
Partner full-time or part-time	1.1891	2.52	3.28
Partner unemployed or non-employed	0.2040	0.63	1.23
Financial stress	−0.2205	−0.71	0.80

[a] In the last five years.
Source: Unemployed respondents in the Work Attitudes Survey who were reinterviewed in the Household and Community Survey (no. = 377).

An important issue for public policy has been the extent to which financial incentives are an important factor motivating the speed with which people return to work. In particular, there has been a concern with the possible disincentive effects of the system of social security benefits. Evidence to date has been rather mixed, but some research has pointed to such an effect. For instance, Nickell *et al.* (1989), analysing data from the late 1970s, found that unemployed men whose benefits represented a relatively high proportion of their previous earnings in work took longer to obtain a job. We examined the effect of the level of

TABLE 4.13. *Determinants of job acquisition, female unemployed*

Log likelihood = −331.9855.
Global chi-squared = 54.36.
Degrees of freedom = 19.
P value = 0.0000.

	Parameter estimates	Parameter estimates/standard error	Exp (coefficient)
Work attitudes			
Employment commitment	0.2818	0.76	1.33
Employment deprivation	−0.1855	−0.88	0.74
Occupational flexibility	−0.2482	−0.87	0.78
Geographical flexibility	0.1173	0.35	1.12
Gender traditionalism	−0.0527	−1.24	0.73
Class and labour market characteristics			
Manual	0.6541	2.16	1.92
Unemployed once before[a]	0.4757	1.27	1.61
Unemployed twice before[a]	1.3140	2.47	3.72
Individual characteristics			
Age <25	−0.5521	−1.39	0.58
Age 25–34	−0.0697	−0.20	0.93
Age 45+	−0.0867	−0.20	0.92
No qualifications	−0.6300	−1.41	0.53
Vocational or O level qualifications	−0.0565	0.15	1.06
Type of unemployment			
Claimant seeker	0.7031	1.62	2.02
Non-registered	1.6290	3.67	5.10
Type of locality			
High unemployment	0.1264	0.50	1.13
Household characteristics			
Partner full-time or part-time	0.3307	1.10	1.39
Partner unemployed or non-employed	−0.8480	−1.42	0.43
Financial stress	−0.1940	−0.65	0.82

[a] In the last five years.

Source: Unemployed respondents in the Work Attitudes Survey who were reinterviewed in the Household and Community Survey (no. = 377).

TABLE 4.14. *Determinants of job acquisition amongst the unemployed seeking work*

Log likelihood = −540.8494
Global chi-squared = 80.29.
Degrees of freedom = 20.
P value = 0.000.

	Parameter estimates	Parameter estimates/standard error	Exp (coefficient)
Work attitudes			
Employment commitment	0.1795	0.61	1.20
Employment deprivation	−0.1764	−0.99	0.75
Occupational flexibility	−0.4799	−2.29	0.62
Geographical flexibility	0.4215	1.77	1.52
Pay flexibility	−0.3695	−1.30	0.69
Gender traditionalism	−0.0423	−1.32	0.78
Class and labour market characteristics			
Manual	0.7870	3.21	2.20
Unemployed once before[a]	0.7904	2.91	2.20
Unemployed twice before[a]	0.6726	2.04	1.95
Individual Characteristics			
Age < 25	−0.5710	−1.76	0.57
Age 25–34	−0.2677	−0.92	0.77
Age 45+	−0.1095	−0.33	0.90
No qualifications	−0.9880	−2.86	0.37
Vocational or O level qualifications	−0.1250	−0.42	0.88
Sex	−0.0277	−0.11	0.97
Type of unemployment			
Non-registered	0.7209	2.87	2.06
Type of locality			
High unemployment	0.0410	0.20	1.04
Household characteristics			
Partner full-time or part-time	−0.6928	2.60	2.00
Partner unemployed or non-employed	−0.1628	−0.60	0.85
Financial stress	−0.1217	−0.50	0.89

[a] In the last five years.

Source: Unemployed respondents in the Work Attitudes Survey who were reinterviewed in the Household and Community Survey (no. = 377).

income from benefits relative to prior earnings for the subsample of those that were in receipt of benefits. Although the estimated effect was in the direction that would be expected if higher replacement ratios were related to a slower return to work, it was not statistically significant either overall or for men and women taken separately.[2] This may imply that the importance of such disincentives varies with the level of unemployment, with individual motives playing a much smaller role in periods of mass redundancy and high unemployment. However, it should be noted also that a benefit effect only emerges consistently in Nickell *et al.*'s work for teenagers, a group that was not represented in our own sample.

More generally, the assumption that the earnings/benefit ratio is a good guide to the effective financial pressure on the household is likely to be misleading, in that it fails to take account of the employment structure of the household and, hence, of the availability of other sources of income.[3] For the main analysis, therefore, we have tested the effects of such financial pressure more directly by taking a measure of financial stress, based on the difficulties that people experienced in making ends meet. As Heady and Smyth (1989) have shown, such reported measures relate well to more objective measures of economic deprivation. However, even this direct experience of financial pressure failed to have any significant effect on the time taken to find work (Table 4.11). Overall, the evidence suggests that financial incentives and pressures are not of central importance in explaining people's chances of finding work.

There may be unmeasured characteristics of the work attitudes of the unemployed that increase their vulnerability to unemployment. If that is the case, one would expect that those that have had several experiences of unemployment would possess them to a greater degree and would find it correspondingly more difficult to find another job than those with a previous experience of continuous employment. In fact, however, far from those with past histories of unemployment taking longer to find work, they have higher probabilities of getting a job. This effect is particularly marked among male manual and female non-manual workers with two or more earlier spells of unemployment.

How is this pattern to be accounted for? One possibility is that past experience of unemployment increases people's skills at searching for a job. They may have been able to take effective action more rapidly in looking for work. An alternative explanation is that the recurrent unemployed are people that are locked into sectors of the labour market where employment is particularly volatile, due to a sharply fluctuating product market and the predominance of employers that rely on quick hire and fire policies. While the rather broad industrial categorization available to us did not permit any strong test of this hypothesis, it is perhaps indicative that such workers are drawn disproportionately from construction and 'other services'.

The only subgroup of the unemployed where it does seem plausible that work attitudes may have had an effect on the probability of getting a job is that of the claimant non-seekers. Unsurprisingly, those that were not looking for work at the time proved to have a significantly lower chance of finding a job. Further, if the equation is run separately for the claimant non-seekers (Table 4.15), longer-term employment commitment verges on being a significant factor influencing the chances of finding work (t coefficient of 1.95). Indeed, those with higher employment commitment had nearly five times the odds of getting a job of those with lower employment commitment.

Yet even among the non-seekers, there were clearly many for whom continued unemployment is difficult to attribute to employment commitment *per se*. It was seen earlier that this relatively small category of the unemployed was drawn disproportionately from specific types of people, in particular from older male workers and from women with children under 5 years of age. In both cases, there are likely to be active constraints on labour market participation that reduce the likelihood that people will have been actively searching for work in the past month. As other studies have shown (White 1983: 114 ff.; Westergaard *et al.* 1989: 114 ff.), older workers may become discouraged from applying by finding repeatedly that employers were unwilling to recruit people close to retirement, and they are also the most likely to be hindered from taking a job by ill health. Similarly, it is well recognized that the lack of adequate child care provision significantly constrains the employment opportunities available to young mothers. Certainly, as can be seen in Table 4.16, the three explanations most frequently given by the claimant non-seekers for why they were not looking for work were their responsibilities for young children, the lack of available jobs, and ill health.

Overall, then, our data suggest that variations in employment motivation provide little explanation of the duration of unemployment for the greater part of the unemployed. However, there are two potential difficulties with the data that need to be

TABLE 4.15. *Determinants of job acquisition amongst the unemployed claiming benefits but not seeking work*

Log likelihood = –52.3490.
Global chi-squared = 22.92.
Degrees of freedom = 18.
P value = 0.1936.

	Parameter estimates	Parameter estimates/standard error	Exp (coefficient)
Work attitudes			
Employment commitment	1.5516	1.94	4.72
Employment deprivation	–0.0893	–0.21	0.86
Occupational flexibility	–0.6313	–1.72	0.53
Geographical flexibility	–1.2392	–0.94	0.29
Gender traditionalism	–0.1841	–1.44	0.33
Class and labour market characteristics			
Manual	–0.3146	–0.43	0.73
Unemployed once before[a]	–0.6606	–0.73	0.52
Unemployed twice before[a]	2.0312	–1.11	0.13
Individual characteristics			
Age < 25	–0.4118	–0.46	0.66
Age 25–34	0.7990	0.74	2.22
Age 45+	–0.5901	1.15	0.55
No qualifications	0.8556	0.75	2.35
Vocational or O level qualifications	0.9792	0.94	2.66
Sex	0.3537	0.42	1.42
Type of locality			
High unemployment	–0.9933	–1.35	0.37
Household characteristics			
Partner full-time or part-time	–0.9899	–0.93	0.37
Partner unemployed or non-employed	–0.0340	–0.03	0.97
Financial stress	–2.0191	–2.70	0.13

[a] In the last five years.

Source: Unemployed respondents in the Work Attitudes Survey who were reinterviewed in the Household and Community Survey (no. = 377).

TABLE 4.16. *Reasons for not looking for work amongst claimant non-seekers*

Reason for not looking for work	Men	Women	Total
Responsibilities for young children	22	55	41
Responsibilities for other dependants	13	2	6
No decent jobs available	16	25	21
Too near retirement	13	6	9
Lack of qualifications	3	8	6
Health	22	17	19
Prefer no paid job	12	4	7
Partner disapproves	7	8	7
Spouse's benefit would be cut	3	14	10
Studying	6	4	5
Other	6	8	7
No.	33	48	81

Note: Multiple response was allowed, therefore percentages can exceed 100%.
Source: The Work Attitudes/Histories Survey, 1986.

considered. The first relates to the time measurement of the variables. For most variables relating to individual and household characteristics, it was possible to backtrack in the life and work history data to establish the person's situation at the outset of their spell of unemployment. For the attitudinal variables, however, measures refer to attitudes at the time of first interview. If the argument is that unemployed individuals are characterized by relatively stable and long-term differences in their underlying pattern of attitudes, reflecting deeper aspects of their personality, then the timing of measurement would not be a matter of any substantial importance. However, it might be argued that attitudes to work will change with longer spells of unemployment and that such change will reduce their initial causal efficacy.

This problem must also be seen in the context of the fact that the cross-sectional survey that forms our point of departure involves a sample of the stock rather than of the flow of the unemployed. A characteristic of a sample of the stock is that it tends to over-represent the longer-term unemployed. If work attitudes are most decisive in the early phases of unemployment and our sample over-represents the longer-term unemployed, an analysis based on the overall sample may underestimate the causal significance of work attitudes. To explore this, we re-estimated the equations for those who had been unemployed for only a relatively short period prior to the interview (three months or less). The results confirmed the previous findings: none of the measures of employment motivation or of job search flexibility emerged as significant determinants of the chances of obtaining a job.

Overall, then, there was little evidence that employment commitment, employment deprivation, or flexibility about job choice had any general impact on re-employment chances. Given the explanatory weakness of attitudinal variables, what factors did account more generally for people's labour market experiences?

Among the factors that increased people's chances of finding work, three stand out as particularly important. First, of the different categories of the unemployed, it was the non-registered that stood by far the best chances of getting a job. Since employment commitment and factors such as age and qualifications have been controlled for, it seems likely that an explanation needs to be sought in the conditions of the labour market rather than in the commitment to work of individuals. The greater proportion of the non-registered were women and they were more likely to be seeking a type of work that had been growing rapidly, namely, part-time work. It was seen earlier that a substantial majority of the non-registered had children under 15, whereas this was the case for only a minority of female claimant seekers. This is likely to account for the fact that the non-registered were three times more likely than the female claimant seekers to be specifically looking for a part-time job. Further, if the nature of the jobs that were obtained between surveys is considered, it is notable that 60 per cent of the non-registered, compared with 19 per cent of the claimant seekers, had taken part-time work.

A second factor that increased chances was related to the employment structure of the household. Unemployed people with a partner in employment had twice the odds of finding a job than people that were single or whose partner was without employment. Although the association is statistically significant only for men, it is in the same direction for women. Since motivational factors have been controlled for, it seems likely that this reflects

differential job search resources, such as access to informal networks that provide information about available job opportunities
and the maintenance of a level of family finance that facilitates
job search. Those with a partner in employment are more likely
to have the resources needed to keep up previous patterns of
social life—whether entertaining at home or engaging in activities
outside the household. Through such sociability, they are more
likely to receive information on the grapevine about available
jobs. At the same time, they will encounter fewer difficulties in
paying for the costs of job search. There is some evidence that
men's job searches involved a wider geographical area. For
instance, 40 per cent of unemployed women compared to only 20
per cent of unemployed men used local shop advertisements as
their main source of information about jobs. The availability of
resources that permitted a geographically more extensive job
search may have been, then, particularly beneficial for men,
explaining the greater strength of the coefficient for the male
unemployed.

Third, there was evidence of a class effect on the likelihood of
finding a job. In particular once other factors have been controlled, manual workers were likely to obtain work more rapidly
than non-manual. It is clear from the separate estimates by sex
that the implications of class position operated in a similar way
for men and for women, although the relationship is somewhat
weaker for women. The greater chances of achieving a job for
manual workers may reflect the fact that unemployment has been
far more prevalent among manual workers and may be regarded,
therefore, as less stigmatic by employers. Higher levels of
turnover in such jobs may also ease the path of new entrants.
However, to the extent that this is the case, although manual
workers may find jobs more quickly, such jobs may prove less
stable in the longer run. Such workers may be particularly susceptible to being caught in a cycle of recurrent unemployment
(Daniel 1983; Harris 1987).

Finally, the most important factor reducing people's chances of
finding a job was that of the absence of qualifications. Those
without qualifications had only half the odds of getting work of
those with qualifications. Given that motivational factors are
controlled for, this would seem to reflect the less favourable
opportunities for work available for such workers. The general

direction of occupational and technical change has been to raise the skill level of work and the qualifications required of employees (Gallie 1991). This structural change in the organization of work is then likely to make the re-entry problems of those without qualifications particularly severe. This is heavily reinforced by the very rudimentary provisions for retraining provided by British labour market institutions.

Overall, the examination of the factors that influenced the likelihood of those unemployed in the first wave of our interviews obtaining work suggests that it is factors linked to the structural conditions of the labour market, rather than to the motivational characteristics of the unemployed themselves, that affect their chances. There was no association between either employment commitment or employment deprivation and the chances of finding work within the sample as a whole. For the greater part, the variables that do appear to influence job chances are those that reflect either the structure of opportunities in the labour market (such as the availability of part-time work, the willingness of employers to recruit unqualified workers) or the availability of mechanisms that provide linkages to information networks about job opportunities (through the contacts and resources made available by having a household member in employment).

7. CONCLUSION

The evidence that we have considered provides some support for the view that there is significant internal differentiation among the unemployed. There were, in the first place, differences by sex, although they were of a rather limited kind. While women appeared to suffer less from the immediate stress of unemployment, they were very similar to men in the importance that they attached to employment in the longer term. Similarly, although women were less likely to be willing to consider geographical mobility in order to find a job, there was no difference between men and women in attitudes to pay or to skill flexibility. Both the lower degree of psychological deprivation due to unemployment and the greater reluctance to be geographically mobile are consistent with the view that women's attitudes to work are affected by their heavier domestic responsibilities. However, these attitudinal differences did not result in women taking longer than men in finding work.

A more marked difference emerged between the different categories of unemployed. In general, the claimant seekers and the non-registered unemployed were very similar. There are no grounds for considering the non-registered as in any sense a less real category of the unemployed. The claimant non-seekers, however, were to some degree distinctive. They had lower levels of employment motivation and they were less likely to be willing to learn new skills in order to find work. Further, this was the one group of the unemployed where longer-term commitment to employment did make a difference to a person's chances of finding work. This must be seen, however, in the context of the social composition of this particular group of the unemployed. It had a higher proportion of older workers, who were more vulnerable to ill health, and a higher proportion of younger mothers, who were faced by a rather inadequate system of child care provision.

With the exception of the claimant non-seekers, the evidence points very consistently to the conclusion that the attitudes to work of the unemployed are not distinctive and are not an important factor accounting for people's vulnerability to unemployment. There was very little difference between the employed and the unemployed in terms of indicators of employment stability such as the frequency of changing jobs or the amount of time that people had spent in their longest job. Those that were currently unemployed were clearly not, on the evidence of their past work histories, inherently unstable members of the work-force. Nor did it seem likely that the position of the unemployed could be explained in terms of their current attitudes to employment. Overall the unemployed were even more likely than the employed to show a strong longer-term commitment to employment. Finally, for the greater part of the unemployed, there was no evidence that differences in either employment motivation or in the flexibility of attitudes to job search affected the time that it took people to find work again. Rather our evidence points to the importance for job chances of the availability of particular types of work, of the resources that can be provided by the household to facilitate job search, and of the structural misfit between the low qualifications possessed by the unemployed and the sharp rise in qualifications required by the changing nature of work in industry.

NOTES

1. The measure of gender traditionalism in attitudes to employment was constructed from a factor analysis of a series of Likert items on women's labour market participation. The factor items which formed the basis of the scale related to views about women's suitability for responsibility at work, whether they should stay at home in times of high unemployment and whether or not men should be still the main bread-winners.
2. The estimates for the replacement ratio (benefits as a percentage of last pay) were, for the whole subsample, coefficient –0.0099 (t statistic, –1.8); for men, coefficient –0.0096 (t statistic, –1.30); for women, coefficient –0.0075 (t statistic, –0.84). Control variables were as in Table 4.11.
3. Where the partner of the unemployed person was in employment, the impact of the unemployment on the household's ability to manage financially was much less severe than where the partner was without paid work. For instance, where the wife was unemployed, but the husband was in full-time employment, 43% said that they were finding it difficult to make ends meet. In contrast, where both partners were unemployed the proportion rose to 80%, and where the husband was unemployed and the wife non-employed to 85%.

5

The Relationship between a Husband's Unemployment and his Wife's Participation in the Labour Force

RICHARD B. DAVIES, PETER ELIAS, AND ROGER PENN

1. INTRODUCTION

It is a well-replicated observation (e.g. Greenhalgh 1980; Layard *et al.* 1980; Joshi 1984) that there is an inverse relationship between husbands' unemployment and the labour force participation of married women; wives of unemployed men in Britain are less likely to be engaged in paid work than the wives of employed men. For example, in the Women and Employment Survey (Martin and Roberts 1984) 33 per cent of wives with unemployed husbands were working compared with 62 per cent of wives with working husbands. One interpretation of this result is that if wives of unemployed husbands had behaved exactly as the wives of working husbands, an additional 29 per cent of them would have been in paid employment. We refer to this summary figure as an 'employment shortfall'.

As Dilnot and Kell (1987) have argued, there could be a direct causal link between the labour force participation of married couples, in that it represents a rational economic response to the regulations governing the payment of transfer income[1] which prevailed in the period spanned by these studies. Another possibility is the 'macho' effect suggested by Barrère-Maurisson *et al.* (1985) in discussing similar results in France. They suggest that there

* Chris Jones at the Institute for Employment Research, University of Warwick, helped to develop IDEAS, the software used for the manipulation of the work and life history survey data. Jon Barry and Brian Francis at the Centre for Applied Statistics, Lancaster University, contributed substantially to the development of the software package SABRE used for the statistical modelling reported in this chapter.

may be reluctance amongst wives of unemployed husbands to work because this could damage the husbands' self-esteem.

Nevertheless, the observed cross-sectional correlation between a husband's unemployment and his wife's non-employment, together with a sound rationale for such a relationship, is only a necessary condition for the assertion that a husband's unemployment can *cause* his wife to give up her job. It is not sufficient to argue that, simply because one observes lower rates of employment among wives in households in which the husband is unemployed, male unemployment is directly associated with lower rates of female labour force participation. As Dilnot and Kell point out, emphasizing the extreme case: 'It is possible that those women married to unemployed men who are at present out of work could never find a job, whatever the structure of the benefit system, because either their personal characteristics are such that no-one would ever want to employ them, or because there are simply no jobs in the area' (1987: 15).

In other words, the heterogeneous nature of the observed sample, in terms of unobserved (and possibly unobservable) characteristics, may give rise to a spurious state-dependent relationship. This is an important issue, for if it can be shown that there is a direct causal relationship, this could imply that the rules which governed the operation of the transfer payment system were both inequitable and inefficient. They may have the unintended effect of increasing, not reducing, family poverty and decreasing net economic output below the level which would prevail in the absence of such rules.

2. EARLIER WORK

Some of the earliest work indicative of a possible relationship between a wife's labour force status and the unemployment of her husband arose from attempts to quantify the extent of 'additional' or 'discouraged' worker effects on female labour supply. The 'additional worker' effect would arise if the reduction in household living standards associated with a rise in male unemployment led to an increase in the labour force participation of women, or to an increase in the hours worked by working women, in an attempt to maintain household living standards.

The 'discouraged worker' effect relates to the impact of a rise in unemployment generally upon the perceived chance of obtaining work and/or the low rewards to working, particularly for those non-working women who have a low expected market wage. Male unemployment rates were usually used to proxy the supply/demand imbalance, given statistical problems arising from the definition and measurement of female unemployment. In other words, as male unemployment rises, the chances that a non-working woman will search for work could be reduced as her perceived probability of finding a job may fall.

From aggregate time-series analysis of regional data, Corry and Roberts (1970, 1974) and Berg and Dalton (1977) estimated that the elasticity of female labour force participation rates with respect to male unemployment was in the range –0.03 to –0.04. Greenhalgh (1977), Grice (1978), and McNabb (1977) find similar results in cross-sectional studies of the labour force participation of married women. For example, in her study of the labour force participation rates of married women in 106 towns in Great Britain in 1971, Greenhalgh indicates that each percentage point increase in the local male unemployment rate is associated with a reduction of 0.7 per cent in the local labour force participation rate. Layard *et al.* (1980), using individual-level data from the 1974 General Household Survey, estimated that the probability of the wife being in paid work was reduced by 30 per cent in households in which there was an unemployed husband. From these studies the view arose that, in terms of the net impact of husbands' unemployment on their wives labour force participation, the 'discouraged worker' effect outweighed the 'additional worker' effect.

The earliest pooled cross-section/time-series analysis of the participation of married women in paid work, drawing upon quarterly information from the Family Expenditure Survey (Elias 1980; Molho and Elias 1984), gave further insight into the nature of the correlation between the participation of married women in paid work and the unemployment of their husbands. These studies showed that a correlation remained after controlling for wage effects, household income, and family structure, and the general supply/demand imbalance in the local labour market. The depressing effect of the husband's unemployment on the wife's employment appeared to be at its strongest when there were young children in the household. These two studies were unique in that they used household information about married couples and controlled for wage and household income effects.

Sociological studies of the relationship between a husband's unemployment and the economic status of his wife have provided more depth and detail to the nature of the relationship, but do little to further our understanding of the dynamics of the processes at work. Barrère-Maurisson *et al.* (1985) discusses the phenomenon among French couples in terms of the effect upon a husband's self-esteem of being 'supported' by a working wife. Similarly, McKee and Bell (1985) reported case-study evidence in which issues of masculinity, authority, marital stability, and pride were quoted as important factors preventing the wife from adopting a 'bread-winner' role when her husband became unemployed. Interestingly, McKee and Bell also reported that couples they interviewed were well aware of the financial disincentive to work arising from the operation of the social security system:

Often wives engaged in an accounting procedure estimating how much they could realistically earn in the labour market and how much would subsequently be deducted from husband's benefits, finding, when expenses for travel, childcare and incidentals, were included a *reduction* in the family's overall standard of living. Few women opted for, or remained in, paid work in the face of these costs. (1985: 393)

Possibly the most detailed study of the impact of a husband's unemployment on his wife's labour force participation is that obtained from the DHSS Cohort Study of Unemployed Men (Moylan *et al.* 1984). This was based upon a national sample of 2,300 men who became unemployed in the autumn of 1978, following up on their labour market experience at one, four, and twelve months after becoming unemployed. The sample was heavily biased towards married men, facilitating a short but detailed longitudinal analysis of the behaviour of the unemployed men and their wives. Some of the key findings from this study are:

1. The wives of men who became unemployed were less likely to have been in employment than wives in general.
2. Changes in wives' employment status during the year could not be accounted for in terms of the characteristics of wives married to men who remained unemployed compared with the wives married to men who returned to work.

3. Some of the changes in wives' employment status seemed to
be systematically related to the type of benefit the family
was receiving.

In particular, the study revealed that only about one in eight
of the wives of the men who remained unemployed for at least
four months, and who were in receipt of Supplementary
Allowance, were themselves employed before their husbands
became unemployed. However, over two-fifths of these women
left employment during this four-month period. As the authors
of this study conclude: 'This provides strong *prima facie* evidence
of a disincentive effect on the wives' behaviour, although there
are other possible explanations which may well explain some of
this difference' (Moylan *et al.* 1985: 132).

Garcia (1989) takes the findings from this study a stage further, incorporating a model of the labour force participation of
the wives of unemployed men within a utility-maximizing framework, subject to the income rules regarding payment of unemployment and supplementary benefit. From this simulation
model, Garcia concludes that only a small part of the difference
between the labour force participation of the wives of employed
versus unemployed husbands may be accounted for by the disincentive effect of the rules relating to transfer payments. Other
factors which he hypothesizes account for the difference include
the local labour market influence (i.e. a 'discouraged worker'
effect), other social status influences on the labour force participation of wives whose husbands are not working, and the possibility of a relationship between the 'employability' of both
husbands and wives in households where the husband is likely
to experience unemployment. In contrast, Kell and Wright
(1990), using cross-sectional information from the 1983 Family
Expenditure Survey and Labour Force Survey, note a 39 per cent
difference between the labour force participation of the wives of
employed men compared with unemployed men and conclude:
'entitlement to social security benefits, and supplementary
benefits in particular, can result in severe disincentives. This factor must be regarded as a major explanation of the low participation rates for women married to unemployed men' (1990: 124).

In summary, these studies indicate that there appears to be a
relationship between a husband's unemployment and his wife's

employment and that this relationship derives from both sample heterogeneity—the wives of men who become unemployed are less likely to be in work at any given point in time than the wives of men who do not experience unemployment—and from cross-couple state dependence—the fact that her husband has become unemployed increases the probability that the wife will give up her job. At issue here is the relative strengths of these influences. Put simply, do we have sufficient evidence of a state-dependent relationship to suggest that the nature of the social security system operated as a significant disincentive for married women to engage in paid employment at or around those times when their husbands were unemployed?

3. PARTNERSHIPS IN THE SOCIAL CHANGE AND ECONOMIC LIFE SURVEYS

The new information which forms the basis of this enquiry is the partnership life and work history data available from the Social Change and Economic Life Initiative (SCELI; see the Methodological Appendix at the end of this book). This information evolved in a complex fashion, giving rise to a non-equal probability sample of married couples in the six localities studied: Aberdeen, Coventry, Kirkcaldy, Northampton, Rochdale, and Swindon. The subjects of the enquiry presented in this chapter consist of the respondents who were contacted in 1986 and (for their partners) 1987 and who were living together in a marital partnership in 1987.

The remainder of this chapter is structured as follows: Section 3.1 describes the characteristics of the married couples as recorded in the surveys, detailing their economic status, ethnicity, occupations, and earnings. Section 3.2 presents some information on the dynamics of the relationship between wives' labour force participation and husbands' unemployment, examining the work histories of men and women living in a marital partnership through a sixteen-year period prior to the survey, focusing specifically upon the unemployment of husbands and the employment of their wives. The issue of whether or not the experience of unemployment is concentrated within a relatively small number of households is examined in more detail in Section 3.3. At this juncture, some of the main factors which govern the dynamics of the relationship between husbands' unemployment and wives' labour force participation are increasingly apparent, but the use of simple cross-tabulations and graphics as analytical techniques becomes inappropriate as the exploration of these dynamic effects progresses. For this reason, Section 4 switches into a multivariate statistical framework. In particular, it describes the method by which we seek to allow for unobserved differences between women in terms of their propensity to engage in paid work. This may sound complex and, indeed, the statistical estimation procedures that are used have some sophisticated features. As has been argued earlier, it is most important to distinguish between influences which are specific to the married couple (e.g. their motivation, preferences, and attitudes to work) and those which depend not so much upon the individuals concerned, but on the economic and social circumstances in which they find themselves (e.g. having an unemployed husband). Our concern is with the extent to which unemployment among married men can be viewed as a direct *cause* of their wives leaving paid employment. Section 5 describes the method we adopted to measure this effect using a simple yet meaningful summary statistic derived from the statistical analysis—the concept of an *employment shortfall*. Section 6 concludes the chapter with an assessment of the various results obtained.

In all of the empirical analyses which follow, the extent of women's labour force participation is measured by recording whether or not a woman is in a paid job (full-time, part-time, or self-employed). In a strict sense, labour force participation would include the unemployed state. That is, a woman who stated she was either employed or unemployed would be regarded as participating in the labour force. In practice, female unemployment is not reported in a consistent fashion between women in different age-groups. Further, the key process we are interested in is whether or not a woman gives up her job when her husband loses his. For these reasons, we regard the labour force participation of married women as synonymous with their employment in full- or part-time work.

3.1. Characteristics of the Partnerships

Table 5.1 gives an overview of the characteristics of the 1,171 partnerships which were identified according to the procedures outlined above. Across all the localities, nearly 80 per cent of the husbands in these partnerships were in paid work, compared with 57 per cent of their wives. The split between the two broad age-groups shown in Table 5.1 indicates that the wives tend, on average, to be slightly younger than their husbands. This was confirmed by examining the age difference between husbands and wives. One in four of all partnerships contains a couple in which the husband is at least five years older than his wife.

Looking across the localities, Table 5.1 reveals that Swindon has a significantly higher rate of employment among the couples identified in the survey. Husbands' employment rates are low in Rochdale and Coventry, reflecting the higher rates of unemployment prevailing in these areas. Coventry and Rochdale have significant proportions of married couples of Asian ethnic origin: over 9 per cent of the Rochdale couples and almost 7 per cent in the Coventry locality.

Table 5.2 presents some information on the manual/non-manual[2] structure of the occupations in which these couples were working in 1987. Clearly, Kirkcaldy stands out as an area in which a much higher proportion of both men and women are in manual occupations. Additionally, Coventry wives are much more likely to be employed in manual occupations than in Aberdeen, Northampton, Rochdale, or Swindon. The bottom half of Table 5.2 compares households in which the husband was employed in 1987 and those in which he was unemployed. Given the small numbers of women who were in paid work in households in which the husband was unemployed, the comparison between the two types of household should be made with caution. There is a general indication that a greater proportion of the working wives in households in which the husband was unemployed in 1987 tend to be employed in manual occupations compared with the households in which the husbands were employed in 1987.

Table 5.3 shows, in cross-sectional format, the relationship between the economic status of husbands and wives. Across all localities, in households in which the husband was employed in

TABLE 5.1. *Characteristics of partnerships, SCEL Household/Community Survey, 1987* (%)

Characteristics of partnership	Locality							All
	Aberdeen	Coventry	Kirkcaldy	Northampton	Rochdale	Swindon		
Economic status in 1987								
Husband employed	79.3	74.7	84.0	83.5	72.7	83.9		79.8
Wife employed	57.5	55.7	56.5	54.2	55.2	63.0		57.2
Age structure								
Husband 20–39	57.0	42.1	44.5	50.5	46.4	46.4		47.8
Husband 40–60	43.0	57.9	55.5	49.5	53.6	53.6		52.2
Wife 20–39	61.1	50.0	50.0	58.8	59.0	53.6		55.3
Wife 40–60	38.9	50.0	50.0	41.2	41.0	46.4		44.7
Ethnic group								
White	100.0	93.2	99.0	96.9	90.7	98.6		96.5
Asian	–	6.8	1.0	1.0	9.3	0.9		3.1
Afro-caribbean	–	–	–	1.0	–	–		0.2
BASE (= 100%)	193	190	200	194	183	211		1,171

Source: SCEL Household/Community Survey, 1987.

TABLE 5.2. *Manual and non-manual occupations of husbands and wives by economic status of husbands, 1987 (%)*

Social class	Locality						
	Aberdeen	Coventry	Kirkcaldy	Northampton	Rochdale	Swindon	All
Husband							
Non-manual	53.5	49.3	38.0	49.4	44.2	48.8	47.2
Manual	46.5	50.7	62.0	50.6	55.8	51.2	52.8
Wife							
Non-manual	69.4	56.4	58.6	75.4	64.3	64.8	65.0
Manual	30.6	43.6	41.4	24.6	35.7	35.2	35.0
BASE (= 100%)	108	102	16	114	98	128	666
Households in which husband unemployed							
Wife							
Non-manual	40.0	40.0	14.3	40.0	25.0	50.0	41.0
Manual	60.0	60.0	85.7	60.0	75.0	50.0	59.0
BASE (= 100%)	10	5	7	5	4	8	39
Households in which husband employed							
Wife							
Non-manual	72.2	59.0	59.6	74.7	66.7	68.2	66.9
Manual	27.8	41.0	40.4	25.3	33.3	31.8	33.1
BASE (= 100%)	90	83	99	99	81	110	562

Source: SCEL Household/Community Survey, 1987.

1987, about 60 per cent of wives were in paid employment. In households in which the husband was unemployed in 1987, only 33 per cent of wives were in paid jobs, a difference which compares well with the findings of Layard *et al.* (1980). Looking across the localities, there is little variation in this proportion for households in which the husband was employed. For the households in which the husband was unemployed, there appears to be some variation across the localities. However, due to the low sample numbers recorded, this may reflect sampling variation rather than any systematic difference between the localities.

The lower half of Table 5.3 presents similar information for these same households in 1982, as long as the couples concerned were in their present partnership in that year. Essentially the same pattern is revealed, with just over 60 per cent of the wives in paid work if their husbands were in paid jobs, compared with 38 per cent of the wives in households in which the husband was unemployed.

Table 5.4 examines the relationship between the economic status of the wives and the *earnings* of their husbands. The information presented in this table is based upon a sample which is approximately half the size of that shown in the preceding tables, reflecting the fact that accurate income information was only obtained from the first of the two linked surveys used in this study. For households in which the husband is in employment, there appears to be an inverse relationship between wives' employment and husbands' earnings; the higher the net monthly income of the husbands, the lower is the proportion of their wives in employment. There is a stark contrast, though, between the economic activity of the wives of non-earning husbands from those who have husbands in employment.

3.2. *The Dynamics of Labour Force Participation among Married Couples*

Apart from the DHSS Cohort Study of the Unemployed (Moylan *et al.* 1984), there has been little empirical evidence to shed light upon the sequence and timing of labour force participation decisions made by married couples. This can be particularly useful in an exploration of underlying causal processes. For example, if a husband's unemployment is directly related to his wife's non-participation in the labour force, we would, in general,

TABLE 5.3. *Economic status of husbands and wives, 1987 and 1982* (%)

Economic status	Locality						
	Aberdeen	Coventry	Kirkcaldy	Northampton	Rochdale	Swindon	All
1987							
Households in which husband employed							
Wife self-employed	1.3	4.9	2.4	0.6	2.3	3.4	2.5
Wife full-time employee	29.4	31.7	35.1	35.2	36.1	35.0	33.8
Wife part-time employee	28.8	24.6	19.0	21.0	26.3	26.6	24.3
BASE (= 100%)	153	142	168	162	133	177	935
Households in which husband unemployed							
Wife self-employed	–	–	–	–	3.7	4.8	1.5
Wife full-time employee	20.0	23.3	25.0	18.8	–	33.3	19.3
Wife part-time employee	24.0	3.3	18.8	6.3	11.1	14.3	12.6
BASE (= 100%)	25	30	16	16	27	21	135
1982							
Households in which husband employed							
Wife self-employed	1.2	2.8	2.4	0.6	3.1	1.2	1.8
Wife full-time employee	32.3	31.0	36.6	32.9	36.9	30.2	33.2
Wife part-time employee	24.8	26.2	23.8	29.7	23.1	31.4	26.7
BASE (= 100%)	161	145	164	155	130	172	927
Households in which husband unemployed							
Wife self-employed	–	–	–	–	–	–	–
Wife full-time employee	16.7	21.4	30.0	40.0	25.0	–	22.1
Wife part-time employee	–	7.1	20.0	20.0	5.0	50.0	16.2
BASE (= 100%)	6	14	10	10	20	8	68

Source: SCEL Household/Community Survey, 1987.

TABLE 5.4. *Economic status of wives by net monthly income of husbands* (%)

Husband's net monthly income is in:	Economic activity of wife				
	Self-employment	Full-time employee	Part-time employee	Other	BASE (= 100%)
1st quartile	3.9	33.8	44.2	18.2	77
2nd quartile	3.7	27.2	43.2	25.9	81
3rd quartile	3.8	32.9	30.4	32.9	79
4th quartile	2.5	20.3	31.6	45.6	79
Refused	–	27.3	18.2	54.5	11
Not known/not stated	2.7	29.1	32.7	35.5	110
Not in employment	0.8	14.0	14.7	70.5	129
TOTAL	2.7	25.3	30.9	41.2	566

Source: SCEL Household/Community Survey, 1987.

expect to see her non-participation during this spell, and not at other times. In this subsection, we begin to explore the timing and sequence of these events for husbands and wives by reconstructing their labour force participation over the past sixteen years.

Some indication of the dynamics of the labour force participation of married women and its relationship to unemployment among their husbands can be gained from Figure 5.1. Each part of Figure 5.1 displays a sixteen-year profile for a group of households, grouped in terms of the age of the married women within them. By 'sampling' the work histories of the couples in each household in a particular month (February was selected to maximize the chance of observing seasonal unemployment), a profile of the labour market status of the couple is established for each household. The employment of the wives and unemployment of their husbands is plotted as a percentage of the number of households in each age cohort. This base number is adjusted in each year, to ensure that each couple was in its current (1987) partnership in each earlier year.[3] All couples who were not in their current partnership have been excluded from the analysis.

Figure 5.1 shows the experiences of employment and unemployment for households in which the wife was aged 35–39 years

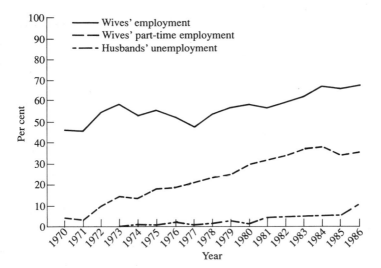

Wives aged 35–39 years in 1986

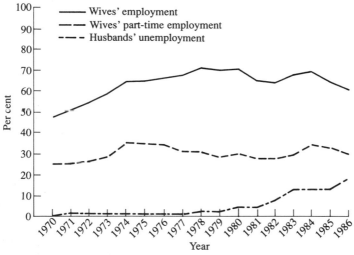

Wives aged 50–54 years in 1986

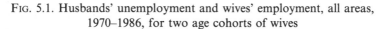

FIG. 5.1. Husbands' unemployment and wives' employment, all areas, 1970–1986, for two age cohorts of wives

in 1987, and the same information for households in which she was aged 50–54 years. These two age-groups were selected to portray the experience of two cohorts who were likely to have completed their family formation plans. The upper chart displays the expected dip in employment associated with family formation in the 25–29 year age range and the increasing proportion of employment among the wives which is held on a part-time basis. The unemployment of their husbands can be seen to increase gradually in the post-1975 period. No relationship between husbands' unemployment and wives' employment is apparent in this graph. The lower chart shows that, for 50–54-year-old married women, their employment rate exhibits a steady increase up to 1979, followed by a slight downward trend in the post-1979 period. This appears to coincide with the significant rise in the experience of unemployment among the husbands of these women, from virtually 0 in 1978 to almost 20 per cent of households by 1986.

In essence, these graphs give no clear indication of an inverse relationship between husbands' unemployment and wives' unemployment except for the older age-group (50–54-year-olds). For the younger age-group analysed, the strong upward rise in employment in their post-family formation period could mask any potential moderating influence upon their employment arising from the fairly low, but increasing, unemployment experienced by their husbands.

3.3. *The Concentration of Unemployment Experience*

There is some evidence of cross-couple state dependency from the longitudinal analysis of age cohorts presented in the preceding subsection, at least among the older age-groups. However, the extent of this cross-state dependence is not clear. Earlier research (Moylan *et al.* 1984) has suggested that the experience of unemployment among married men may be concentrated in particular households. There is a need to disaggregate this analysis further to determine the extent to which the experience of unemployment is concentrated among particular groups of households consisting of married couples.

One simple approach is to assume that the best indicator of whether or not a household is likely to have experienced unem-

ployment in previous years is their current experience of unemployment. Thus, households were divided into two groups, those
in which the husband was unemployed in 1986 and those in
which he was not unemployed at this time. Figure 5.2 compares
the sixteen-year profile of employment of the wives of men who
were unemployed in 1986 with that of the wives of men who
were not unemployed in 1986. By definition, therefore, in 1986
we observe no unemployment in the upper chart and 100 per
cent unemployment in the lower chart. Looking back in time, we
observe the extent to which husbands in each of these two groups
will have experienced employment or unemployment at some earlier date.

This comparison is most revealing. What is interesting is that,
in all earlier years for households in which the husband was not
unemployed in 1986, very little unemployment is experienced in
the earlier years. By contrast, the lower chart on this figure
reveals that the earlier experience of the unemployment of husbands is primarily focused within those households in which
there is current experience of unemployment. It can be seen that,
not only is there a clear correlation between the rise in male
unemployment and the fall in female employment, but there is
also evidence that the employment profile for the wives whose
husbands were unemployed in 1986 is about 15 to 20 percentage
points lower than the corresponding profile shown in the upper
chart in Figure 5.2.

4. STATISTICAL MODELLING OF PARTNERSHIP WORK HISTORY DATA

The analyses conducted in Section 3 have given some indication
that husbands' unemployment depresses their wives' employment.
Simple cross-sectional tabulations appear to demonstrate this (see
Table 5.2), but no causal relationship can be implied from such
analysis. Men who are more likely to experience unemployment
could be married to women who are less likely to work. Equally,
married men and women who live in areas of low labour demand
could experience high levels of male unemployment and low levels of female labour force participation. Moving on to a simple
dynamic analysis by viewing the experience through time of

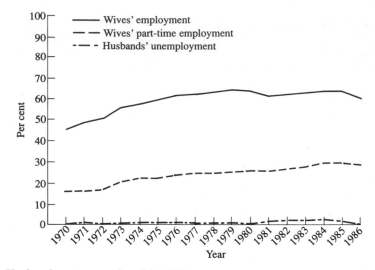

Husbands not unemployed in 1986

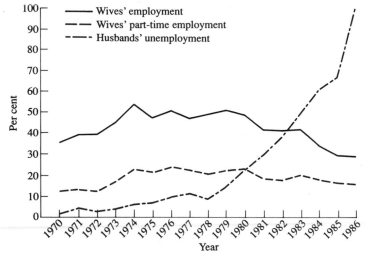

Husbands unemployed in 1986

FIG. 5.2. Husband's unemployment and wives' employment, all areas, 1970–1986, by whether or not husband was unemployed in 1986

employment and unemployment among married couples (Figures 5.2 and 5.3) does give some indication that rising unemployment among husbands is associated with lower employment among their wives, but it is clear also that a variety of influences can be compounded in such analysis. Family formation and the presence of young children are major factors which influence whether or not a woman works, as are her age and qualifications. Such factors, which affect the opportunity for women to engage in paid work, we refer to as *observed heterogeneity*. The final part of Section 3 indicates clearly that the experience of male unemployment through time is concentrated within relatively few households and, within such households, there does seem to be a link between the increasing experience of unemployment among married men through the 1980s and the decline in employment among their wives. The fact that certain households experience a disproportionate share of unemployment could result from *residual heterogeneity*, differences between households in terms of their likelihood of experiencing unemployment arising from unobserved (and, possibly, unobservable) factors such as motivations and work preferences.

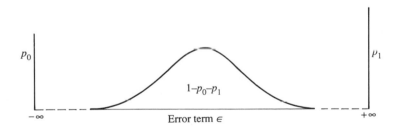

Fig. 5.3. Representation of residual heterogeneity as Normally distributed with end-points (the 'mover–stayer' formulation)

The challenge we address in this section is to distinguish true state dependence from heterogeneity; personal and labour market characteristics may influence the employment status of both partners and therefore generate a spurious cross-couple state dependence. A measure of control for such characteristics is possible using the graphical methods of the previous section. These indicate that the state dependence effect is reduced but not eliminated by disaggregating the graphs by locality and wife's age. The problem with control by disaggregation is, of course, that the number of observations in each disaggregate category rapidly become too small and, in this context, the graphs become irregular and impossible to interpret.[4] The advantage of statistical modelling is that many control variables may be included simultaneously in the analysis. Moreover, with microlevel longitudinal data it is even possible to exercise some control for unmeasured effects. This may be critically important for avoiding misleading results when state dependence effects are of interest (Heckman and Singer 1984; Davies and Pickles 1985).

The second objective of the statistical modelling is to assess whether any true cross-state dependence between husband and wife's employment status is consistent with the operation of the social security benefits regime. In particular, the social security disincentives for wives to have paid work generally became more severe after their husbands had been unemployed for a year (Dilnot and Kell 1987). A corresponding 'twelve month' effect should be evident in the data if the lower rates of employment of wives with unemployed husbands are at least in part a rational response to these disincentives.

4.1. Analytical Framework

The SCELI partnership data allow us to construct a response variable sequence S_i for each wife i consisting of monthly binary outcomes ($y_{i\tau_i}, y_{i,\tau_i + 1}, y_{i,\tau_i + 2}, \ldots, y_{it}, \ldots y_{iT}$), coded 1 if the wife is in paid employment, 0 otherwise, and running from marriage in month τ_i to the 1987 survey date in month T. For each month t and wife i, we may also construct a vector of values $\mathbf{x}_{it}$ for explanatory variables. These explanatory variables will include both control variables and variables summarizing the husband's employment status.

The conventional logistic regression model for binary response gives the probability of observed outcome y_{it} as

$$P(y_{it}) = \exp[y_{it}(\beta'\mathbf{x}_{it})]/[1 + \exp(\beta'\mathbf{x}_{it})];$$

where β is a vector of unknown regression coefficients (parameters) measuring the systematic relationship between the explanatory variables and the response. Such a model could be derived by a random utility approach as proposed, for example, by Zabalza (1982). However, quite apart from the tautology some suspect in such derivations, this may give a misleadingly rigid theoretical context for the proposed analysis. The logistic regression model provides a convenient and flexible representation within which the effects of interest may be disentangled and could therefore be consistent with any number of theoretical perspectives on the participation of married women in the labour market. More importantly, the model does assume that the direction of causality runs from the husband's employment status to that of the wife; the male is implicitly taken to be the primary wage earner with the wife having a subordinate and secondary role. Martin and Roberts (1984) provide some empirical support for this approximation.

To include an explicit representation of the effects of omitted variables, we extend the logistic regression model to give the 'internal heterogeneity' (Allison 1987) formulation

$$P\ (y_{it}) = \exp\ [\,y_{it}\ (\ \beta' x_{it} + \epsilon_i)\ ]/[1\ +\ \exp\ (\ \beta' x_{it} + \epsilon_i)],$$

where ϵ_i is an individual specific error term. The presence of these error terms greatly complicates the calibration of the model because, for sound statistical reasons, they may not be estimated simultaneously with the regression parameters and must be eliminated in some way from the model.[5] The approach corresponding closest to standard statistical practice is to assume that the errors are Normally distributed in the population and to integrate (average) them out of the sequence probabilities.[6] We will refer to this as a Normal-logistic model. It is identical to the logistic variance component model used by Anderson and Aitkin (1985) in a study of interviewer effects.

Statistical models are often quite robust to violations of Normal error term assumptions but longitudinal models of this type appear to be a notable exception. Indeed, it has been long recognized (e.g. Massy *et al.* 1970: 62; Spilerman 1972) that parameter distributions such as the Normal tend to underestimate the number who are 'stayers' in the social process under investigation. In this instance it is plausible to argue that some married women will have a 0, or very low, probability of ever taking paid employment or, at the other extreme, of ever not working, and this could not be accommodated by the declining tails of a

Normal distribution. This problem may be addressed by including a 'stayer' component in the Normal-logistic formulation, allowing empirically estimated proportions of the population to be in the two extreme categories.[7] It is equivalent to assuming that the error terms have the distribution shown in Figure 5.3. The Normal distribution is augmented by finite probabilities at plus and minus infinity on the logit scale corresponding to paid employment probabilities of 1 and 0, respectively. The result is a sophisticated 'mover–stayer' model, which Davies and Crouchley (1986) demonstrate has greatly enhanced flexibility in representing the residual heterogeneity due to omitted variables.

Table 5.5 summarizes the basic calibration results for a variety of models. These are termed 'Conventional Logistic', 'Normal-Logistic', and 'Normal-Logistic with end-points', corresponding to the types of model discussed in the three preceding paragraphs. It should be noted that each model includes the explanatory variables discussed in the next section. The number of partnerships investigated in each locality is fairly modest but the data sets are large because every month of a marriage contributes a set of observations to the analyses. The log-likelihoods of the calibrated models consequently have large negative values. The conventional logistic model ignores the information on temporal continuity in the data and treats each outcome as independent. This is sometimes referred to as a 'pooled cross-sectional model' (Allison 1982). The considerable improvement in the log-likelihoods on introducing a Normal error indicates appreciable heterogeneity between wives in their employment status even after accounting for the effects of the explanatory variables.[8] The additional parameter in the Normal-logistic model measures the standard deviation of the Normal error distribution, and the estimated values in Table 5.5 provide further evidence of the extent of the residual heterogeneity, and a salutary reminder of the low levels of explanation typically achieved by analyses of social phenomena. For example, a scale parameter of 1.3 indicates that, for a group of women with identical values of the explanatory variables and with average employment probability of 0.5, about 5 per cent would be expected to have actual employment probabilities outside the range from 0.07 to 0.93. The results in Table 5.5 also support the contention that end-point probabilities can improve the representation of heterogeneity.[9]

TABLE 5.5. *Summary of model calibration results*

	Localities						
	Aberdeen	Coventry	Kirkcaldy	Northampton	Rochdale	Swindon	All
No. of partnerships	174	163	188	162	155	186	536[a]
No. of observations (months of marriage histories)	30,742	33,117	40,960	30,799	27,613	35,793	105,898
Conventional Logistic Model							
Log-likelihood	-15,624.7	-17,188.9	-22,326.1	-16,685.2	-14,324.7	-19,641.9	-57,328.0
Normal-Logistic Model							
Log-likelihood	-10,201.8	-11,887.2	-15,616.0	-10,804.9	-9,898.7	-12,443.3	-38,184.9
Scale parameter	1.43	1.18	1.34	1.31	1.41	1.52	1.37
Normal-Logistic Model with end-points							
Log-likelihood	-10,095.9	-11,823.2	-15,493.6	-10,727.2	-9,787.8	-12,296.9	-37,796.4
Scale parameter	1.25	1.07	1.03	1.26	1.30	1.38	1.11
End-point probabilities							
0	0.057	0.065	0.062	0.031	0.083	0.062	0.064
1	0.052	0.032	0.034	0.088	0.114	0.106	0.072

[a] The 'All localities' analyses were restricted to partnerships for which the wife was the original respondent. This enabled wives' educational qualifications to be included as explanatory variables.

4.2. Substantive Results

Having established the superiority of the Normal-Logistic models with end-points over a conventional logistic formulation, we now direct attention at the substantive results from these models. Table 5.6 lists the main explanatory variables together with parameter estimates and their standard errors for the various localities. The parameter estimates shown in Table 5.6 were all derived from maximum likelihood estimation of the Normal-Logistic with end-points model, summary statistics for which were given in the bottom four rows of Table 5.5. The variable of interest, the husband's employment status, is represented by a block of dummy variables for different durations of unemployment with employment providing the reference group. The selection of control variables, although inevitably constrained by available data, was strongly influenced by previous discussion in the literature, particularly Joseph (1983) and Joshi (1984). Asian wives tend to have a low level of labour force participation and, as quite different processes may be operating on both the supply and the demand side, Asian partnerships were excluded from the analyses reported. As will be evident from Section 3.1, this mainly affected Coventry and Rochdale.

It is emphasized that the dummy variables representing the presence in the household of children of different ages are defined strictly as specified in Table 5.6. Thus, for example, the total effect of a child less than 1 year old is given by the sum of the parameter estimates for <1 year, <5 years, and <11 years old. The expectation is that each of these dummy variables will have large negative coefficients, indicating not only that young children reduce the probability of the mother having paid employment but also that this effect declines appreciably with the increasing age of the youngest child. The values obtained are clearly consistent with this expectation.

The results for the variable representing the total number of children is less straightforward to interpret. Although the probability of the mother working appears to decrease, as expected, with the number of children in two localities, it is estimated to increase in three and overall. However, the size of the effect is generally modest in comparison with the dummy variables indicating the presence of young children.

TABLE 5.6. *Parameter estimates for Normal-Logistic model with end-points*

	Localities						
	Aberdeen	Coventry	Kirkcaldy	Northampton	Rochdale	Swindon	All
Intercept	2.37 (0.02)	1.67 (0.02)	−0.25 (0.02)	1.12 (0.02)	1.74 (0.03)	1.78 (0.02)	1.41 (0.02)
Husband's unemployment duration							
0 month	−	−	−	−	−	−	−
1–6 months	0.15 (0.08)	−0.36 (0.10)	−0.05 (0.06)	−1.51 (0.09)	−1.45 (0.11)	−1.66 (0.08)	−0.09 (0.04)
7–11 months		0.01 (0.17)	−0.19 (0.12)		−1.44 (0.12)		−0.18 (0.10)
1–2 years	−1.43 (0.06)	−0.88 (0.08)	−0.81 (0.10)	−1.96 (0.27)	−2.22 (0.15)	−0.98 (0.07)	−0.74 (0.06)
> 2 years		−0.89 (0.03)	−2.71 (0.03)		−3.32 (0.09)		−1.36 (0.02)
Age of youngest child							
< 1 year	−1.31 (0.04)	−1.27 (0.04)	−1.08 (0.03)	−1.56 (0.03)	−1.19 (0.02)	−1.27 (0.03)	−1.28 (0.02)
< 5 years	−2.12 (0.01)	−2.40 (0.01)	−2.09 (0.01)	−2.03 (0.01)	−1.74 (0.02)	−2.26 (0.01)	−1.94 (0.01)
< 11 years	−1.96 (0.01)	−1.76 (0.01)	−1.31 (0.01)	−1.87 (0.01)	−1.26 (0.02)	−1.28 (0.01)	−1.85 (0.01)
11+	−	−	−	−	−	−	−
No. of children	−0.09 (0.01)	0.30 (0.01)	0.63 (0.01)	0.51 (0.01)	−0.17 (0.01)	0.00 (0.01)	0.29 (0.01)
Age							
Husband's age	0.15 (0.01)	−0.38 (0.01)	0.01 (0.01)	−0.04 (0.01)	0.38 (0.01)	−0.09 (0.01)	0.09 (0.01)
(Husband's age)$^2 \times 10^{-2}$	−0.18 (0.01)	0.63 (0.01)	−0.05 (0.01)	−0.07 (0.01)	−0.55 (0.01)	−0.04 (0.01)	−0.13 (0.01)
Wife's age	0.11 (0.01)	0.60 (0.01)	−0.10 (0.01)	−0.12 (0.01)	0.02 (0.01)	0.15 (0.01)	0.09 (0.01)
(Wife's age)$^2 \times 10^{-2}$	−0.20 (0.01)	−0.99 (0.01)	0.14 (0.01)	0.20 (0.01)	0.02 (0.01)	−0.09 (0.01)	−0.16 (0.01)
Time							
Calendar year $\times 10^{-1}$	−0.25 (0.07)	−1.33 (0.07)	6.08 (0.06)	2.17 (0.07)	1.87 (0.10)	3.07 (0.05)	2.96 (0.03)
(Calendar year)$^2 \times 10^{-3}$	0.79 (0.04)	1.07 (0.05)	−3.60 (0.04)	−1.11 (0.04)	−1.07 (0.07)	−1.65 (0.03)	−1.58 (0.02)

Notes: The response variable is wife's employment status (1 = in paid employment; 0 = not in paid employment). Standar errors are in parentheses.

A dash (−) indicates the reference group.

It is well known that failure to control adequately for temporal effects in a longitudinal model can result in misleading inference about state dependences. The additional error structure of the model provides limited assurance in this regard because the individual-specific error terms are assumed to be constant over time and cannot be fully effective in controlling for time-varying omitted effects. Husband and wife's ages were therefore entered as quadratics into the model to ensure some flexibility in representing the systematic relationship with wife's employment status. The overall pattern is that of paid employment declining after wives reach middle age, but there is complex variation between localities and between the effects of the wife's own age and that of her husband. A quadratic was also used for the calendar year variable, which carries the heavy burden of summarizing the effects of secular change in the employment participation of married women and the effects of local labour market changes. The results all indicate increasing rates of paid employment for married women over recent decades.

A particular feature of the survey data collected in the Rochdale locality is information on the educational qualifications of both partners. These were included as control variables in the Rochdale analyses, serving as a proxy for earning potential as well as ease of obtaining a job and 'taste for market work' (McNabb 1977). The parameter estimates are shown separately in Table 5.7a and reveal the expected higher levels of paid employment for wives with educational qualifications. The effects of the husband's educational qualifications are more difficult to interpret. In so far as educational qualifications are correlated with income, the negative coefficients for the higher qualifications are consistent with the phenomenon noted in Section 3.1: the higher the income of the husbands, the lower the proportion of their wives in employment. But the large positive coefficient for 'other significant qualifications' appears to contradict such a relationship. One possibility is that wives' employment probabilities are lower at either end of the husbands' educational qualification spectrum for different reasons; for husbands with higher qualifications, the lower level of wives' employment may be due to lack of financial pressure, while for husbands with no educational qualifications it may be due to absence of opportunities and limited taste for market work.

TABLE 5.7. *Additional parameter estimates for Rochdale and all localities analyses*

(*a*) *Highest educational qualification: Rochdale and all localities analysis*

	Higher education	O/A level and equivalent	Other significant qualifications[a]	None (reference group)
Rochdale				
Wife	0.75 (0.04)	0.62 (0.06)	1.09 (0.04)	—
Husband	−0.21 (0.05)	−0.24 (0.03)	0.72 (0.03)	—
All localities				
Wife	−0.04 (0.06)	−0.07 (0.03)	−0.30 (0.05)	—

[a] Clerical and commercial qualifications; apprenticeships, HGV, and PSV licences; and professional qualifications without examinations.

(*b*) *Locality effects: all localities analysis*

Aberdeen (reference group)	Coventry	Kirkcaldy	Northampton	Rochdale	Swindon
—	0.05 (0.02)	−0.71 (0.02)	0.22 (0.02)	−0.06 (0.02)	−0.43 (0.02)

For the other localities, educational qualifications are only available for the partner, male or female, who happened to be the original respondent. By restricting the analysis of the combined data from all localities to partnerships in which the wife was the original respondent, it was possible to include the wife's educational qualifications as a control variable. There are insufficient partnerships to adopt this approach in the analyses for the individual localities. With parameter estimates (see Table 5.7*a*) suggesting lower rates of paid employment for wives with educational qualifications, the results are inconsistent with expectations and raise doubts about the efficacy of the 'all localities' analysis. The main limitation of this model is that the distinctive characteristics of the different labour markets are represented by a simple block of dummy variables (see Table 5.7*b*). In principle, more complex inter-labour market variations could have been modelled by the inclusion of interaction terms, but the massive size of the data set prevented this approach within available computer resources.

Apart from this reservation about the analysis of the combined data, there does not appear to be anything untoward about the performances of the control variables in the seven models calibrated. Their general effects are largely as expected and variations between localities are more a matter of detail than an indicator of a notable discrepancy. We may therefore turn with some confidence to assess the results for the main variable of interest, namely, the husband's unemployment duration.

Most of the localities provide unequivocal evidence of the expected 'twelve month' effect. In Aberdeen and Kirkcaldy the husband's unemployment has no significant impact on the wife's employment status for the first twelve months but has a highly significant negative effect after that period; in Coventry and for the combined localities analysis, there is some indication that the husband's unemployment reduces the probability of his wife having paid work even during the first twelve months, but the effect is appreciably and significantly more pronounced for longer unemployment durations; and in Rochdale the effect is substantial during the first twelve months but significantly stronger afterwards. Some difficulties were experienced in calibrating the models for Aberdeen, Northampton, and Swindon because of the scarcity of unemployment spells in the work histories of the husbands. As a result, it was necessary to adopt a coarser categorization of unemployment duration, as shown in Table 5.6. The results for Northampton suggest an increase in the husband's unemployment effect after twelve months, although the increase is not statistically significant. Only Swindon is anomalous and this could well be due to the atypical behaviour of a few individuals.

5. EMPLOYMENT SHORTFALL

In this section, we return to more readily understood characteristics of the data to complete our investigation into the relationship between husbands' and wives' employment status. The statistical modelling results of Section 4 have revealed the systematic relationships of interest in the data and we now apply these relationships to separate out the different factors contributing to the employment shortfall of married women. The technique we adopt is that of sample enumeration, widely used for prediction in transportation research but generally unfamiliar elsewhere.[10]

By applying the calibrated model to the data at a specific point in time and summing the calculated outcome probabilities, an estimate is obtained of the number of wives in paid employment. This exercise is undertaken separately for partnerships with employed and unemployed husbands, and subtracting the results gives the gross shortfall at that point in time. This is the estimated proportion of wives with unemployed husbands who would be in paid employment if, in aggregate, they behaved the same as wives whose husbands are working.[11] The model is then used to estimate how the wives of unemployed men would behave if there were no cross-couple state dependence. This is achieved by repeating the sample enumeration with the block of dummy variables for husband's unemployment duration set to 0. Any resulting shortfall is therefore attributable to the control variables and heterogeneity provision rather than any true state dependence. Subtracting this 'spurious' shortfall from the gross shortfall gives the net effect due directly to the husband's unemployment.

The numbers of unemployed husbands was too small for effective analysis in the three localities with low rates of unemployment. Even for the other three localities, there was some concern about the low number of unemployed husbands at any point in time. The results in Table 5.8 are therefore based upon combined analysis of February 1985 and February 1986 data.

These results are important because they not only confirm but also quantify the conclusion already reached that there are both true and spurious state-dependence effects underlying the low levels of paid employment by the wives of unemployed husbands. Thus, for example, the gross shortfall of 26.7 per cent for Coventry is reduced to 18.9 per cent just by the set of control variables included in the conventional logistic model. With full control for heterogeneity by the Normal-logistic model with endpoints, the shortfall attributable to the direct effect of the husband's unemployment is estimated at just 8.2 per cent. Thus, although about 27 per cent fewer of the wives of unemployed husbands are in paid employment, only about 8 per cent of this shortfall appears to be a consequence of their husbands' unemployment. Some caution should be exercised in generalizing from these precise figures because the sampling variations and hence the precision of the estimates are unknown.[12] There is also con-

TABLE 5.8. *Employment shortfall percentages from calibrated models*

| | Localities | | | |
	Coventry	Kirkcaldy	Rochdale	All
No. of husbands not working	50	34	33	51
No. of husbands working	248	309	241	883
Conventional Logistic Model				
Wives with husbands not working				
Gross shortfall	26.7	31.7	45.8	26.8
Net shortfall	18.9	28.4	26.5	15.3
Normal-Logistic Model with end-points (net shortfall)				
Wives with husbands not working	8.2	23.4	21.5	9.9
Normal-Logistic Markov Model with end-points (net shortfall)				
Wives with husbands not working	10.8	16.5	20.0	8.5
Wives with husbands working	0.2	0.2	0.8	0.2
All wives	2.0	1.8	3.1	0.7

siderable variation between localities. But the general pattern is evident with, over all localities, only about 10 per cent shortfall due to true cross-couple state dependence.

A limitation of these analyses is that they do not attempt to explore fully the dynamics of employment behaviour. For example, a husband's unemployment may have quite a different effect on a wife's continuation in employment from its effect on a wife not currently working. At the very least, any unemployment effect from the husband will be superimposed upon a process which includes strong inertial elements attenuating response. Thus a wife in employment is unlikely to respond immediately to her husband's unemployment. In addition to any commitment to her job, she may be concerned about the difficulty of returning to the labour market at a later date and she may anticipate, or at least hope, that her husband will shortly obtain employment. Conversely, a wife who did not work while her husband was unemployed may be reluctant to change the life-style to which she has become accustomed and, if she does seek employment, may find it takes some time to obtain a job. Such temporal dependences become stronger the shorter the time intervals used in the analysis (Chamberlain 1985) and, in the context of employment, considerable temporal dependences must be expected with time intervals of just one month in length. A further set of Normal-logistic models was therefore calibrated including a Markov component to provide a parsimonious representation of wives' employment status inertia. This component was simply a dummy variable taking the value 1 if the wife was in paid employment during the previous month and 0 otherwise.[13]

The sample enumeration calculations are considerably more complicated for this model with evaluation of the 'predicted' employment status figures at the time-points of interest requiring successive monthly application of the model starting from the month of marriage. The results are included in Table 5.8. There are some changes in the estimated employment shortfall figures for the wives with unemployed husbands, although, with the exception of Kirkcaldy, we suspect that these changes are within sampling variation. The main new insight provided by the Markov analysis is that it is now possible to estimate an employment shortfall effect for the wives of employed husbands; because of inertial factors, some wives who would otherwise be working remain without paid employment after their husbands cease to be unemployed. This effect is generally small, although nearly 1 per cent of wives in Rochdale with working husbands fall into this category. In the final row of Table 5.8, the net shortfalls for wives with and without working husbands are aggregated to give the estimated percentage of all wives who are not in paid employment as a direct consequence of their husbands' unemployment. The values vary from 0.7 per cent of wives over all localities to 3.1 per cent of wives in Rochdale. The overall consequences of the cross-state dependence are fairly modest.

6. CONCLUDING COMMENTS

As expected from the results of earlier studies, a far larger proportion of the wives of working husbands in the SCELI partnership data were themselves in paid work than the wives of unemployed husbands. Descriptive analyses provide prima-facie evidence of both a true cross-couple state dependence in employment status and a spurious relationship due to heterogeneity. The conclusions are confirmed and quantified by the formal statistical analyses. Less than half the observed discrepancy in wives' employment status is due to true cross-couple state dependence. Nevertheless, this may be a substantial effect, amounting to about 20 per cent of the wives of non-working husbands in Kirkcaldy and Rochdale not in paid employment as a direct consequence of their husbands' unemployment. Over the six localities, the figure is about 10 per cent of wives with unemployed husbands. This is equivalent to about 0.7 per cent of all married women living with their partners. The large variations between localities caution against interpreting these figures as other than very general indicators of the overall situation in Britain. On the other hand, our confidence in the basic results is greatly strengthened by replication across localities. True cross-couple state dependence in employment status was not an isolated phenomenon during the period covered by this study and there is very strong circumstantial evidence that, at least in part, it was a rational response to the social security regime in existence over the time period investigated.

The extent to which the causal mechanism derives from an

economic process and the extent to which it stems from more complex motivating influences associated with the social roles adopted by married couples remain unresolved. The important conclusion drawn from this study is that there exists such cross-couple state dependence, not to the degree previously thought to be evident, but important enough to warrant further investigation.

NOTES

1. For example, in the 'pre-1988' benefits regime, in a family of 2 adults and 2 children in receipt of supplementary benefit on account of the long-term unemployment of the husband, the net increase in household income from a decision by the wife to increase her weekly hours of work from 0 to 30 hours is £4, given that above £4, each £1 of her income reduces her husband's entitlement to supplementary benefit by £1.
2. The manual/non-manual distinction is made with reference to the social class categories of the 1980 Classifications of Occupations, where non-manual is defined as social class categories I, II, and III (non-manual).
3. For example, the number of 1986 partnerships in existence at earlier years is as follows:

Age of wife in 1986 (years)	No. of couples for whom 1986 partnership was in existence in				
	1970	1975	1980	1983	1986
35–39	72	142	161	169	180
50–54	85	87	91	92	98

4. It appears that Moylan *et al.* (1984) limited their attempts at control to one variable at a time for similar reasons.
5. The problem here is ensuring *consistent* estimation of the structural (i.e. the β) parameters. Roughly speaking, consistency means that the parameter estimates approach the true values of the parameters as the sample size increases. This is usually regarded as the minimum requirement of an acceptable estimation procedure. Consistency is prejudiced when, as in this model, the number of error terms or 'nuisance parameters' increases without limit as the sample size increases (Neyman and Scott 1948).

6. Formally, the probability of response sequence S_i, conditional on the error term ϵ_i, is given by

$$P(S_i \mid \epsilon_i) = \prod_{t=\tau_i}^{T} P(y_{it}),$$

and the unconditional probability is given by

$$P(S_i) = \int P(S_i \mid \epsilon_i) f(\epsilon_i) d\epsilon_i,$$

where $f(\epsilon_i)$ is the probability density function of the error terms. With a Normal distribution, this integration has to be performed numerically, giving

$$P(S_i) = \sum_{j=1}^{n} = P(S_i \mid \alpha\xi_j) \, \rho_j,$$

where n is the number of quadrature points (taken to be 8 for all the analyses in this paper), ξ_j and ρ_j are the location and mass, respectively, of the jth quadrature point, and α is the scale parameter, necessary because the quadrature points assume a Normal distribution with unit variance. A more general integrated likelihood approach is to adopt a non-parametric characterization of the error-term distribution, as recommended, for example, by Heckman and Singer (1984), Alternatively, in a conditional likelihood approach to this problem (Andersen 1970) the error terms are eliminated by appropriately reformulating the model to focus solely upon variation within sequences. Both these alternatives would avoid any concern about whether an assumed parametric distribution, such as the Normal, is sufficiently flexible but the additional computational demands would be excessive for the large data sets in this study.

7. Formally, the sequence likelihood is

$$L_i = p_0 \left[\prod_{t=\tau_i}^{T} (1 - y_{it}) \right] + p_1 \left[\prod_{t=\tau_i}^{T} y_{it} \right] + (1 - p_0 - p_1)P(S_i),$$

where p_0 and p_1 are the probabilities of being a 'stayer' in state 0 and 1, respectively, and $P(S_i)$ is as defined in n. 6.

8. A likelihood ratio test is not strictly appropriate because the conventional logistic model lies on the boundary of the parameter space of the Normal-logistic model. Nevertheless, likelihood ratio χ^2 test statistics exceeding 10,000 with one degree of freedom (i.e. increases of over 10,000 in twice the log-likelihood with only one additional parameter) are impressive by any standards.

9. Again, a likelihood ratio test is not strictly appropriate but, with χ^2 test statistics exceeding 100 with just two degrees of freedom, there is unequivocal evidence that end-point parameters significantly improve the model.

10. The typical situation (see e.g. Hensher and Johnson 1981) is that of a logistic regression model of choice between public and private transport calibrated on a sample of commuters and including cost and travel time explanatory variables. Sample enumeration is then used to predict the proportion of the sample that would change their mode of transport to work if policy variables such as public transport fares were changed. Under a variety of random sampling schemes (some involving weighting) this proportion is a consistent estimate of the proportion of the population as a whole. Davies (1992) gives an account of sample enumeration methods applied to female employment participation.

11. In a cross-sectional analysis with a logistic regression model, this proportion would be identical to the observed discrepancy between the wives of employed and unemployed husbands. The longitudinal analysis smooths out short-term fluctuations and there will tend therefore to be a difference between the observed and estimated discrepancies in any specific month. To minimize the impact of random variation on the results, the sample enumeration calculations are based on the estimated discrepancy.

12. The asymptotic theory has not yet been developed for estimating standard errors. In principle, resampling methods could be used but the massive computing resources required render this approach impractical for this large study.

13. Formally, the model is rewritten as

$$P(y_{it}) = \exp \left[y_{it}(\beta' x_{it} + \gamma y_{i,t-1} + \epsilon_i)\right] / \left[1 + \exp (\beta' x_{it} + \gamma y_{i,t-1} + \epsilon_i)\right],$$

where γ is an additional parameter measuring the strength of the Markov effect. The problem of initial conditions (see Heckman 1981) was ignored because, as indicated in n.3, most of the sequences are several years long.

6

The Effects of Labour Market Position, Job Insecurity, and Unemployment on Psychological Health

BRENDAN BURCHELL

1. INTRODUCTION

Often, when considering the impact of unemployment on the individual, we are not so much concerned with the simple lack of a job itself, but the impact of worklessness on the quality of life. Unravelling this link is a complex task. For instance, the economic consequences of unemployment do not simply depend on the loss of the wage. They are a complex function of the unemployment insurance or benefits available, and also the duration of the spell of unemployment and the difference in pay and prospects between the jobs that precede and follow the spell of unemployment (e.g. whether the individual has experienced a loss of seniority or a downgrading because of the spell of unemployment).

In a similar vein, it may be too simplistic to consider the psychological damage caused by unemployment in a way that would suggest that all of the unemployed suffer from psychological ill health and none of the employed do. While there is indeed good, well-documented evidence that, on aggregate, the unemployed suffer worse psychological health than the employed, this view hides the damage done to many employees by their labour market position. It also overestimates the importance of work *per se* for psychological health.

To prove that the effect of unemployment on psychological

* In addition to the valuable contributions from the three editors of this book, I would also like to thank Lynda Burchell, John Devereux, Colin Fraser, Jill Rubery, and Frank Wilkinson for their help in preparing this chapter.

health is indirect or, to put it another way, is neither a necessary nor a sufficient condition, two types of evidence are directly relevant. One can think of employment status (with or without paid work) and its effect on psychological health (beneficial or harmful) as a two-by-two contingency table (see Table 6.1). Empirical investigations of individuals or groups usually fall into two of the four cells that are supportive of the simple link between employment and psychological health—either 'without work and poor health' (cell 4) or 'working and good health' (cell 1). The other two possibilities (or cells) stand to challenge the theory: people without paid work and in good psychological health or people with paid work but whose labour market activity is nevertheless harmful to their psychological health.

TABLE 6.1. *Labour market effects on psychological health*

Employment status	Beneficial	Harmful
With paid work	Cell 1	Cell 2
Without paid work	Cell 3	Cell 4

If the poor psychological health generally found among the unemployed is only one specific instance of a more general phenomenon in high-unemployment labour markets, this will have implications both for theories of psychological health among the unemployed and for theories which suggest that societies are becoming more polarized.

The evidence for more widespread effects of high-unemployment labour markets will be considered separately in the next two sections. First, there are the studies that have shown that, under some conditions, groups of unemployed individuals can enjoy good psychological health (i.e. cell 3). Then evidence will be presented, both from the literature on labour markets and psychological health and from empirical analysis of the Social Change and Economic Life Initiative (SCELI) data, that the unemployed are not the only group to suffer psychologically from their labour market situation (i.e. cell 2).

2. UNEMPLOYMENT AND GOOD PSYCHOLOGICAL HEALTH

Interesting initial (even if weak) evidence of how worklessness is not necessarily associated with poor psychological health was given in a provocative paper by Fryer and Payne in 1984. Their evidence came from very detailed case-studies of eleven carefully selected individuals who were very well adapted to unemployment in most ways.[1] These individuals had in common an ability to structure and fill their own lives and work towards goals which they set themselves. They concluded that a small proportion of the population have the personal resources to continue to identify and pursue goals of personal significance outside normal paid employment, and thus protect their psychological health through such activity.

Further evidence of the nature of the psychological environment that allows men to be able to undergo periods without paid work but to avoid harmful psychological consequences comes from a study that compared groups of men from two factories that were facing falling order books (McKenna and Fryer 1987). One group was made redundant and the other group was (following union negotiation) laid off on a rolling basis. The data were collected in one period where one group of men, because of the coincidence of lay-off, holidays, and maintenance shut-down, went for approximately twelve weeks without work. The two groups of men, redundant and laid-off, were thus both without work, claiming benefit, and in other objective ways in a similar position. The groups differed greatly, though, in their adjustment to worklessness. The laid-off workers planned how they would spend their spare time, for instance decorating their homes, repairing cars, gardening, taking up new sporting activities, and going on holidays. They typically bought in the materials that they needed before their lay-off, and were usually successful in carrying out their plans before their return to work. Five weeks after the lay-off these men were, if anything, slightly better in their perceived health than a control group of men who had remained at work in the factory.

By contrast, the men who had been made compulsorily redundant had considerably worse perceived health. Due to relatively large redundancy payments they did not have immediate financial problems. However, they typically spent many days watching television and reported feeling bored. When interviewed it was their fear of the uncertainty about their future that these men mentioned frequently as one of their main worries. They did not know whether they would be working or still unemployed in a few weeks' time. The researchers concluded that it was the inability to plan for the future that caused the problems for the redundant group.

Fineman's (1983, 1987) qualitative surveys and follow-ups with white-collar males who had suffered redundancies have also come up with some instances of men who seem to cope better with unemployment than with poor jobs. For instance, in one telling quote a mathematics graduate who had experienced several poor, insecure jobs between spells of unemployment finally decided that life was less stressful in unemployment than in such unsatisfactory and unpredictable jobs: 'I've done absolutely nothing about finding work. Since unemployment my life has been much more pleasant' (1987: 273).

To conclude this section, there is some evidence that under some circumstances individuals can be unemployed yet remain in good psychological health. There are probably other groups that also fare well in unemployment, but who have not yet been subject to investigation; perhaps the 'idle rich' would fall into this category too. However, although benefiting from unemployment is a logical possibility, the environmental conditions that would facilitate good psychological health are probably scarce in Britain in the 1990s, and look like remaining the exception rather than the rule.

3. EMPLOYMENT AND POOR PSYCHOLOGICAL HEALTH: THE CASE OF JOB INSECURITY

There is a large literature on psychological health and employment, for instance linking stressful jobs with anxiety and stress-related illnesses such as heart disease. By contrast, the link of interest in this section is that between position in the labour market and psychological health. More particularly, under what situations do individuals occupy cell 2 in Table 6.1, that is, being employed but suffering psychological damage attributable to their position in the labour market?

There are several studies that have explored the links between more general changes in the economy and psychological health, for instance the work of Brenner (1979), in which he uses aggregate data from England and Wales for the period from 1936 to 1976. Brenner found that the level of unemployment had a powerful effect on age-specific morality rates throughout this period. From this he argues that economic-related stress plays a major role in determining the health of the population. More detailed analysis of US data (Brenner 1973) suggests that economic downturns are directly instrumental in creating psychological problems rather than, say, leading the community to be less tolerant of individuals with chronic problems. For instance, the increases in psychiatric admissions rates in New York during economic depressions were only observed among individuals of working age, and not in senility-related admissions. However, given the many problems involved in drawing inferences from macro-data about phenomena occurring at the microlevel, conclusions from that sort of study will, unfortunately, have to remain tentative (see Warr 1985 for a detailed critique). However, for studies using other methodologies, there had, to date, been a complete lack of British data available, and one has had to look to other labour markets for evidence.

Detailed analysis of survey data from the United States allowed competing models to be tested to uncover the mechanism by which economic factors can affect the psychological health of individuals. For instance, in a survey of 4,000 principal wage earners in the USA, Dooley *et al.* (1987), established that perceived job security was the single most important predictor of scores on a checklist of psychological symptoms. Thus, respondents feeling insecure in their job (measured by asking whether they expected a change in their employment for the worse or whether anything had happened recently to make them feel less secure in their job) was a highly significant factor in causing symptoms of mild depression in the general population. Furthermore, when looking at the risk of an individual being in the top quintile of the sample on their symptom checklist score (a commonly used criterion for potential clinical 'cases'), perceived job insecurity was again the most important of all their stress-related predictors, increasing the risk of severe symptoms by a factor of 2.63.

In the same data set, objective job security was also measured by calculating the extent to which the industrial sector that each individual was working in was contracting or expanding at the time of the interview (the field-work period being four years between 1978 and 1982). In a panel design part of the study, 600 of the initial respondents were later reinterviewed; their change in objective security was used in a regression analysis to predict changes in psychological well-being. Although this measurement would clearly have contained a large amount of error variance by measuring security at the level of industries rather than firms or individuals, there was nevertheless a highly significant relationship. An improvement in the economic prosperity of the worker's industrial sector (whether or not the worker had changed industrial sector between interviews) led to fewer psychological symptoms being reported.

More detailed analysis of survey data from the United States allowed competing models to be tested to uncover the mechanism by which economic indicators can affect the psychological health of individuals. Using data collected from a telephone survey of 500 individuals in the Los Angeles area between 1978 and 1980, Catalano and Dooley (1983) tested three different models to see whether:

1. economic *contraction* increases the incidence of *undesirable* job and financial events, which in turn increase the incidence of illness and injury,
2. economic *change per se* increases the incidence of *undesirable* job and financial events and therefore of illness and injury, or
3. economic *changes per se* increase the incidence of *all* job and financial events and therefore of illness and injury.

The survey included measures of both desirable and undesirable life events. Economic change variables were derived from several monthly indices such as the unemployment stocks and flows and changes in the sizes of the industrial sectors. The rolling nature of the survey meant that these were constantly changing, thus providing the variation in the independent variable. The dependent measure for these analyses was a dichotomous variable derived by asking the respondents whether they had been ill or injured over the last three months (it is assumed that any link between economic activity and illness must be stress-related).

Loglinear models found that the first of these three possibilities received the greatest support, but the link was only really proved for the middle third of the sample on their socio-economic status variable.

A study by Oliver and Pomister (1981) of US automotive workers found that job insecurity was associated with Beck Depression Inventory scores for workers who had personally experienced a lay-off in the year before the survey, but not for the rest of the sample. Unfortunately, though, the reliability of this finding might be questionable; a response rate of 11 per cent from the mailed questionnaire was further reduced to 7 per cent who provided sufficient details to be used in the final analysis. If accepted at face value, however, this supports Fineman's observations that job security becomes far more salient an issue for those who have lost jobs in the past themselves. This is best illustrated by some of the quotations he gives from white-collar workers who had been made redundant in the late 1970s but were back in employment when he recontacted them:

It was bloody hard work being unemployed and this job is worse than my previous one in terms of what I do and job title. But unemployment has left me thinking more about security than the prospects of my job—something that never used to bother me. (Fineman 1987: 273–4)

I constantly think about the vulnerability of my job, at my age, in this recession. (Fineman 1987: 227)

I suppose I now have to see the security of the job as being more important than the actual work and prospects. (Fineman 1983: 79)

Swedish data have also provided some evidence of a causal link between job insecurity and stress-related morbidity. Knox *et al.* (1985) found an indirect link between employment security and resting systolic blood pressure, with relative body weight being the intermediate step in the link. James (1984) found support for the link between systolic blood pressure and job insecurity using a sample of Black North American employees. Support for the link between job insecurity and heart disease has also come from the preliminary analyses of a German study (Siegrist *et al.* 1986).

It is possible, however, that these surveys confounded job insecurity with other undesirable aspects of jobs. Most of the theories and empirical evidence on relative advantage in the labour market point to the fact that jobs that are bad in some ways (for example, insecurity) are more likely to be bad in other ways (for example, low pay, low intrinsic satisfaction, and high stress) (Blackburn and Mann 1979). Frese (1985) tested many alternative hypotheses using very detailed data on job stresses and strains collected from a sample of German blue-collar workers. It was found that, while job security was not independent of other job stressors, it did have an independent effect on job strain as measured by psychosomatic complaints. Objective measures of stress factors by observers and co-workers doing the same job were used to reduce the risk of methodological contamination in correlating two subjective measures. Prior variables such as age, socioeconomic status, and motivations to over-report stress or strain (termed 'political exaggeration') were also controlled for, but did not eliminate the link between job characteristics and psychosomatic complaints. The reverse causality hypothesis was eliminated with causal path analysis of longitudinal data. Finally, the effect was found to hold for both stress over-reporters and stress under-reporters (determined by comparing their own stress scores with the observer and group 'objective' measures). The treatment of the data went just about as far as is possible with a non-experimental design to prove a causal link between job stress, job insecurity, and psychological ill health in that particular sample.

Further evidence of this link between perceived insecurity and psychological ill health has been provided by Kasl and Cobb (1982), who found that the threat or anticipation of unemployment was as bad as unemployment itself. Once employees had been given notice of redundancies, the period before the actual lay-off was often more stressful than the unemployment that followed. Burn-out, a stress-related syndrome, has also been linked to job security by Wade *et al.* (1986), and Landsbergis (1988).

We should, however, be very cautious about generalizing from this type of evidence. There is evidence that links between economic or labour market variables and psychological health may be very situation- or culture-specific. Perhaps most importantly, job insecurity becomes potentially much more threatening in times of higher unemployment, and it must be borne in mind that many studies conducted in the 1970s were set in labour markets with much lower rates of unemployment. Furthermore, some studies have shown how job insecurity has a differential effect on distinct groups of employees. For instance, Axelrod and Gavin (1980) found that the pattern of correlations between an 'Anxiety–Depression–Irritation' (ADI) scale, job dissatisfaction, and psychosomatic symptoms and stress measures (such as job insecurity) were very different for managers of white-collar workers from those found among managers of blue-collar workers in the same mining plant. For instance, job insecurity was very highly correlated with the ADI scale and job dissatisfaction for the blue-collar managers (0.47 and 0.66 respectively) but not for white-collar managers (0.10 and 0.13 respectively). Although we should be wary of accepting this as a generalized finding from just one plant, it shows nicely the importance of context. As Gergen (1973) has argued and Amir and Sharon (1984) have demonstrated, social-psychological findings do not occur in a vacuum but can only be understood and reliably replicated in a given social context within a given culture. This is not to say that those differences are not predictable. For instance, Shapiro (1977) predicted that job security would be more important for less-educated, lower-income, and lower-social-class employees, as it was a value associated with the lower end of Maslow's hierarchy. The assumption is that for employees in the more advantageous parts of the labour market, food, shelter, and security needs will have been superseded and replaced by strivings for higher-order needs such as self-fulfilment. While Shapiro received support for this hypothesis, controlling for income, education, and class reduced but did not eliminate differences between Black and White workers. He concludes that not all cultural differences are economically determined in this instance. Having sounded this cautionary note, however, empirical studies of the Eurobarometer do show that adverse reactions to unemployment show remarkable consistency between countries (Marsh and Alvaro 1990).

To be able to understand the way in which job insecurity affects an individual, one must first appreciate the way in which the individual perceives the threat. Jacobson (1987) attempted to arrive at such an appreciation by using a qualitative 'personological' approach to measure the reaction of Israeli civil servants after an announcement that 3 per cent of all jobs were to be cut.

Before this it had widely been believed that government jobs were totally secure. In in-depth interviews the experience was described by the majority as 'externally imposed', 'unpredictable', 'bewildering', and 'disrupting'. They labelled their emotional experiences as (in order of frequency of mention) 'demoralization', 'suspicion and external anger', 'hope', 'helplessness', 'stress', 'desire to cope', and 'self-anger'. The interesting points about these reactions are their diversity (perhaps not surprising only two weeks after the announcement), but also the overlap between many of these and the feelings experienced in mild forms of neuroses.

Greenhalgh and Rosenblatt (1984) too, in a review of much of their own research into job insecurity, found that feelings of powerlessness played a central role, but they also pointed to a second facet of job insecurity that affects its impact: the severity of the threat. This can range from, at its most severe, permanent job loss with little chance of regaining one's position in the labour market to loss of one relatively small aspect of one's job, such as the temporary loss of a promotion opportunity.

The severity of threats to job security will vary greatly between different labour markets. For instance, risk of job loss would be more threatening in high-unemployment situations, or where the incumbent felt less able to find another job as good as his or her current one.

Taken together, there is a considerable amount of evidence that some employees do not enjoy the psychological benefits of their position in the labour market that are implicitly assumed in psychological models of unemployment and health. While not commonly remarked upon, a theme that can be discerned in this literature is the harmful effects of job insecurity. The next question to be addressed, therefore, is whether these findings were replicated in the British data collected in SCELI. The implications for psychological theories, the polarization debate, and policy will be discussed in the final section.

4. EMPIRICAL EVIDENCE FROM A BRITISH LABOUR MARKET

By reviewing a very disparate set of studies reported in the literature, a pattern of evidence linking employment insecurity to psychological stress has been uncovered. However, none of the evidence can necessarily be generalized directly to British labour markets in the latter half of the 1980s. The surveys conducted as part of the SCELI programme give an ideal opportunity to explore the relative psychological well-being of unemployed individuals and employees. However, in this chapter, rather than treating employees as a homogeneous group, they will be disaggregated into groups depending upon the characteristics of their position in and trajectory through the labour market. The first analysis to be presented here will use the 616 employed respondents from the Northampton area.[2] The second analysis is of a longitudinal nature, using data from a follow-up survey of 30 per cent of the original sample who were recontacted approximately eight months later. To overcome the problems posed by the smaller sample, similar data that were collected simultaneously in six local labour markets (Aberdeen, Coventry, Kircaldy, Northampton, Rochdale, and Swindon) were pooled.

Along with the other topics in the questionnaire, a very short version of the General Health Questionnaire (GHQ) was included; the four items with the highest item–whole correlations were selected from the usual twelve-item version (using the tables provided in Banks *et al.* 1980). This scale measures mild depression by asking questions about, for instance, loss of confidence and an inability to enjoy oneself. The scale used here was square-rooted to remove a mild upward straggle in the distribution of scores. Job security was measured in three forms in the questionnaire. First, respondents were asked how likely they thought it was that they would lose their job and become unemployed in the next twelve months. Secondly, they were asked whether their employer saw their job as being permanent, fixed-term, or temporary. Thirdly, respondents were asked to rate each job in the history section on a four-point scale depending on how secure they thought it was when they first obtained that job.

If we treat the sample as a whole, perceived job security can be shown to have a direct effect on GHQ scores, along with several other labour market variables related to job security. The problem with this sort of analysis is that it assumes that the effects of each variable are the same for the whole sample. Even many neoclassical labour market economists now accept that the labour market is segmented to some extent, with each sector having very different characteristics. At its simplest, the labour market is more realistically conceived as being two or more relatively autonomous markets, a primary and one or more secondary sectors. The primary sector consists of well-paid, skilled jobs, the secondary sector of the less-skilled, poorly organized labour where productivity is not rewarded to the same extent as in the primary segment.

One problem of studying labour market segmentation and psychological health is in deciding how to form these groups. There are no simple criteria for defining either precariousness in the labour market or membership in a particular labour market segment. Rather, membership of the secondary labour market can be thought of as being defined by a constellation of concurrent attributes. In medical terms this would be called a syndrome rather than a specific invariant manifestation of a condition.

In the absence of *a priori* considerations, a cluster analysis was performed using fifty-six labour-market-related variables to divide the very heterogeneous sample of employees into more homogeneous subgroups representing different labour market sectors. The variables used in the clustering reflected the work histories of the respondents, the level of rewards for their current job, the content and status of their current job, their perceptions and satisfactions with both their current and aspired-to future jobs, and several variables reflecting the situation outside the labour market and the nature and size of their employer. GHQ scores indicating psychological well-being were not used to cluster the sample. Five clusters were identified, each very different from the others on many variables (see Burchell and Rubery 1989, 1990 for further details of this stage of the analysis).

The main features of the outcome can be gauged from a brief description of each of the five groups in terms of the variables used to define the clustering:

Group 1: 'the primary segment'. This was the largest group (40 per cent of the total sample), and, by almost all objective criteria, the most advantaged. They were predominantly male (78 per cent), well-paid, in high-social class jobs, and most of their previous job quits had been to get better jobs and had resulted in pay promotions.

Group 2: 'stickers'. This group (comprising 31 per cent of the sample) was a little older than the other groups (43 years

compared to a sample mean of 38), and predominantly female
(62 per cent). They were the most satisfied group with respect to
all aspects of their jobs, even though their pay, fringe benefits,
and skill levels were considerably lower than group 1. They were
the least likely to state that they would like to change jobs, and
saw the internal labour market[3] as being more advantageous
than all of the other groups.

Group 3: 'female descenders'. Of the 13 per cent of the sample
in this group, 96 per cent were female. This group had the highest amount of domestic interference in labour market activity (as
measured by working part-time, past job quits for domestic reasons, past periods of full-time housework, having to look after
children, etc.). They received the lowest pay, and had the highest
proportion of job changes to same- or worse-paid jobs. For half
of them their last change of job had been to a worse-paid job
than the one that they had held previously.

Group 4: 'young and mobile'. This small group (5 per cent)
was 80 per cent male. They were, on average, a few years
younger than the other groups (mean age = 30 years). Their perceived chances of getting better jobs were the highest of all the
groups. They were most likely to see those jobs as being with
other employers, and thought the advantage of being an insider
within a firm was minimal. They were most likely to have moved
to better-paid jobs when they changed jobs in the past, but were
not the most likely to say that they liked their current jobs better
than all previous jobs.

Group 5: 'labour market descenders'. This group of only 4 per
cent of the sample consisted of 83 per cent males. They seemed
to have nothing going for them. They had all had a job change
in the past that had involved a drop in the social-class rating of
their job, and most had at some time been sacked or made
redundant. They were also the most likely to have been unemployed in the past. They stand out most in their current jobs
because of their lack of perceived job security. Similarly, they
were particularly dissatisfied with their job security, as well as
being the most dissatisfied group with their jobs overall. Most of
them had been looking for jobs in the last year, and almost all
said they would be keen to change jobs if plenty of jobs were
available.[4]

When the GHQ scores of each of the five groups were compared with a one-way analysis of variance, there were large, statistically significant (F (df = 4, 575) = 7.2, $p < 0.001$), and predictable differences (see Figure 6.1). In particular, the 'labour market descenders' had the worst psychological health of the five groups, and the two most stable groups (1 and 2) had the best psychological health. Figure 6.1 shows that the unemployed individuals in the sample and the employees in cluster 5 were not significantly different, although the unemployed did have very slightly higher GHQ scores.[5] Rather than being homogeneous in their psychological well-being, employees showed large, predictable differences depending upon their labour market experiences.

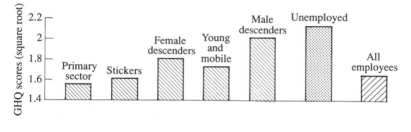

Fig. 6.1. GHQ scores for clusters and unemployed

A simple comparison between the highest- and lowest-scoring clusters of employees reveals that this difference (0.56) is larger than the difference between the mean for all employees and the mean GHQ score for the 146 unemployed individuals who were interviewed (0.37).

The second survey, conducted some eight months after the first (see the Methodological Appendix at the end of this book) was of limited usefulness in answering questions about what happens to the different clusters over time. As there were already only a small number (22)·of employees in the group of particular interest for present purposes, the 'labour market descenders', the 26 per cent resampling fraction for employees reduced this number to a mere 7. Could any conclusions be drawn about their continued labour market participation from such a small number?

Surprisingly the answer is *Yes*. The mean GHQ score for the 'labour market descenders' group was still so much worse than that for the other four groups combined (a difference of approximately one standard deviation) that the difference was statistically reliable ($T (141) = 2.61$, $p = 0.005$, one-tailed). Their labour market position was still more precarious than the other groups taken together. For instance, while only 12 out of the 121 employees who were still employed when reinterviewed at the second survey (10 per cent) felt that they might lose their jobs and become unemployed in the next twelve months, 3 of the 5 employees from cluster 5 who answered the question felt threatened in this way. Furthermore, while none of the 139 employees from clusters 1 to 4 became unemployed in the period between the two surveys, 1 of the 7 employees from cluster 5 did ($p < 0.025$ (one-tailed) for both of these results using Fisher's Exact Test). Thus, not only do these differences in labour market disadvantage continue into the future, but so do their psychological consequences.

Unfortunately, though, care must be taken in drawing causal conclusions from studies such as these. The cross-sectional nature of the design (cross-sectional in the way the groups were defined, that is) gives little indication of the extent to which it may have been individual characteristics such as poor psychological health that led to the precariousness of these employees' position in the labour market. The second set of analyses overcomes this problem and leads to the conclusion that there is a direct *causal* link between job insecurity and poor psychological health.

The results to be presented here for the second analysis use only those respondents who were both unemployed at the time of the first survey and selected for interview again at the time of the second survey. From all six areas there were 365 respondents who fell into this category, 200 men and 165 women. Unemployment, it will be recalled, was defined in SCELI as being out of work and either having looked for work over the last four weeks or claiming either unemployment benefit or supplementary benefit on the grounds of unemployment.

The sample is rather different from that in the previous analysis, since only those individuals who had been recently unemployed are being considered here. Many of the individuals in this more select sample would be similar to those in clusters 3 and 5 in the first analysis, as this is where much of the unemployment is accounted for. However, this does not detract from this analysis, as the critical findings refer to changes within respondents over time, not simple cross-sectional differences between groups.

The measure of job security was again the question that asked 'Do you think that there is any chance at all of you losing your job and becoming unemployed in the next twelve months?' but this time asked during the second interviews. There were several reasons to suggest that this question was an accurate reflection of their job security. First, it correlated very highly with other similar questions about their perceived job security and the nature of their contract of employment. Secondly, of those employees who responded affirmatively to this item when it was asked in the first survey, only 69 per cent were still in the same job at the time of the second survey,[6] compared to 80 per cent who had said that there was no chance of their losing their job in the next twelve months. Furthermore, those who answered yes were over three times as likely to be unemployed at the time of the second interview (6.5 per cent) as those who answered negatively (1.9 per cent).

Of the 200 men in the sample who were unemployed at the time of the first survey, 144 (72 per cent) were still unemployed at the time of the second survey, 29 (14 per cent) had found insecure work, and 27 (13 per cent) had found secure work. The corresponding figures for the 165 women were 97 (59 per cent) still unemployed, 25 (15 per cent) insecurely employed, and 43 (26 per cent) securely employed. It is interesting to note at this point that insecure employment was over twice as common among those re-entering the labour market from unemployment as among the work-force as a whole (see Table 6.2). This is consistent with the data presented by Dex (1988*a*, table 3.25) and Daniel (1990), who showed that a high proportion of the destination jobs of the unemployed are seasonal or temporary in nature.

The main hypothesis, however, was that security of employment was itself a significant causal factor in psychological well-being. To test this a repeated-measures analysis of variance was used, with GHQ scores at the time of both the first and the second interviews as the dependent variables, time as the 'within subjects' factor, and employment status at the time of the second interview (securely employed, insecurely employed, or still unemployed) as the 'between subjects' factor. A significant time by

TABLE 6.2. *Percentages of employees reporting that there was 'any chance at all of losing your job and becoming unemployed in the next twelve months'*

Type of employee	Men		Women	
	%	No.	%	No.
Employees re-employed between the two surveys	52	56	37	68
Employees with less than 1 year's tenure in current job in the first survey	41	208	27	324
Employees with more than 1 year's tenure in current job in the first survey	21	1,739	14	1,485
All employees in the first survey	24	1,983	16	1,836

employment status interaction effect would show that the *change* in GHQ scores was contingent on *changes* in employment status.

As exploratory analyses showed that the patterns of GHQ scores of the male and female respondents were quite different (resulting in a three-way interaction of sex by employment status by time), the results for men and women will be presented separately for simplicity.

Figure 6.2 shows the mean GHQ scores for the men. The interaction between employment status and time was highly significant (F (2, 198) = 5.2, p = 0.006). As a more precise test of the difference between the securely re-employed and the insecurely employed groups, the analysis was repeated with only those two groups. Again it revealed that the *securely* re-employed group showed a significant improvement in GHQ scores relative to the *insecurely* re-employed group F (1, 55) = 7.29, p = 0.009), who, as the figure shows, had only a very slight improvement in GHQ scores.

The results for the women tell a rather different story, as can be seen from Figure 6.3. Again there was a significant (albeit weak) interaction between employment status and time (F (2, 162) = 3.06, p = 0.049), but here the difference lay between the group who remained unemployed and the other two groups, with no significant interaction between the two re-employed groups (F

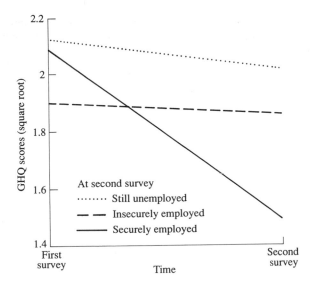

FIG. 6.2. Changes in GHQ scores for men unemployed at first survey

(1, 66) = 0.61, non-significant). It was tempting at this point to divide the re-employed women into more homogeneous subgroups to see whether those groups with patterns of labour market participation more similar to men also reacted to job insecurity in a manner more similar to men. After all, as the cluster analysis demonstrated, and as has been argued elsewhere (Burchell and Rubery 1990; Hakim 1991), the implicit assumption in much early theorizing on labour market segmentation (e.g. Barron and Norris 1976) that women can be treated as a homogeneous group is not supported by supply-side analyses. Unfortunately, however, the number of women in the securely re-employed and insecurely re-employed groups made further subdivision too unreliable. Nevertheless, if women with children under the age of 16 are excluded from this analysis, there is some (non-significant) evidence that the securely re-employed women fare better than the insecurely re-employed women—but further investigation must await more data.

The small sample sizes also thwart a full control of potentially confounding variables, but the longitudinal nature of the design

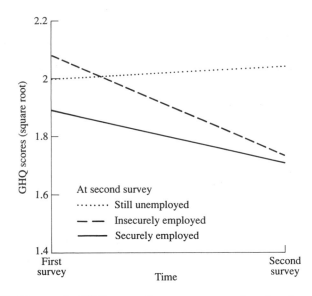

FIG. 6.3. Changes in GHQ scores for women unemployed at first survey

makes it less prone to spurious relationships and counter-explanations than cross-sectional analyses. However, the obvious contender, low pay, which is often treated as synonymous with insecurity as a main feature of secondary labour markets, does not offer an alternative explanation for the pattern of GHQ results for either men or women. Although there was some evidence that the securely re-employed individuals were paid marginally more than the insecurely re-employed ones, entering hourly pay as a covariate into these analyses did not detract from the security effects reported here.

As further checks, for both sexes the between-group differences observed at the time of the first survey (when all these respondents were unemployed) were *not* statistically significant. The slight falls in GHQ scores for the unemployed and insecurely re-employed men, and the slight drop for unemployed women, were not significant either.

Thus, for men at least, the psychological benefits of re-employment were moderated by the security of the jobs that they obtained. Those who entered insecure jobs showed only a negligible improvement in their psychological health, whereas those who entered secure employment showed a very marked improvement in their GHQ scores. For women, psychological benefits of re-employment accrued irrespective of the security of the jobs that they obtained.

5. DISCUSSION

To return to the original question set out at the beginning of the chapter, Is there evidence that the negative psychological consequences of high levels of unemployment extend beyond those individuals who are unemployed themselves? The answer is *yes*, and the evidence here shows that those men who are in insecure employment at the disadvantaged end of the labour market suffer approximately the same level of psychological disadvantage as the unemployed themselves. There is also evidence that under some circumstances the unemployed may not suffer psychologically at all. However, this is a very occasional phenomenon that is unlikely to affect more than a small proportion of the unemployed. The two exceptions described here are those who have a secure future through a guarantee of certain re-employment or those unusual individuals who have been able to find a rewarding role outside paid work, while simultaneously managing to cope without a wage.

6. PSYCHOLOGICAL THEORIES OF UNEMPLOYMENT AND WELL-BEING

Social psychological theories of the effects of unemployment can be divided into two types: ones that focus primarily on the deprivation of work *per se*, and others that focus more broadly on the individual's position in the labour market. These can be called 'work' theories and 'labour market' theories respectively.

The results presented here cannot be easily accounted for with current theories of the effects of unemployment. M. Jahoda's (1982) theory of the manifest and latent consequences of unemployment has been the most influential of the work theories, but for present purposes Warr's vitamin model (1987) is similar in its essential features. Jahoda lists five categories of experience (for example, a time-structure on the day and enforced interpersonal contact) that individuals who work benefit from psychologically, and that the unemployed usually go without. Furthermore, she argues, it is not primarily the lack of the wage but rather the lack of these types of experience that causes the psychological problems experienced by the unemployed. The main focus for these theories is the objective features of the day-to-day lives of individuals. Yet, for both insecurely employed and securely employed individuals, the tasks involved in their everyday lives are probably very similar. In the same way, McKenna and Fryer's (1987) redundant and laid-off men (described earlier in this chapter) were identical in their objective circumstances, yet their own interpretations of and reactions to their situation were very different. What was different there was their perception of the future—their feelings of security or insecurity.[7]

In some ways it is possible to view insecurity as providing an additional term in models like Jahoda's that suggest that the loss of certain 'categories of experience' cause the psychological problems of the unemployed. However, what these models have overlooked is that, under some circumstances, individuals can construct their lives so as to provide themselves with these categories of experience when they are not provided by work; however this control over their day-to-day activities is lost when they face insecurity over their future. The evidence of those in insecure jobs and presumably experiencing *both* Jahoda's categories of experience *and* reduced well-being is not explicable from within Jahoda's model.

Neither are the findings presented here easily interpreted in terms of a model that equates the effects of unemployment with the direct economic consequences of the loss of the wage; referred to as a 'vulgar Marxist' perspective by Fraser (1981). There is the possibility, however, that the threat of job loss might be equated directly with the threat of poverty in the assumptive worlds of the insecurely employed.

A model that is directly compatible with these findings, however, is agency theory (Fryer and Payne 1984, 1986; Fryer 1986). Agency theory argues that it is the interruption to the actor's plans and strategies that usually causes the negative psychological consequences of unemployment, rather than anything intrinsic to the work itself. While there are some people who have the personal resources to maintain an environment conducive to good psychological health even under very threatening conditions (for example, Fryer and Payne's sample of eleven men who managed to turn unemployment into a very active and positive experience), most people need a certain amount of security in order to be able to maintain a psychologically meaningful existence. Most jobs, particularly better jobs, provide that security. However, increasingly deregulated labour markets that are conducive to casualization of labour (see Burchell 1989; Rubery 1989) are likely to narrow the distinction between employment and unemployment. Larger numbers of employees may find themselves suffering from frustration and distress because they do not have adequate resources, social power, or psychological preparation to cope with the insecurity and uncertainty associated with casualized labour markets.

It is also important to consider the experience of unemployment in terms of the labour market experiences of the individual before the onset of unemployment. Bakke's studies in the 1930s emphasized that the jobs that preceded periods of unemployment were typically unskilled jobs in contracting industries and characterized by threat, subservience, and external control (Bakke 1933; O'Brien 1985). These are the conditions least likely to enable individuals to cope successfully with unemployment. From this point of view, insecure employment can be seen to be threatening not only in its own right but also in the way it fails to prepare people psychologically for its common sequel, unemployment.

Agency theory also gives us an insight into why women seem to be less affected by job insecurity than men. Inasmuch as many women rely on a male partner's wage as the main income for their household, they may not see threats to their own job security as putting them in as much jeopardy. Furthermore, as many women tend to have labour market careers that are secondary to their domestic commitments (Hakim 1991), they may realize that it is more likely that they will lose their job due to their domestic situation rather than their employer. Scott and Burchell (forthcoming) found that a third of all women's job quits were for domestic reasons, compared to less than 10 per cent of men's. Other analyses of the SCELI data (e.g. Burchell *et al.* 1989; Horrell *et al.* 1989) have also found that women (perhaps because of the way in which their skills are undervalued) tend to see their jobs as being more easily replaced by other jobs of equal worth. We would expect that women pursuing a career that was more central to their life than their domestic commitments would react to job insecurity in a manner more similar to the men in the sample. Unfortunately, the small numbers in the groups of re-employed individuals made such comparisons inconclusive, leaving this as a question for future research.

Other studies have also found strong evidence for the key role that predictability of the future plays in maintaining the psychological health of men. For instance, Payne *et al.* (1983) found that two-thirds of unemployed men stated that not knowing what was going to happen to them in the future months was a major problem.

The interesting thing about agency theory is that it is not specific to unemployment. It would predict that the psychological health of anyone facing insecurity similar to that often found among the unemployed would be similarly affected. Inasmuch as the number of people who have felt their jobs to have been threatened is much greater than the number of people who are actually unemployed any one point in time (see Table 6.2), the implications of this theory may be that the psychological damage done by high rates of unemployment is not confined to the unemployed, but rather extends to the even greater number of employees who feel the threat of unemployment. This is indeed what has been found in the empirical evidence presented here. As M. Jahoda (1989) argues, the traditional, reductionist social psychology that is concerned with the individual while ignoring the complexity of social institutions is inadequate if psychology is to become relevant to the complex phenomena that affect us, such as those experienced in the labour market.

The evidence that job insecurity has increased markedly in prevalence in recent times is mixed (Rubery 1989). While surveys of employers have reported increasing numbers of temporary and casual workers being taken on, the Labour Force Survey and Workplace Industrial Relations Survey provide little evidence of any sustained trend in employees classifying themselves as being in 'seasonal, temporary or casual jobs' or 'under contract for a specific period of time' rather than 'permanent jobs'. However, there are other, less easily measurable threats to job security than those that originate directly from the lack of a permanent contract of employment, for instance bankruptcies, plant closures, and dismissals. A further difficulty in using official statistics to measure levels of job insecurity is that there may well be differences between objective and subjective levels of security. Hartley (1989), for instance, found high levels of confidence among employees in an ailing manufacturing plant. Paradoxically, reported feelings of job security increased further among the survivors of successive rounds of redundancies right up to the final closure of the factory. Furthermore, as it is the perceived rather than the actual level of job security that has the immediate psychological impact, that is what should be measured.

An insidious feature of labour market insecurity is that, like unemployment, it is self-perpetuating. The data in Table 6.2 suggest that unemployment and insecure re-employment may form a vicious circle, excluding a sector of the work-force from re-entry into stable employment.

Proponents of the European Social Charter (e.g. Muckenberger and Deakin 1989) have argued that insecurity is not a necessary feature of labour markets. For instance, a highly regulated labour market might afford employees a high level of employment security even in times of high unemployment. Yet, the 1985 Conservative Government Department of Employment White Paper entitled 'Employment: The Challenge for the Nation' explicitly states that there is a direct trade-off between labour market regulation and unemployment. This justified their attempts to reduce unemployment through removing 'red tape'.

A large amount of Government (and European Community) regulation accumulated in times of fuller employment. Whatever the merits of particular items, the total effect, imposed across the whole of industry, is often now to deter employers—especially smaller ones, without the time and staff to master the complexities—from taking on workers; and the careful pursuit of externally-guaranteed protection against disadvantage for every individual circumstance can thus yield, for many people, the severest disadvantage of all—the lack of a job. (p. 20)

The social psychology of job insecurity might have to take over from the social psychology of unemployment as the research topic for the 1990s.

NOTES

1. The economic benefits of employment were the main exception to this. Several members of the sample did report financial problems or worries.
2. Only one locality was used because this analysis relies heavily on many of the team-specific questions which were asked only in Northampton.
3. Employees' perceptions of the internal labour market were measured by asking them whether they saw the best opportunities of advancement as being with their current employer or with another employer.
4. The other 7% of the sample were excluded because they formed clusters of less than six individuals (i.e. less than 1% of the sample). In the cases that were inspected closely this was because either they had very unusual patterns of responses on the variables, or they had clearly been flippant in their responses.
5. Additional analyses showed that these disadvantaged employees actually had slightly (but again not significantly) worse psychological health than the unemployed if the direct effect of poverty on psychological health was controlled for.
6. There was some considerable variation around this time interval between interviews. The median duration was 248 days (8.2 months), but the lower and upper deciles were 166 days (5.4 months) and 293 days (9.6 months). While there was a small, predictable effect that the unemployed respondents from the first survey who were recontacted sooner were more likely to still be unemployed, this does not detract from the main results reported here.
7. It is also likely that the two groups of men in McKenna and Fryer's study differed in another important way, their perceived social status—a quality that is held to be significant in a number of social-psychological theories of unemployment including Jahoda's (1982), Warr's (1987), and Kelvin and Jarrett's (1983). But it could be argued that this, in turn, is further evidence that orientation towards the future, rather than the present, is the critical determinant of the psychological functioning of the individual.

7

The Psychological Consequences of Unemployment:
An Assessment of the Jahoda Thesis

JONATHAN GERSHUNY

The fact that unemployment leads to psychological distress is now well documented in the literature (Warr 1987). Not only have a wide range of studies revealed a consistent cross-sectional association between employment status and well-tested measures of psychological health such as the General Health Questionnaire (GHQ), but longitudinal studies have demonstrated clearly the chronological sequences necessary to confirm causality. People's psychological health has been shown to grow worse when they move from employment to unemployment and to recover when they return to a job. However, what is less clearly established are the precise mechanisms that lead to psychological stress.

Two major arguments have been advanced. The first is that the major source of the distress produced by unemployment is financial. Typically unemployment leads to a sharp fall in living standards and to chronic insecurity about whether the household budget can be balanced. However, this dominant emphasis on the financial consequences of unemployment has been challenged by Marie Jahoda (1982), who suggests that the implications of unemployment for personal stability are much wider-ranging. As well as its manifest function of producing income, employment has an equally important set of latent functions. As Jahoda puts it:

an analysis of employment as an institution makes it possible to specify some broad categories of experience, enforced on the overwhelming majority of those who participate in it: the imposition of a time structure, the enlargement of the scope of social experience into areas less emotionally charged than family life, participation in a collective purpose and identity, and required regular activity. These categories of experience are not at the whim of a good or bad employer, but follow necessarily from the structural forms of modern employment. (1982: 59)

If the central thrust of Jahoda's argument is correct, it raises nonetheless some important questions about the types of factor that might mediate the experience of unemployment. As Jahoda notes, there is no inherent reason why such categories of experience should be provided uniquely by employment. In earlier societies, for instance, such psychological functions may have been provided by rituals, religious or community practices (1982: 59). However, she is firmly of the view that the distinctive characteristic of industrialized societies is the all-pervasive effect of employment conditions in structuring time experiences (1982: 59–60). Yet, it might be argued that other institutions may still structure time and activity in advanced societies. In contrast to the inter-war period, which formed the central experience out of which Jahoda's ideas emerged, the post-war era saw a tendency towards the reduction of the working day in employment and, due to the rise of domestic technologies, a reduction in the time that had to be spent on domestic labour (Gershuny and Jones 1987). It seems plausible that this produced an increase in the relative importance of leisure to people's lives and identities. A central empirical question, then, must be whether in the mid-1980s it was possible for the unemployed to meet many of the psychological functions previously provided by employment through continued or even increased participation in community leisure activities and in the patterns of sociability that derived from them.

A second issue is whether the implications of unemployment for the categories of experience that Jahoda highlights are generally applicable or gender-specific. The reverse side of the common finding that women in employment bear a double burden, in that they retain their responsibilities for the domestic work of the household, is that they are likely still to have a clearly defined set of valued activities when unemployed. Further, since a high proportion of women will have experienced, at some point, a period of temporary withdrawal from the labour market for child-rearing, they may have chosen, or have been obliged to develop, more extensive networks in the community for coping with the everyday problems of non-employed life. In short, there is the possibility that unemployed women would have stronger sources of positive identity when out of work and more effective support networks, shielding them to some degree from the severity of the impact of unemployment. It will be seen in Chapter 8 that in a proportion of unemployed households, men are likely to have adapted to unemployment by increasing their own share of domestic work. Certainly, it seems probable that one change from the 1930s has been greater flexibility about socially acceptable gender roles, even if the overall amount of change in behaviour remains unimpressive. This raises the question of whether it has been easier for men in the 1980s to adapt to the psychological pressures of unemployment by finding a new source of activity and sense of purpose in the home.

This section is concerned to examine first the extent to which unemployment does generate psychological distress through changes in the individual's environment other than those involving financial loss and, secondly, the extent to which different patterns of sociability and domestic organization may mediate the impact of unemployment. A difficulty in testing the Jahoda framework, however, is that various categories of experience are only impressionistically defined and there is nothing like an agreed or tested set of indicators. The operationalization of the concepts that we have adopted here must be regarded as experimental. Five statements were designed to tap the key components of the categories of experience. Respondents were asked to indicate how much they agreed or disagreed with each, with respect to the way that they had spent their days in the previous week. Their answers were in terms of a five-point scale ranging from agree strongly to disagree strongly. The items were:

1. I had time on my hands that I did not know what to do with.
2. Most days I met quite a range of people.
3. I was doing things that were useful for other people.
4. I had certain responsibilities at particular times most days of the week.
5. I felt respected by the people I met.

According to Jahoda's argument that the categories of experience are derived primarily from the workplace in modern societies, those in employment should show generally positive responses to statements 2, 3, 4, and 5, and generally negative responses to question 1. Those outside employment may gain access to some or all of the categories of experience, either as a result of some extra-economic structural circumstances (such as their responsibility for the care of young children) or from their own initiative (for instance, participation in voluntary community activities). But given that they do not have access to these experiences as a matter of course as those with paid jobs do, they would be expected to show a lower level of access to the categories of experience. Does this expected pattern hold true?

Table 7.1 presents the proportion that agreed with each of these statements by employment status and sex. It is immediately apparent that the unemployed differ from those in work very much in the way that Jahoda suggested. They were substantially more likely to have time on their hands, and they were less likely to have met a range of people, to have felt that they were doing something useful, to have had responsibilities at particular times, and to have felt respected. The pattern of the unemployed was rather closer to that of the non-actives, except that the unemployed were considerably more likely to have felt that they had time on their hands and they were less likely to have felt that they were respected.

To what extent do the nature of out-of-work roles and activities mediate the deprivation in categories of experience generated by loss of employment? A first approach to this is to examine the pattern for men and women. If non-work roles can mediate significantly, then it could be expected that unemployed women would retain greater access to the categories of experience than unemployed men. Although the pattern for men and women is similar in general outline, there are some notable differences in emphasis. Whereas a majority of men (58 per cent) complained that they had had time on their hands, this was the case for only a minority of women (31 per cent). Conversely, women were much more likely to feel that they had been doing something useful (56 per cent compared with 36 per cent for men) and that they had responsibilities at particular times. Unemployed women had a level of activity and a sense of purpose to their activity that was much closer to that of people in employment than was the case for men. This provides some support for the view that the more substantial responsibilities that women undertake in the domestic sphere provide a sense of identity and a patterning of

TABLE 7.1. *Jahoda items by employment status*

Jahoda items	% agree					
	Self-employed	Employed	Unemployed	Non-active	Gamma	Significance
Men						
Time on hands	9	10	58	39	-0.51	0.00
Meet range of people	69	59	42	44	0.27	0.00
Doing something useful	69	62	36	44	0.30	0.00
Responsibilities at particular time	83	77	51	53	0.35	0.00
Feel respected	59	49	43	50	0.09	0.02
Women						
Time on hands	17	8	31	19	-0.22	0.00
Meet range of people	69	66	40	38	0.37	0.00
Doing something useful	66	69	56	51	0.21	0.00
Responsibilities at particular time	90	83	75	74	0.15	0.01
Feel respected	59	51	37	43	0.13	0.00

Source: The Household and Community Survey, 1987.

activity that helps to some degree to offset certain of the psychological consequences of unemployment that have been identified in studies focusing on the male unemployed.

If this is the case, does increased involvement by men in the domestic division of labour mediate the effects of unemployment? As will be seen in Chapter 8, there was evidence of an increase in male involvement with unemployment, although the majority of households remained relatively traditional in the way household work was organized. To examine the impact of the organization of domestic work, a summary index of the Jahoda categories was constructed by summing the negative responses to the first item and the positive responses to the remaining four items. There was, in fact, no statistically significant relationship between the degree of sharing of domestic work and the overall extent of male access to the Jahoda categories of experience. This suggests either that the extent of change had been too modest to compensate for the deprivation due to loss of work, or that the adoption of relatively new role patterns does not provide the same sense of structure and meaning that comes when these patterns are better established.

A second possibility is that the loss of access to the categories of experience is mediated by the level of extra-household sociability. To test this, an index of sociability was constructed[1] and then divided into three equal categories of low, medium, and high sociability. As can be seen in Table 7.2, there was a strong overall association between the level of sociability and the Jahoda score, with access to the categories of experience rising with higher levels of sociability. The pattern for the unemployed is less strong, although still statistically significant. It would appear to be only when unemployed people have relatively high levels of sociability that there is a marked improvement in their experience. However, it is clear that, even in this case, sociability outside work is not able to remove the effects of not having a job. For both men and women, the most sociable category of the unemployed still fell short of the Jahoda score for the least sociable category of the sample for their sex taken as a whole.

The final issue to be examined is whether access to the Jahoda categories of experience is important in determining people's vulnerability to more serious types of psychological distress. The interview schedule included a short version of the GHQ.[2] This consisted of the four items with the highest correlations with the

TABLE 7.2. *Jahoda scores by sociability*

Sociability	Mean Jahoda score			
	All men	Unemployed men	All women	Unemployed women
Low	2.93	2.06	3.12	2.78
Medium	3.19	1.88	3.31	2.61
High	3.34	2.57	3.45	2.92
Significance	0.00	0.02	0.001	0.51
Mean	3.16	2.14	3.27	2.75

Source: The Household and Community Survey, 1987.

overall twelve-item version (Banks *et al.* 1980). This short version of the GHQ would not be appropriate as a clinical guide at an individual level, but, used in the aggregate, it does provide a useful basis for comparing the states of psychological adjustment of various socio-economic categories.

The answers to the individual statements representing particular categories of experience provide only a low level of prediction of the GHQ. Moreover, statement 3 ('useful for other people') provided what initially seemed anomalous results: both low and high answers are associated with relatively poor psychological adjustment, while the medium answers were associated with relatively good psychological adjustment. The reasons for this will be discussed later. For present purposes, it was decided to proceed with a version of the aggregate index of access to the categories of experience in which this item was excluded.

Table 7.3 shows a first approach to the examination of the association between the index of access to the Jahoda categories of experience and psychological well-being for the questionnaire sample as a whole. A very clear linear relationship emerges for both men and women; men with low access to all the categories have a mean GHQ score of 4.81 (i.e. 3.46 + 1.35) which represents relatively poor psychological adjustment, whereas those with high access to all categories have a mean score of 3.07, representing relatively good psychological adjustment. The equivalent range for women goes from 5.6 to 3.23. In both cases the associations are very clearly significant; the lower the access to the Jahoda categories the worse the psychological adjustment (i.e. the higher the GHQ score). But in both cases a very small part of the total variation in GHQ in explained (4 per cent for men, 3 per cent for women).

Plainly much of the variation in the GHQ scores for the sample as a whole is to be explained by something other than the Jahoda categories. And even the minimal level of explanation assigned in Table 7.3 presumably includes some of the effects of employment status (which Table 7.1 demonstrated to be associated with the Jahoda categories). Income may also be associated with access to both the Jahoda categories and the GHQ scores. Does the Jahoda variable maintain any explanatory power once the influence of these other variables is accounted for?

Table 7.4 provides variance decomposition parameters for two

TABLE 7.3. *Men's and women's GHQ by levels of access to Jahoda categories of experience*

Variable + category	Men (Grand mean 3.456)		Women (Grand mean 3.68)	
	No.	Unadjusted effect parameters	No.	Unadjusted effect parameters
Access to categories of experience				
0	71	1.35	30	1.92
1	214	0.31	201	0.10
2	297	0.10	354	0.20
3	412	−0.11	447	−0.05
4	374	−0.39	366	−0.35
Multiple R^2		0.036		0.026
Multiple R		0.188		0.160
Significance of F		0.000		0.000

Source: The Household and Community Survey, 1987.

TABLE 7.4. *Explaining SCEL men's and women's GHQ scores*

Model 1

Source of variation	Sum of squares	Significance of F
Men		
Main effects:		
Income	105.010	0.000
Employment	157.958	0.000
Covariates		
Categories of experience	85.085	0.000
2-way interactions:		
Income/employment	165.518	0.004
Explained	513.571	0.000
Residual	5,373.083	
TOTAL	5,886.654	
Women		
Main effects:		
Income	214.644	0.000
Employment	114.301	0.000
Covariates:		
Categories of experience	100.344	0.003
	53.323	0.001
	53.323	0.001
2-way interactions:		
Income/employment	132.374	0.057
Explained	400.341	0.000
Residual	6,333.676	
TOTAL	6,734.017	

Model 2

Source of variation	Sum of squares	Significance of F
Men		
Main effects:		
Income	105.010	0.000
Employment	157.958	0.000
Covariates:		
Categories/unemployed	28.716	0.008
Categories/non-employed	51.458	0.000
Categories/employed	32.068	0.005
2-way interactions:		
Income/employment	154.692	0.009
Explained	529.901	0.000
Residual	5,356.752	
TOTAL	5,886.654	
Women		
Main effects:		
Income	214.644	0.000
Employment	114.301	0.000
Covariates:		
Categories/unemployed	24.153	0.023
Categories/non-employed	31.788	0.009
Categories/employed	9.500	0.153
2-way interactions:		
Income/employment	134.544	0.051
Explained	414.629	0.000
Residual	6,319.387	
TOTAL	6,734.017	

attempts to provide a more general picture. Both models are hierarchical: all the variance in GHQ associated with income is extracted before employment status is entered into the analysis, and the Jahoda categories variable is entered after employment. Consider first the men. Income explains 1.8 per cent of the variance (i.e. 105/5,887), employment 2.7 per cent, and interactions between these 2.8 per cent of the variation in GHQ (a total of 7.3 per cent); both of these variables and the interactions between them are significant at the 0.001 level. Model 1 uses the Jahoda categories index as a covariate; this explains only a further 1.4 per cent of the variance. So less than half of the influence estimated in Table 7.3 remains once the effects of income and employment are taken into account. The approach adopted for model 1, however, has the limitation of assuming that the effect of the Jahoda categories is the same for employed and for unemployed people. Model 2 makes separate estimates of the effects of the Jahoda categories for unemployed, non-employed, and employed people. Each of the three separate effects are clearly statistically significant. Together they account for 1.9 per cent of the variance in GHQ: still a very small effect.

Moreover, the effect is yet smaller for women. Adopting the same hierarchical approach, income and employment together account for 5 per cent of the variance in GHQ. And once this variance has been extracted, only 0.8 per cent remains to be associated with the Jahoda categories using model 1, and model 2 raises this to just below 1 per cent. On the basis of these results, it might be tempting to conclude that the Jahoda effects are negligible.

But Tables 7.5 and 7.6 show that the impact of the categories of experience varies substantially by employment status. It gives the Multiple Classification Analysis effect parameters for the models described in Table 7.4 (though these versions of the models are not hierarchical). It can be seen that, for both men and women, those with higher incomes are in general happier than others (though this effect almost disappears when we control for employment status). Men and women in employment show, in general, substantially better psychological adjustment than the unemployed, and rather better adjustment than the non-employed. This effect remains strong even once the influences of income and the Jahoda categories have been controlled for.

Table 7.5. Explaining women's GHQ scores: effect parameters (grand mean = 3.682)

Variable + category	No.	Unadjusted effect parameters	Adjusted for independent + covariates	
			Model 1 effect parameters	Model 2 effect parameters
Income (£ per month)				
1 0–500	526	0.30	0.19	0.19
2 500–1,000	551	-0.05	0.01	0.01
3 1,000–1,500	223	-0.29	-0.22	-0.22
4 1,500+	92	-0.71	-0.61	-0.63
Single				
Part-time employed	40	1.04	0.86	0.64
Full-time employed	104	-0.33	-0.32	-0.59
Unemployed	77	0.82	0.54	1.11
Non-employed	73	0.07	-0.17	0.06
In couples				
Part-time employed	331	-0.18	-0.10	-0.36
Full-time employed	311	-0.26	-0.08	-0.34
Unemployed	83	0.45	0.36	0.97
Non-employed	373	0.07	-0.01	0.24
			Regression coefficients	
Access to Jahoda categories				
Categories/unemployed			-0.190	-0.361
Categories/non-employed				-0.249
Categories/employed				-0.110
Multiple R^2			0.040	0.042
Multiple R			0.199	0.204

Source: The Household and Community Survey, 1987

TABLE 7.6. *Explaining men's GHQ scores: effect parameters* (grand mean = 3.445)

Variable + category	No.	Unadjusted effect parameters	Adjusted for independent + covariates	
			Model 1 effect parameters	Model 2 effect parameters
Income (£ per month)				
1 0–500	442	0.33	0.10	0.10
2 500–1000	589	−0.04	0.02	0.03
3 1,000–1,500	227	−0.48	−0.29	−0.30
4 1,500+	97	−0.13	0.07	0.05
Single				
Part-time employed	8	−1.70	−1.60	−1.77
Full-time employed	161	0.08	0.04	−0.11
Unemployed	70	0.63	0.37	0.65
Non-employed	27	1.07	0.89	2.10
In couples				
Part-time employed	11	0.01	0.07	−0.09
Full-time employed	870	−0.24	−0.16	−0.33
Unemployed	138	0.83	0.59	0.88
Non-employed	70	0.33	0.16	1.38
			Covariate regression coefficients	
Access to Jahoda categories				
Categories/unemployed			−0.224	−0.302
Categories/non-employed				−0.599
Categories/employed				−0.161
Multiple R^2			0.059	0.064
Multiple R			0.243	0.252

Source: The Household and Community Survey, 1987.

The influence of the Jahoda categories is estimated in the form of regression coefficients. For the men, these coefficients are all significant at the 0.005 level; the overall coefficient for model 1 is –0.224 (i.e. a high level of access to each additional Jahoda category brings a reduction of 0.224 in the GHQ score). Model 2 provides separate estimates for employment categories—the effect for employed people is –0.161, while that for unemployed people is nearly twice as large (–0.306). The women's pattern is similar: for the Jahoda categories overall –0.190, for the employed –0.110, and for the unemployed –0.361. But though the overall coefficient is significant at 0.005, the unemployed coefficient is only significant at 0.05, and that for the employed is not significant at this level.

The general pattern is nevertheless reasonably clear. Controlling for the influence of other variables, the Jahoda categories have a significant influence and (certainly for men, probably for women) access to the Jahoda categories has a larger positive effect on psychological well-being for the unemployed (and for the non-employed) than for the employed.

Further, by focusing down on the unemployed as a group, the significance of the Jahoda categories emerges rather more sharply. Table 7.7 shows the mean GHQ of unemployed men to be 4.28, which compares quite well with the estimate of 4.32 that we may derive by adding the men's unemployment effect from model 2 (0.88) in Table 7.6 to the overall men's mean from the same source (3.44). Even before controlling for the influence of other variables (i.e. model 1), there is a nearly monotonic effect of the Jahoda categories, improving psychological adjustment through just about two and a half GHQ units as one moves through the range of the Jahoda index. Once the other variables are controlled for (i.e. model 3), the influence becomes very nearly linear. The 7 per cent of variance explained by the Jahoda variable on its own is hardly diminished by adding in the extra variables, leaving the model explaining overall a respectable 22 per cent of the variance in GHQ. As can be seen in Table 7.8, the pattern for unemployed women is similar, although the effect of the Jahoda categories is less strong. In this respect, there are similarities between unemployed and non-active women.

Relatively low levels of explanation are to be expected, given that the short version of the GHQ is a rather noisy indicator and

TABLE 7.7. *Explaining the GHQ scores of unemployed men, married or cohabiting* (mean = 4.28)

Variable and category	No.	Effect parameters		
		Model 1	Model 2	Model 3
Age				
20–33	21			–0.26
34–46	72			0.02
47–60	44			0.09
Educational qualifications				
None	71			0.21
CSE/O level	38			–0.13
A level	14			–0.06
Higher/further	14			–0.65
Social class				
Service	25			0.38
Intermediate	34			0.21
Working	78			–0.21
Household income (£ per month)				
£0–500	97		–0.20	–0.19
£500–1,000	32		0.24	0.18
£1,000–1,500	6		2.01	2.10
£1,500+	2		–0.32	–0.05
Age of youngest child			**	*
0–5	52		0.64	0.71
6–10	19		0.96	0.83
11–18	31		–0.62	–0.73
None	35		–0.94	–0.86
Count of Jahoda categories		**	*	*
0	23	0.94	1.04	1.00
1	34	0.16	0.12	0.19
2	37	–0.17	–0.10	–0.09
3	30	–0.04	–0.18	–0.22
4	13	–1.51	–1.54	–1.49
R^2		0.07	0.20	0.22

* Significant at 0.05.
** Significant at 0.005.

Source: The Household and Community Survey, 1987.

TABLE 7.8. *Explaining the GHQ scores of unemployed and non-employed women, married or cohabiting*

Variable and category	Unemployed			Unemployed or non-employed		
	No.	Model 1	Model 2	No.	Model 1	Model 2
Mean		4.31	4.31		3.9	3.9
Household income (per month)			*			**
£0–500	30		−0.07	169		0.01
£500–1,000	39		−0.58	209		−0.04
£1,000–1,500	11		−1.48	58		−0.36
£1,500+	3		−2.06	20		−1.74
Missing	77		0.61	151		0.41
Age of youngest child						
0–5	40		1.36	231		1.89
6–10	9		−0.31	53		0.22
11–18	14		0.28	57		−0.05
None	97		−0.57	266		−0.29
Count of Jahoda categories			**		**	**
0	9	2.91	2.94	25	1.70	1.89
1	36	−0.03	0.08	124	0.19	0.22
2	51	−0.02	−0.06	183	0.04	−0.08
3	45	−0.69	−0.75	185	−0.09	−0.11
4	19	0.37	0.38	90	−0.46	−0.44
R^2		0.10	0.18		0.03	0.06

* Significant at 0.05.
** Significant at 0.005.

Source: The Household and Community Survey, 1987.

that the questionnaire-based Jahoda measure does not look directly at individuals' patterns of activity. Our experimental work suggests that it may prove possible to use some of the more direct information on activity patterns from the diaries to establish proxies for the Jahoda categories. For example, it may be surmised that a lack of 'time-structure' may correlate with very large amounts of time devoted to watching television (on the argument that 'channel-hopping', as opposed to planned viewing, is an essentially unstructured activity). In practice, having controlled for employment status, television viewing time does explain on its own around 5 per cent of the variance in GHQ.

The construction of another proxy suggests an answer to the apparently anomalous behaviour of the 'useful activity' item in the original statements used to measure aspects of the Jahoda categories of experience. This can be operationalized through the diary evidence in terms of the time devoted to communal activities and to caring activities for other adults or children. These include many of the categories that constitute regular unpaid domestic work. Participation in such activities may contribute to people's general feelings of well-being. But there is also evidence, at least for women, that high levels of work in these areas may give rise to considerable dissatisfaction (e.g. Oakley 1974). Thus, in respect to this particular category, a countervailing Oakley effect might be set against the Jahoda effect. It may be that some of those respondents who felt strongly that they had been engaged in 'useful activity' did so on the basis of very high levels of unpaid work which gave rise to dissatisfaction and relatively poor psychological adjustment. Preliminary work on the diary material does indeed suggest that there is a U-shaped relationship between unpaid work time and GHQ scores.

Our provisional conclusions at this stage can be stated as follows: (1) Jahoda does seem to be quite correct that her categories are strongly associated with paid employment. (2) Access to these categories of experience does correlate significantly with levels of psychological adjustment, though only a very small proportion of is variance can be explained in terms of the categories (particularly where the effects of other variables have been extracted first). (3) The effect of access to the Jahoda categories on GHQ is significant for both men and women, though the influence seems to be rather smaller in the case of women. (4) The effect is rather more important for unemployed people. For instance, those unemployed men with the lowest access to categories of experience are estimated to have a corrected mean GHQ score of 5.28 as against the average for full-time employed men of 3.12, whereas those (few) men reporting the highest level of access to the categories have a corrected mean GHQ score of 2.79—substantially below the employed men's average.

NOTES

1. See pages 250 and 251 of this volume. People were asked who they were with when they last engaged in sporting, cultural, and social activities outside their households. A measure of sociability was constructed in which the score increased with the number of different types of people from outside the household involved in the activity. This number was then weighted by the frequency with which the person carried out that activity.

2. The General Health Questionnaire is discussed in Chapter 6 of this volume. Larger GHQ scores indicate poorer psychological adjustment, whereas lower GHQ scores indicate better psychological health.

8

Unemployment, the Household, and Social Networks

DUNCAN GALLIE, JONATHAN GERSHUNY, AND CAROLYN VOGLER

UK
J64
D10
J12

1. INTRODUCTION

Most research on the social consequences of unemployment has tended to focus on its implications for the individual. In particular, it has shown that the loss of work leads to a marked rise in anxiety and depression (Warr 1987). However, some of the earliest qualitative studies (Bakke 1935, 1940*a,b*; Komarovsky 1940) also suggested that unemployment had major implications for the quality of household relations and for the relationship between the household and the wider community (Jahoda *et al.* 1972). In particular, it was seen as leading to a shift in roles within the household and to the increased social isolation of unemployed people. Both of these factors were seen as reinforcing the psychological distress generated by unemployment.

A salient finding of the inter-war studies was that unemployment placed greater responsibility for financial management on the female partner (Bakke 1940*b*). At the same time, it posed significant problems for male gender identity, given the identification of the male with the bread-winning role. More recent discussion has focused on the implications of unemployment for changes in the pattern of domestic work. The evidence here is very inconsistent. Some studies have suggested that unemployment is unlikely to lead to significant renegotiation of domestic roles (Pahl 1984; Morris 1985). Research using time budget data (Thomas *et al.* 1985; Gershuny *et al.* 1986), however, points to a rather more marked change in male participation in household tasks with unemployment.

A second area of interest has been the relationship between unemployment and involvement in social networks. Inter-war studies painted a fairly uniform picture of the social withdrawal of the unemployed, attributable to psychological distress, the stigma of unemployment, and the lack of the material resources necessary for maintaining social relationships (Jahoda *et al.* 1972; Bakke 1935). Post-war studies, however, while not directly comparable, suggested that the unemployed retained a rather higher level of sociability (Warr and Payne 1983) and that this was particularly the case for women (Martin and Wallace 1984).

The nature of the relationship between unemployment, domestic organization, and social networks may have important implications for theories of the psychological consequences of unemployment. These generally assume that the activities of the unemployed in the household and in the community only aggravate psychological distress. This view was encouraged by the emphasis in the inter-war literature on the collapse of community activities and the passivity of the unemployed within the household. If, however, in the 1980s unemployment is associated with a significant renegotiation of the division of domestic labour, or with the preservation of regular patterns of interaction within the local community, the question is raised whether the unemployed may be able to find compensations for the loss of employment in their domestic and community lives.

Previous studies have tended to suffer from severe methodological limitations, using small samples of unknown representativeness, and failing to provide comparable information about those in employment. The evidence from the Social Change and Economic Life Initiative (SCELI) allows us to examine these issues in a more systematic way, drawing on the 1987 Household and Community Survey, which provides partnership data on 1,200 couples and on approximately 600 single people (see the Methodological Appendix at the end of this book for further details). This allows a direct comparison of the employed and the unemployed. The quality of the evidence is greatly enhanced by the fact that, on many of the key issues, information about household organization was collected from both partners independently. Finally, the study enables us to use both questionnaire and time budget approaches to the measurement of patterns of domestic work and leisure activity.

This chapter focuses on three principal issues. First, it will examine the implications of unemployment for the way in which financial decision-making and domestic work is organized in the household; secondly, it will consider whether unemployment affects patterns of leisure activity and sociability; and thirdly, it will assess the extent to which patterns of household organization and sociability mediate the psychological impact of unemployment. One of the central conclusions is that the effects of unemployment are not *sui generis*, but are heavily mediated by the social location of the individuals who experience it.

2. UNEMPLOYMENT AND THE ORGANIZATION OF THE HOUSEHOLD

How far can unemployment be seen as leading to a greater sharing of financial management and a more equal division of domestic tasks? The literature contains two broad interpretations of the effects of unemployment. One view emphasizes its potential for breaking down traditional gender roles: male unemployment is seen as potentially conducive to greater equality in domestic roles, or even role reversal, as men's bread-winning role is undermined while their availability for domestic tasks is increased. The second perspective, however, emphasizes the way in which the experience of unemployment may reinforce and indeed strengthen traditional gender roles, as one or both partners seek to reaffirm or protect the husband's threatened masculine identity.

In approaching these issues, it is important to note from the outset that the unemployed were in quite diverse household situations. A large number (33 per cent of men and 47 per cent of women) were single people. Among those who were married, there were differences in the employment status of the spouse. A majority (57 per cent) of unemployed married[1] men had economically inactive wives, and a further 15 per cent had wives that were also unemployed. The remainder divided roughly equally between those with wives in full-time employment (15 per cent) and those with wives in part-time work (13 per cent). Among unemployed married women, the pattern was very different. The great majority (72 per cent) had husbands who were in full-time employment, while the remainder had partners who were also unemployed. It is important to assess whether the effects of unemployment on internal household processes are mediated by the type of household structure.

2.1. Unemployment and the Management of Household Money

How far is unemployment associated with greater equality in the management of household money? Previous studies have suggested that, in households where the husband is unemployed, the wife is much more likely than in other households to manage the entire household budget—the female whole-wage system (Morris 1988, 1990). The reason for this is thought to be that, where financial pressures are very severe, control over expenditure is most effective when it is undertaken by one partner. Given her greater responsibility for collective expenditure, the burden of managing an inadequate income most commonly falls to the woman.

Respondents were asked two questions on money management. The first asked people to say which of a set of possible financial arrangements came closest to the way in which they currently organized their own household finances. The examples were chosen to reflect Jan Pahl's (1989) classification of allocative systems into the female whole-wage system, the male whole-wage system, the housekeeping allowance system, and the joint pool.[2] Respondents were then asked who had ultimate responsibility for organizing household money and paying bills—the male partner, the female partner, or both equally. Answers to the two questions correspond very closely indeed, except among those claiming to use the joint pool, who could be divided into three roughly equal groups on the basis of their answers to the second question. In roughly a third of pooling households, men had ultimate responsibility for managing money (the male pool), in roughly a third wives had this responsibility (the female pool), and in the remaining third it was shared jointly (the equal pool).

Table 8.1 compares the methods of money management used in households with an unemployed member with those used in households where no one was unemployed. In contrast to the picture provided by previous (impressionistic) literature, there were no statistically significant differences between the two types of household. When husbands were unemployed, however,

TABLE 8.1. *Methods of financial allocation used in households in which one or both partners were unemployed* (%)

Allocatory system	Neither unemployed	One or both partners unemployed	Husband unemployed	Wife unemployed
Female whole wage	27	28	32	19
Male whole wage	10	8	7	11
Housekeeping allowance	12	11	11	10
Equal pool	20	19	21	16
Male pool	15	17	16	18
Female pool	16	17	13	26
TOTAL	100	100	100	100
No.	1,077	170	109	75

Source: The Household and Community Survey, 1987.

couples were marginally more likely to use the female whole-wage system, whereas, when wives were unemployed, couples were more likely to use the female pool.

Unemployment, in short, seemed to have had little influence over household financial organization. This conclusion was confirmed by a direct question about whether or not people had changed their financial arrangements as a result of unemployment. Only 9 out of 109 unemployed men and 1 out of 75 unemployed women had changed their method of financial allocation since becoming unemployed. Amongst the 9 men who had changed, there were no clear patterns of change. Only 1 man had changed from some form of pooling to the female whole-wage system.

Systems of money management used in unemployed households thus appear to pre-date the current experience of unemployment. As can be seen from the regression analysis in Table 8.2, the main determinants of the female whole-wage system were the husband's social class and both partners' socialization and qualifications. After controlling for these factors, husband's unemployment had no independent effect on the use of the female whole-wage system.

2.2. The Domestic Division of Labour

Is male unemployment associated with a shift towards greater equality in the division of labour within the home or does it reinforce traditional gender roles? Three measures of the domestic division of labour were available: first, perceptions of who was ultimately responsible for ensuring that the family had an adequate income and that the housework was done properly; secondly, perceptions of who usually undertook various household tasks; and thirdly, time budget data for the week following the survey.

Data from all three sources showed a consistent pattern. When wives were unemployed domestic organization was relatively traditional; especially when the husbands were in full-time employment. When husbands were unemployed, however, the division of labour tended to be less traditional than when husbands were in employment. But the extent to which this was the case was strongly affected by the wives' employment status; the most

TABLE 8.2. *Logistic regression of the female whole-wage (FWW) system* (no. = 1,079)

Variables	Estimate	Standard error	Odds ratio	Chi-squared	Degrees of freedom	Significance
Husband in class 7	0.6456	0.1618	1.9	27.9	1	<0.001
Husband's parents used FWW	0.4823	0.1512	1.6	15.2	1	<0.001
Wife higher class than husband	0.6647	0.2032	1.9	5.3	1	<0.05
Wife's parents used FWW	0.3366	0.1517	1.4	4.7	1	<0.05
Wife in class 7	0.5145	0.1724	1.7	10.1	1	<0.01
Wife has vocational/O levels	0.5628	0.1898	1.8	6.1	1	<0.02
Husband has vocational/O levels	0.4263	0.1843	1.5	5.2	1	<0.05
Constant	−2.040	0.1562	0.13			

Source: The Household and Community Survey, 1987.

conventional division of labour occurred where wives were non-employed or in part-time work, while the least conventional patterns were found where wives were in full-time employment. It must be remembered, however, that most unemployed men were living with non-employed wives—a situation in which change was least likely.

Wives in full-time employment, for example, had ultimate responsibility for housework in 85 per cent of households where husbands were in employment, compared with only 54 per cent of households where husbands were unemployed. Where wives were economically inactive, however, the difference was much smaller: they were responsible for housework in 96 per cent of households where husbands were in employment, compared with 87 per cent of households where husbands were unemployed.

The data showing how particular domestic tasks in the household were carried out provides a similar picture. Task performance was measured by asking both respondent and partner who usually did the housework, the washing-up, the cooking, and washing the clothes (Table 8.3). A summary indicator of traditionalism in the domestic division of labour was then constructed by allocating a score of 2 to each traditional response and a score of 1 to each non-traditional response. Scores were summed across the four items producing a domestic division of labour index in which high scores indicated traditional gender roles and low scores less traditional patterns. The overall index score for all households where the male partner was unemployed was 6.7, compared with 7.2 where the male was employed and 7.4 where he was self-employed. The differences between the scores of the unemployed and the employed were significant at the 0.01 level. Again, however, the extent of sharing in households with an unemployed person varied considerably depending on the partner's employment status (Table 8.3). The most traditional households were those in which wives were unemployed while husbands were in full-time work (with a score of 7.3), while the least traditional were those in which husbands were unemployed while wives were in full-time employment (which scored 5.5). Those in which husbands were unemployed while wives were non-employed, in part-time work, or also unemployed themselves fell between the two extremes.

Finally, the same overall pattern emerges in the time budget

TABLE 8.3. *Household labour market position and organization of domestic work* (% giving traditional answers)

Domestic division of labour	Husband full-time				Husband unemployed			
	Wife full-time	Wife part-time	Wife non-employed	Wife unemployed	Wife full-time	Wife part-time	Wife non-employed	Wife unemployed
Broad Responsibilities								
Responsibility for housework	85	96	96	100	54	83	87	82
Responsibility for income	44	81	96	100	36	29	83	70
Task performance								
Washing up	43	63	78	71	26	47	62	59
Vacuuming	69	88	91	86	29	70	79	60
Washing clothes	93	94	99	96	78	98	94	79
Cooking	78	89	93	88	51	65	73	86
Overall index of domestic division of labour	6.8	7.3	7.5	7.3	5.5	6.7	7.0	6.9

Note: High scores indicate traditional gender roles and low scores less traditional. Women have traditionally been responsible for housework and childcare as well as actually doing the washing-up, vacuuming, washing clothes, and cooking. Men have traditionally been responsible for income.

Source: The Household and Community Survey, 1987.

data, although the numbers are reduced (only half the original respondents returned completed diaries) and, as a result, differences between households are often not statistically significant. As can be seen in Table 8.4, unemployed wives with husbands in full-time employment stood out as doing the largest proportion of the total washing-up, cleaning, washing clothes, and cooking in their households. Conversely, wives who were in full-time employment while husbands were unemployed stood out as doing the smallest proportion of the total in their households. Households in which husbands were unemployed while wives were non-employed, in part-time work, or also unemployed themselves fell between the two extremes.

Male unemployment appears, then, to be linked in a consistent way to the domestic division of labour. But are these patterns the result of changes accompanying unemployment or do they simply reflect a continuation of the situation before unemployment? In order to investigate the extent to which unemployment itself had been the cause of change, respondents and partners who defined themselves as unemployed were asked whether they had changed the way in which they organized domestic tasks since becoming unemployed and, if so, which partner had increased his or her share of the work.

Approximately half of both unemployed men and unemployed women reported that unemployment had brought about a change in the way that domestic work was organized in the household. Where it was the man who had become unemployed, change was strongly related to the wife's employment status, being most likely to occur when wives were in full-time employment and least likely when wives were non-employed (Table 8.5). The overwhelming majority of unemployed men with partners in full-time employment (82 per cent) had changed their level of involvement in domestic work since becoming unemployed, 62 per cent doing a lot more and 20 per cent a little more of the domestic work. When wives worked part-time, 71 per cent of unemployed husbands claimed that the way household tasks were organized had changed in the direction of greater male involvement, with 43 per cent doing a lot more and 28 per cent doing a little more of the domestic work. When wives were non-employed, however, husbands were much more likely to report no change in the domestic division of labour (64 per cent), although a small minority (26

TABLE 8.4. *Domestic division of labour by household labour market situation, time budget diary estimates*

Husbands' and wives' employment status	Proportion of tasks done by wife			
	Washing up	Cleaning	Washing clothes	Cooking
Husband full-time, wife full-time	0.41	0.64	0.90	0.48
Husband unemployed, wife full-time	0.12	*	0.77	-0.08
Husband full-time, wife part-time	0.54	0.71	0.92	0.67
Husband unemployed, wife part-time	0.15	0.64	1.00	0.26
Husband full-time, wife non-employed	0.62	0.76	0.90	0.65
Husband unemployed, wife non-employed	0.42	0.58	0.75	0.47
Husband full-time, wife unemployed	0.54	0.84	0.84	0.68
Husband unemployed, wife unemployed	0.57	0.63	0.48	0.56

Source: The Household and Community Survey, 1987.

TABLE 8.5. Changes in the domestic division of labour since husband's unemployment (%)

Changes in domestic division of labour	Husband full-time		Husband unemployed		
	Wife unemployed	Wife non-employed	Wife unemployed	Wife part-time	Wife full-time
No change	48	64	50	29	17
Wife lot more	38	1	*	*	*
Wife little more	8	1	3	*	*
Husband little more	2	26	3	28	20
Husband lot more	4	8	44	43	62
	100	100	100	100	100
No.	34	55	12	16	15

Source: The Household and Community Survey, 1987.

per cent) claimed that they did a little more of the domestic work. Change was also less common where both partners were unemployed (50 per cent reported no change), although 44 per cent of husbands claimed they were doing a lot more of the domestic work. These patterns were unrelated to the presence or ages of children, or to husband's age. Finally, where the wife had become unemployed, but the husband remained in work, change took the form of reverting to a more traditional pattern of domestic work.

In short, the experience of unemployment seemed to produce changes in the domestic division of labour, although both the extent and direction of change were strongly mediated by the spouse's employment status. In the small number of households where husbands were unemployed while the wives were in full-time employment, the data indicate a distinct move to greater equality in gender roles, thus supporting the role reversal thesis. Overall, however, the magnitude of the change does not appear to have been large: in the majority of households where husbands were unemployed, the data indicate a shift in, rather than a fundamental change in, traditional patterns. And when wives became unemployed couples reverted to a more traditional division of labour.

Overall, the evidence indicates that unemployment had no effect on the way in which couples organized money, although changes were detected in the domestic division of labour. This implies that the general principles underlying change in the domestic division of labour may be rather different from those underlying change in systems of money management. The domestic division of labour appears to be susceptible to gradual changes around the edges in response to wives' full-time employment and husbands' unemployment. Systems of money management, however, appear to be much more entrenched and less amenable to change; they are more constrained by class and socialization and less flexibly related to patterns of labour market participation.

3. LEISURE ACTIVITIES AND SOCIABILITY

In this section we turn to activities outside the household. A recurrent theme in qualitative studies has been that unemployment leads to social withdrawal and social isolation. In part this is attributed to the lack of the financial resources needed to take part in the usual range of social activities, and in part it is seen as a result of the loss of self-confidence of the unemployed and their desire to avoid social contacts that might well be further damaging to their self-esteem. In this section, we shall be concerned to see, first, whether unemployment leads to a significant reduction in people's participation in leisure activities and, secondly, whether it affects their sociability, that is to say, the extent to which they engage in activities with other people outside the immediate household.

3.1. Unemployment and Leisure Activities

Respondents were asked how often they engaged in different types of leisure activity. The responses were broadly grouped into sporting, cultural, social, and other activities. 'Sporting' included activities such as swimming, playing a sport, or watching live sport. 'Cultural' covered activities such as attending leisure activity groups, evening classes, and church services, or going out to a cinema, theatre, or concert. 'Social' included paying a social visit to someone's home, having someone round to one's own home, and going out to a pub or club. Finally, 'other' activities involved activities like walking, gardening, reading, and watching television.

To provide a measure of the frequency of each activity, the response categories were given the following weights: an activity that was carried out once a week or more was given a weight of 1, fortnightly a weight of 0.5, monthly a weight of 0.25, and every few months a weight of 0.07. As can be seen in Tables 8.6 and 8.7, there was considerable variation in the frequency with which activities were carried out. The most common activities were watching television, reading, and walking. Visiting, entertaining, and going to the pub took place on average about once a fortnight. Going out to the theatre, concerts, or the cinema were very rare indeed.

Were the unemployed significantly different from other people in the frequency with which they engaged in such activities? To assess this, a summary index of each individual's activity pattern was computed by summing the scores on the different items. This

TABLE 8.6. *Leisure activities by employment status, men* (no. = 1,503)

Activity	Self-employed	Employed	Unemployed	Non-active
Library	0.07	0.13	0.16	0.29
Swim	0.09	0.12	0.09	0.09
Play sport	0.35	0.37	0.28	0.22
Watch sport	0.26	0.31	0.32	0.29
Theatre	0.04	0.04	0.02	0.05
Cinema	0.05	0.05	0.05	0.04
Pub	0.62	0.57	0.54	0.42
Church	0.12	0.12	0.13	0.12
Visit	0.45	0.49	0.60	0.46
Entertain	0.44	0.42	0.54	0.47
Garden	0.47	0.50	0.38	0.46
TV	0.96	0.96	0.95	0.96
Read book	0.70	0.75	0.65	0.75
Walk	0.43	0.54	0.65	0.59
Leisure group	0.15	0.14	0.09	0.14
Evening class	0.02	0.06	0.03	0.06
Overall activity Index	5.27	5.57	5.46	5.50

Source: The Household and Community Survey, 1987.

provides little evidence of any general tendency of the unemployed to withdraw into inactivity, the overall leisure activity levels of the unemployed were very similar to those of the employed. Among men, the mean activity score for the unemployed (5.46) was a little lower than that for the employed (5.57); while among women, the pattern was reversed, with the unemployed showing slightly higher scores than the employed (5.58 compared with 5.48). In neither case, however, did these differences reach statistical significance. This similarity in activity levels between the employed and the unemployed did not just reflect the frequency of relatively private activities such as watching television or gardening, since an index based solely on the sporting, social, and cultural items produced the same results. There is some indication, however, of differences in patterns of activity. For instance, the unemployed were less likely than the employed to play a sport or to go to the pub, but they were considerably more likely to visit other people at home or to have people

TABLE 8.7. *Leisure activities by employment status, women* (no. = 1,527)

Activity	Self-employed	Employed	Unemployed	Non-active
Library	0.19	0.16	0.21	0.18
Swim	0.24	0.16	0.15	0.13
Play sport	0.19	0.15	0.08	0.08
Watch sport	0.20	0.17	0.12	0.15
Theatre	0.05	0.06	0.05	0.04
Cinema	0.07	0.05	0.06	0.03
Pub	0.35	0.38	0.31	0.24
Church	0.31	0.18	0.20	0.19
Visit	0.67	0.61	0.74	0.66
Entertain	0.46	0.52	0.61	0.62
Garden	0.44	0.36	0.33	0.41
TV	1.00	0.97	0.98	0.96
Read book	0.87	0.85	0.79	0.76
Walk	0.59	0.58	0.75	0.66
Leisure group	0.30	0.21	0.14	0.16
Evening class	0.13	0.08	0.05	0.04
Overall activity Index	6.04	5.48	5.58	5.29

Source: The Household and Community Survey, 1987.

round. This suggests that there was a displacement of activities towards those that involved less expenditure. It is still very far, however, from the conventional picture of the unemployed as passive and withdrawn.

Men and women also differed in their activity patterns. Overall, men had somewhat higher scores than women. But unemployed women were more involved in leisure activities than unemployed men. This possibly reflected differences in the types of leisure activity in which men and women typically engaged. Men were more likely to spend time going to the pub. Women, in contrast, were more likely than men to visit others and to have people round to their own homes. Men's activities may have been more costly and therefore particularly vulnerable with unemployment. For women, the key resource may have been time rather than money, with, unemployment facilitating a slightly higher level of activity.

Activity patterns also differed depending on whether people were single or had partners (Table 8.8). Overall, single people had higher activity levels than those in partnerships; but they also appear to have been most constrained by unemployment. For both men and women, the activity scores of unemployed single people were lower than those of the employed, and, for men, this difference was statistically significant.

TABLE 8.8. *Overall leisure activity scores by partnership status*

Employment status	Single people		In partnership	
	Men	Women	Men	Women
Self-employed	6.24	4.74	5.14	6.23
Employed	5.95	6.09	5.50	5.34
Unemployed	5.30	5.77	5.54	5.41
Non-active	6.25	5.51	5.09	5.25
All	5.83	5.85	5.44	5.34
Significance employ/unemploy	0.02	0.17	0.79	0.73
No.	287	310	1,216	1,216

Source: The Household and Community Survey, 1987.

As well as comparing activity patterns of people in different employment statuses, we asked people whether they felt that they had changed the frequency with which they did each activity since they became unemployed. As can be seen in Table 8.9, the most common pattern was that people had continued to carry on their activities very much as they had before they had become unemployed. In so far as people had changed their activities, the general direction of change depended on the type of activity in question. There had been a decline in going out to a pub or a club (34 per cent for men and 30 per cent for women) and in visits to the theatre, concerts, or cinema. In contrast, there had been a rise in the frequency with which people visited others at home and received visits. This was particularly the case for women, with 54 per cent saying they visited others more and 47 per cent that they entertained more. Overall, the evidence from people's own accounts confirms the picture that emerged from the previous comparison of activity patterns. While patterns of activity may have changed somewhat in type, it seems unlikely that there

TABLE 8.9. *Changes in activities with unemployment*

Activity	Men			Women		
	More	Same	Less	More	Same	Less
Library	22	74	4	26	68	6
Swim	14	76	10	19	70	11
Play sport	18	73	10	5	87	8
Watch sport	19	71	10	3	88	9
Theatre, concerts	3	85	12	3	82	16
Cinema	7	79	14	7	68	25
Pub	14	53	34	11	59	30
Church	4	96	—	9	86	6
Visit	37	54	8	54	41	5
Entertain	21	72	7	47	47	6
Garden	33	63	5	27	66	7
TV	65	32	3	62	33	5
Read book	44	55	2	51	43	6
Walk	50	46	4	56	42	2
Leisure group	5	91	4	13	82	5
Evening class	3	95	3	4	90	6

Source: The Household and Community Survey, 1987.

was any overall decline in unemployed people's involvement in leisure activities. People had cut back on more expensive forms of entertainment, but had increased those that were cheaper.

3.2. Leisure Activities and Daily Time Use Patterns

Despite maintaining similar levels of activity outside the home, the unemployed still experienced an increase in 'vacant' or 'passive' time as compared with people in employment. Many qualitative studies have emphasized the tendency of the unemployed to withdraw into largely passive activities, but there have been few attempts to estimate the extent to which this occurs.

This issue was explored with the time budget data collected from a subset of respondents and partners for the week following the survey. The activities described in the time diaries were coded in a way which made it possible to compare respondents' behaviour in the diary week with their descriptions of leisure activities given in the interview. The main point to note is that the very different techniques gave an essentially similar picture of the contrast between employed and unemployed people's leisure styles.

In order to estimate the amount of 'passive' time experienced by the unemployed, a variant of multiple regression (Multiple Classification Analysis) was used in which the amount of time spent in various activities was taken as the dependent variable. Since patterns of time use are known to be affected by age and income, these factors have been controlled for in providing estimates of the difference between the employed and the unemployed in the time spent on each type of activity.

The initial analysis showed that unemployed men had, on average, an additional six hours to fill in their day, while unemployed women had an additional four and a half hours. How much of this time gap was spent in relatively passive ways and how much was spent on more constructive activities? The approach adopted is inevitably somewhat arbitrary, but we have chosen to try to estimate the likely upper limit of passive time use. For this purpose, passive time can be taken to include time spent on sleep, eating, and personal care, as well as 'passive leisure' activities such as watching television, listening to the radio, reading newspapers, and just sitting around.

The evidence confirms the impression given by qualitative case-studies that the unemployed filled some of their spare time by sleeping longer (Tables 8.10 and 8.11). However, by far the greater amount of additional time was spent in passive leisure. Unemployed men spent approximately two hours more than the employed on passive types of leisure and unemployed women approximately one and a half hours more. The single most salient leisure difference between the unemployed and the employed was the amount of time spent watching television. The unemployed spent approximately twice as much time on this as the employed.

Taken overall, the total additional time spent on passive forms of time use by unemployed men compared to those in employment added up to 187 minutes, out of an overall time gap of 374 minutes. For women, the additional amount of passive time summed to 134 minutes, out of an overall time gap of 268 minutes. In short, for both sexes, roughly half of the extra time in the day that had to be filled as the result of being without employment was 'passive' time.

TABLE 8.10. *Comparison of time use, men, employed and unemployed, controlling for income and age* (hours and minutes)

Activity	Full-time employed	Unemployed	Difference, unemployed–employed
Employment-related	6.14	42	−5.32
Unpaid Work	2.22	3.41	+1.19
Personal Care	59	3.41	+13
Eating	1.08	1.27	+19
Sleep	7.39	8.13	+34
Trips	39	48	+9
Sport	11	11	—
Walks	5	12	+7
Civic	8	9	+1
Spectator*	5	5	—
Sociability with costs	31	34	+3
Free sociability	28	45	+17
Passive leisure	2.54	4.55	+2.01
Active leisure	37	66	+29

* Watching sport, going to theatre and cinema.

Source: The Household and Community Survey, 1987.

The overall picture from the time use data was thus consistent with the data derived from the questionnaire information, but the time duration data gave us a clearer picture of the balance of the activities of the unemployed. While unemployment did not lead to an absolute decline in the overall level of activities outside the home, the unemployed still had many more hours of the day to fill than the employed. A large part of the additional time that unemployed people had as a result of joblessness was spent in relatively isolated and passive activities (sleep, personal care, television).

3.3. Sociability and Social Support

To what extent did leisure activities provide a bridge between the household and the wider community? To assess this, people were asked whom they were with when they last did each particular activity. Where they were with others, companions from the same household were distinguished from companions outside the household. Our central concern was with the extensiveness of extra-household sociability. The activities that were most likely to generate extra-household sociability were the sporting, cultural, and social activities. A simple measure of sociability was constructed from these, in which the score increased with the number of different types of people from outside the household involved in the activity. This number was then weighted by the frequency with which the person carried out that activity.

The sociability index discriminated more sharply between those with a job and those without than had been the case for the activity index. Among both men and women, the employed and the self-employed had markedly higher scores than the unemployed. For men, the mean sociability score fell from 1.64 among the employed to 1.12 among the unemployed; for women it fell from 1.31 to 1.05. As can be seen in Table 8.12 the extent of extra-household sociability was associated with whether or not a

TABLE 8.11. *Comparison of time use, women, employed and unemployed, controlling for income and age* (hours and minutes)

Activity	Full-time employed	Unemployed	Difference, unemployed – employed
Employment-related	4.28	1.08	−3.20
Unpaid work	3.47	4.12	+25
Personal care	1.06	1.15	+9
Eating	1.13	1.27	+14
Sleep	7.48	8.11	+23
Trips	37	39	+2
Sport	8	7	−1
Walks	6	9	+3
Civic	8	9	+1
Spectator*	4	3	−1
Sociability with costs	24	25	+1
Free sociability	36	45	+9
Passive leisure	2.47	4.15	+1.28
Active leisure	48	1.04	+17

* Watching sport, going to theatre and cinema.
Source: The Household and Community Survey, 1987.

TABLE 8.12. *Extra household sociability by partnership status*

Employment Status	Single people		In partnership	
	Men	Women	Men	Women
Self-employed	2.57	2.22	1.15	1.25
Employed	2.81	2.31	1.41	1.09
Unemployed	1.68	1.36	0.84	0.77
Non-active	2.29	1.62	0.60	0.85
All	2.44	1.90	1.26	0.99
Significance of difference between				
employed and unemployed	0.00	0.00	0.001	0.057
No.	287	310	1,216	1,216

person was single or in a partnership, the overall level being much higher among single people. However, the difference in sociability between the employed and the unemployed was greater for single people than for couples. Further, for both single people and those in partnerships, the difference was greater for men.

The fact that the unemployed typically had a lower level of extra-household sociability than the employed does not necessarily mean that lower sociability was caused by unemployment. It might be that the unemployed tended to participate less in activities with people outside the household before they became unemployed, due to other unmeasured background characteristics. To explore this, respondents were asked whether there had been any change in the frequency with which they saw their friends. It is clear from Table 8.13 that there was no general tendency for contact with friends to decline, as would be suggested by the 'social withdrawal' thesis. Rather, those reporting a change divided almost equally between those who saw more of their friends than before and those who saw less. The pattern was very similar for both men and women. This provides some support for the view that the lower sociability of the unemployed is less an effect of unemployment itself than of other unmeasured background variables.

However, not only was the general level of sociability of the unemployed lower, but there was also a considerable difference in

TABLE 8.13. *Change in frequency in seeing non-household friends with unemployment* (%)

Change in frequency	Men	Women	All
A lot more	15	15	15
A bit more	13	15	14
Same as before	44	44	44
A bit less	15	13	14
A lot less	13	14	14
No.	172	136	308

Source: The Household and Community Survey, 1987.

the structure of their social networks. For the majority of the employed these consisted primarily of other people in work, whereas this was the case for only a minority of the unemployed (Table 8.14). The highly segregated nature of the friendship networks of the unemployed was particularly marked for men. For instance, 86 per cent of self-employed and 85 per cent of employed men said that all or almost all of their friends were in work, compared with 32 per cent of the unemployed and 42 per cent of the non-employed. Among the male unemployed, 53 per cent were in networks where half or more were unemployed and indeed 39 per cent said that this was the case for all or almost all of their friends. Among unemployed women on the other hand, the proportions were 39 per cent and 17 per cent respectively. Since the female unemployed were not much more likely than men to have a high proportion of employed people in their networks, it is likely that there was a greater tendency for them to associate with people that were non-active.

These differences in the extensiveness and composition of social networks were related to differences in the effective social support that people could depend upon. Respondents were asked whether there was anybody outside their household they could rely upon to help if they were feeling depressed, if they needed someone to keep an eye on their home while they were away, if they needed to borrow money to pay an urgent bill, or if they wanted help in finding a job. The majority of people, whatever their employment status, could rely on some degree of support

TABLE 8.14. *Friendship networks by employment status* (%)

Friends' employment status	Men				Women			
	Self-employed	Employed	Unemployed	Non-active	Self-employed	Employed	Unemployed	Non-active
Those reporting friends all or almost all employed	86	85	32	42	60	78	37	46
Those reporting half or more of friends unemployed	3	8	53	18	20	7	39	21

Source: The Household and Community Survey, 1987.

for the first of these categories, although only 40 per cent thought they were likely to get help in finding a job (Table 8.15). The unemployed, however, were less likely than either the self-employed or the employed to have someone to rely on in any of these situations. Indeed, if they were feeling depressed or needed help in looking after the house, or finding work, they appeared to have the weakest support network of any category.

A composite index of the strength of an individual's support network was created by giving a score of 1 for each situation where support was available and a score of 0 where it was not. The scores were then summed, giving a range between 0 and 4. The unemployed clearly emerged as having weaker support networks. Some 61 per cent of the unemployed had scores of 3 or 4, indicating a relatively strong support network, compared to 71 per cent of the employed, 67 per cent of the self-employed, and 66 per cent of the non-actives. However, the nature of the household made a difference to the amount of support an unemployed person could rely upon. For instance, where the unemployed person was a woman with a husband in full-time work, the strength of her support system was higher than where both partners were in full-time employment. Above all it was where the husband was unemployed and the wife was either unemployed or non-employed that the level of support fell heavily, especially for the male partner.

Finally, the level of support that a person could rely upon depended heavily upon the composition of their social network. The higher the proportion of friends that were unemployed, the less likely they were to have a strong support system. Over 70 per cent of those with networks in which less than half of their friends were unemployed had strong support networks. In contrast, where the majority of a person's friends consisted of other unemployed people, less than 40 per cent had a strong support network. The segregation of the unemployed into social networks that consisted largely of other unemployed people thus increased their vulnerability in the face of psychological and financial hardship and was likely to have made it more difficult to escape from unemployment itself.

Overall, then, the data suggested that the unemployed maintained *levels* of leisure activity that were very similar to those of the employed, although there was some displacement of *types* of

TABLE 8.15. *Social support outside household* (%)

Those having someone to rely on to:	Self-employed	Employed	Unemployed	Non-active	All
Help if depressed	77	85	76	86	83
Look after home	96	93	87	91	92
Lend money	74	74	66	64	71
Help find a job	42	42	29	40	40

Source: The Household and Community Survey, 1987.

activity towards those that were less costly. They also had lower levels of sociability with people outside the household than people in employment. There was some evidence, however, that this may not have been a direct effect of unemployment, but a reflection of other background characteristics of the unemployed. Unemployment had a more notable effect on the composition of social networks. The unemployed tended to be relatively segregated, in networks in which a far higher proportion of their friends were unemployed than was the case for employed people. This appears to have directly contributed to the relative weakness of the social support that was available to them. Unemployed friends were less likely to be in a position to offer strong psychological support or effective assistance in meeting financial problems or the difficulties of finding a job. The nature of the social networks of the unemployed offered relatively few opportunities for alleviating the stress of unemployment and helped to lock the unemployed into a position of labour market disadvantage.

4. THE HOUSEHOLD, SOCIAL NETWORKS, AND THE EXPERIENCE OF UNEMPLOYMENT

The evidence that has been examined so far suggests that unemployment leads to some (albeit limited) adaptation of household roles. Further, while the unemployed had lower levels of sociability than the employed, they retained more active social lives than would appear to have been the case in the inter-war period. This raises the question of whether such household and social factors can significantly affect people's experience of unemployment. Were unemployed people who shared household tasks less vulnerable to distress than those in households with more traditional patterns of gender relations? Were people who led a more active social life able to find satisfaction in their non-work activities which helped to compensate for the lack of a job?

The view that people may be able to compensate for the loss of employment through greater involvement in domestic work or more active patterns of sociability assumes that these create particularly high levels of satisfaction with out-of-work life. Respondents were asked to indicate their satisfaction with different aspects of their lives on a scale running from 0 (very dissatisfied) to 10 (very satisfied). As can be seen in Table 8.16, unemployed men were markedly less satisfied with their family lives than were employed men (a difference significant at the 0.001 level). Among women, on the other hand, there was no difference at all. Did greater involvement by men in domestic tasks increase satisfaction with family life among the unemployed? There is no evidence this was the case. The satisfaction scores for men in less traditional households were actually lower than those in more traditional households, although the difference was not statistically significant. It seems that the pressures that unemployment imposed on men's identity in the family were far too strong to be compensated for by adjustments in the organization of domestic work.

Turning to satisfaction with social life, there is again a highly significant effect of unemployment and, this time, it is evident for men and for women. The unemployed were much less satisfied with their social lives than the employed (Table 8.17). It was the case that unemployed people who had extensive social contacts outside the household were more likely to be satisfied than those with more restricted sociability, suggesting that there is some scope for adaptation. But the most notable point is that even the most sociable of the unemployed were still less satisfied with their social lives than the least sociable of the employed. This may reflect qualitative differences in types of social activity due to financial pressures.

In short, greater involvement in domestic organization and higher levels of sociability were not in themselves sufficient to ensure that the unemployed could find equivalent satisfaction in their family and social lives to that of people in employment. This makes it unlikely that they would be able to compensate for the stress of unemployment through changes in their domestic and social lives.

This can be examined more directly by looking at the implications of household factors and patterns of social activity for the psychological distress associated with unemployment. Psychological distress was measured by a reduced four-item version of the General Health Questionnaire (GHQ) based on the items that correlated best with the overall index. This confirmed the well-established finding that the unemployed had poorer psychological

TABLE 8.16. *Satisfaction with family life by sex and domestic division of labour*

	Self-employed	Employed	Unemployed	Non-active
Men	8.64	8.40	7.80	8.49
Women	9.00	8.56	8.56	8.34
Men in households where division of domestic labour is:				
Traditional	8.65	8.37	7.98	8.14
Less traditional	8.58	8.49	7.47	9.00
Women in households where division of domestic labour is:				
Traditional	9.30	8.54	8.56	8.39
Less traditional	8.14	8.60	9.00	8.02

Note: Lower scores indicate lower satisfaction with family life. Differences between the employed and unemployed were significant at the 0.01 level for men, but were not significant for women. The score differences between traditional and less traditional households were not significant at the 0.05 level, except among non-active men.

Source: The Household and Community Survey, 1937.

TABLE 8.17. *Satisfaction with social life by sex, partnership status, and sociability*

	Self-employed	Employed	Unemployed	Non-active
Men				
All	7.29	6.91	5.60	6.89
In partnerships	7.30	6.83	5.48	6.96
Single	7.24	7.30	5.81	6.70
Sociability				
Low	6.96	6.67	5.35	6.61
Medium	6.96	6.60	5.21	7.69
High	8.02	7.38	6.44	6.50
Women				
All	7.52	6.72	5.61	6.26
In partnerships	7.41	6.81	5.89	6.28
Single	8.25	6.31	5.30	6.14
Sociability				
Low	8.40	6.72	5.32	6.05
Medium	7.38	6.65	5.65	5.80
High	6.92	6.80	5.81	7.11

Note: Lower scores indicate less satisfaction with social life. Score differences by employment status and sociability were significant at the 0.01 level.
Source: The Household and Community Survey, 1987.

health than the employed; it was also worse than that of the non-actives. Whereas unemployed men had an average score of 4.3, the score for employed men was only 3.27. Unemployed women had a score of 4.26, while the score for those in employment was 3.49. Further, men in partnerships were particularly likely to experience distress when unemployed, whereas, among women, it was those that were single that appear to have suffered most (Table 8.18).

Did the level of involvement in domestic activities help people to adjust psychologically to unemployment? Unemployed men who were more involved in household work had higher psychological distress scores than those who were less involved (and unemployed women had lower psychological distress scores in households with a traditional division of labour). However, these differences were not statistically significant and the safest conclusion is that the organization of household work did not mediate the psychological impact of unemployment.

What were the implications of higher levels of sociability? Men who were particularly likely to engage in activities with people outside the household had lower scores for psychological distress than those with either low or medium levels of sociability. However, even the most sociable category of unemployed men had worse scores than any category of the employed. Among women, the least distressed category were those with medium levels of sociability, while those with high sociability had the highest stress scores. This may reflect gender differences in the extent to which men and women spend their time at home and in their ability to cope with the social isolation this may involve. But it is important to note that once employment status has been controlled for, sociability had no statistically significant effect on either men's or women's psychological well-being.

It would seem, then, that neither the adaptation of household roles nor the preservation of more active patterns of sociability could remove the psychological deprivations caused by unemployment. Even the most active and sociable of the unemployed had worse psychological health than those in employment. The financial and psychological pressures of unemployment appeared to reduce quite fundamentally the quality of life, even for those who adopted patterns of non-employment activity that might be

TABLE 8.18. *Psychological distress scores by sex and partnership status*

	Self-employed	Employed	Unemployed	Non-active
Men				
All	3.24	3.27	4.30	4.00
In partnerships	3.17	3.23	4.40	3.81
Single	3.71	3.47	4.12	4.50
Women				
All	3.07	3.49	4.26	3.72
In partnerships	3.04	3.43	4.05	3.27
Single	3.25	3.76	4.51	3.74

Note: Psychological distress scores are derived from the four highest loading items of the GHQ (General Health Questionnaire) measure. Higher scores indicate greater psychological distress. The effect of employment status is significant at the 0.01 level, both overall and within partnership status categories.

Source: The Household and Community Survey, 1987.

expected to have given them the best chance of compensating for lack of employment.

5. CONCLUSION

The evidence that has been examined casts doubt on a number of common perceptions of the impact of unemployment on household organization, leisure activities, and sociability. Unemployment had no effect on the way in which couples organized money within the household; systems of money management appeared to be rooted in longer-term factors such as class background and earlier socialization and showed few signs of change in response to unemployment. There was more evidence of change in the domestic division of labour, but this was heavily mediated by the labour market situation of the household. It was only where unemployed men were living with partners in full-time employment that there was any substantial modification of traditional gender roles. For the majority there would appear to have been only a modest increase in men's involvement in domestic work.

With respect to leisure activities and sociability, the data suggest that the image of the unemployed that emerged from the inter-war studies needs substantial qualification in the circumstances of the 1980s. There was little sign of the withdrawal into passivity and social isolation that was highlighted in the earlier studies. The overall levels of leisure activity of the unemployed were very comparable with those of the employed, and the majority of the unemployed reported that they had continued to pursue their leisure activities as frequently as before they became unemployed. There were indications, however, of a tendency for activities to be displaced towards those that were least expensive, and it is clear that the continuation of past levels of leisure activity was quite compatible with a significant increase in the amount of 'vacant' or 'passive' time that was experienced in the course of the day.

The unemployed were more distinctive in their lower levels of sociability, although there was some evidence that this may have reflected longer-term background characteristics rather than the impact of unemployment *per se*. The most striking difference between the employed and the unemployed lay in the nature rather than the extensiveness of their networks. The unemployed were in relatively segregated networks in which their friends also tended to be unemployed. They therefore had weaker social support systems to help with both psychological and material problems. These networks may be a significant factor locking the unemployed into a situation of labour market disadvantage.

NOTES

1. The term married is used to include cohabiting couples.
2. For an extended discussion of these systems see Vogler (1989). In the 'Female Whole Wage System' husbands hand over the whole of their wage packet (minus their personal spending money) to wives who are responsible for managing all the household money. In the 'Male Whole Wage System', however, husbands are responsible for managing all the household finances. In the 'Housekeeping Allowance System' husbands give their wives a fixed sum of money for housekeeping expenses and then retain control over the rest of the money themselves, while in the 'Pooling System' both partners are responsible for managing expenditure from a common pool.

9

An Examination of the Relationship between Marital Dissolution and Unemployment

RICHARD LAMPARD

1. INTRODUCTION

Much evidence exists showing a relationship between male unemployment and marital dissolution. Payne (1989) notes that in 1985 the proportion of widowed, divorced, and separated men aged 16–64 who were unemployed was approximately twice the proportion of married men aged 16–64 who were unemployed. (Source: OPCS General Household Survey, 1985). Other authors, such as Ross and Sawhill (1975), Daniel (1981), Haskey (1984), Eekelaar and Maclean (1986), Warr (1987), and Liem and Liem (1988), have also referred to data which suggests that there may be a causal connection between male unemployment and marital dissolution.

Why should unemployment be related to married couples splitting up? The financial and psychological stresses associated with unemployment have been shown to have negative effects on family life (e.g. Fagin and Little 1984; Popay 1985). It would seem likely that these stresses could also lead to an increased risk of marital breakdown, though Mattinson (1988) argues that loss of work and unemployment 'turn' marriages 'bad' which were already unsatisfactory but in which work had helped to contain immaturities or problems in couples' ways of relating.

Poverty can also increase the risk of marital breakdown. Burgoyne et al., for example, state that: 'the stresses associated with poverty—insecure employment, financial hardship and unsatisfactory housing—exacerbate the inevitable tensions of early married life' (1987: 22). One should therefore be cautious

* The author is grateful for all the comments and suggestions that he has received relating to this paper, and is especially grateful to Catherine Marsh, Máire Ní Bhrolcháin, and David Cox.

about ascribing a high rate of marital dissolution among the unemployed to unemployment itself rather than to other more general factors such as poverty. It is worth noting that Haskey (1984) derived a standardized divorce rate for the male unemployed which was nearly identical to the rate that he derived for unskilled male workers. Furthermore, the critical issue may be insecurity rather than unemployment; Burchell (in Chapter 6) suggests that the psychological consequences of unemployment are similar to the psychological consequences of insecure employment, a hypothesis supported by the study of a factory closure by Beale and Nethercott (1985), which suggested that 'the threat of redundancy was a stress equal to, if not greater than, the actual event'.

Cross-sectional data, however, cannot be used to examine the causal direction of the relationship between marital dissolution and unemployment, whereas a survey such as the Social Change and Economic Life Initiative (SCELI), which collected data both on work histories and on life histories, can in theory be used for such a purpose. (It is worth remembering that there is a third possibility, namely, that the correlation between marital dissolution and unemployment could be a spurious one induced by the joint dependency of both on other variables.)

Any detailed examination of the relationship between marital dissolution and unemployment needs to distinguish between pre-dissolution unemployment and post-dissolution unemployment. It makes sense to divide the examination into two analyses, the first with marital dissolution as the dependent variable and pre-dissolution unemployment as an independent variable, and the second with post-dissolution unemployment as the dependent variable and the dissolution event and pre-dissolution unemployment as independent variables. Furthermore, since one can reasonably assume that male unemployment and female unemployment are not qualitatively identical, the second analysis needs to be repeated for each sex.

The risk that a couple's marriage will dissolve is likely to be dependent on characteristics of *both* the spouses. However, most surveys, SCELI included, do not collect data on ex-spouses. The resulting data sets therefore contain information only on *one* spouse for each recorded dissolution. One can therefore either repeat for each sex the first of the two analyses described in the paragraph above or perform a single analysis and allow some or all of the independent variables to have effects dependent on the sex of the respondent.

Marital dissolution, male unemployment, and female unemployment all suffer to some extent from definitional problems. Female unemployment is even more difficult to define than male unemployment (see Cragg and Dawson 1984; Marshall 1984; Callender 1985). In the SCELI work histories, the respondents were left to decide themselves whether they had been unemployed or non-employed (e.g. a housewife) during any particular period when they were not employed. One result of this was that a significant number of women who had declared themselves to be housewives at the date of the main survey retrospectively reclassified themselves as having been unemployed during the identical period when they updated their work histories in the Household and Community Survey (similarly, some other women reclassified themselves from having been unemployed to having been housewives).

From a sociological perspective (as opposed to a legal perspective), marital dissolution precedes the 'decree absolute' by a significant period in most · cases where a couple eventually becomes legally divorced. The most obvious other landmark to use as an estimate of the point at which a marriage really breaks down is the date at which the couple ceases to live together. An examination of Table 4.8 in OPCS Marriage and Divorce Statistics, 1987, together with the distributions of the durations of pre-divorce separation of the SCELI respondents, indicates that separation pre-dates petitions for divorce in a large proportion of cases.

Approximately 60 per cent of the SCELI respondents whose first marriage had ended in divorce explicitly reported themselves as having separated from their spouses before they became divorced. (Since the marriages of individuals who have already been divorced once are disproportionately likely to end in divorce, it makes sense to restrict attention to first marriages.) However, of the 40 per cent who did not report a distinct separation date, just over a fifth (i.e. about 8 per cent of the total) could be seen to have separated from their spouses in or before the calendar years preceding the years of their divorces. A large number of respondents (approximately 23 per cent of the total) did not report a distinct separation date but could be seen to have separated from their spouses in the calendar years of their divorces. The above distinctions are made on the basis of the data collected by SCELI on living arrangements, which includes information on whether a respondent was living with a partner or not. Unfortunately, only the year (and not the month) when a change in living arrangements occurred was recorded.

If the date of a respondent's separation is used as an estimate of the date at which their marriage broke down, then consistency forbids treating the marriages of respondents who declare themselves to be separated from their spouses as intact. The possibility exists that some respondents who define themselves as separated will achieve reconciliations with their spouses, but a comparison of the distribution of the duration of separation for these individuals with the distribution of the duration of the pre-divorce period of separation for those respondents whose first marriage ended in divorce indicates that it is likely that separation will lead to divorce in the vast majority of cases. The existence in the SCELI sample of a small number of respondents who had been separated for a considerable length of time without being divorced suggests that a further small minority were permanently separated from their spouses at the survey date.

The choice of the date of separation as an estimate of the point of marital breakdown also allows those respondents who were widowed having separated from their spouses but not having been divorced to be included in the sample of 'broken first marriage' respondents.

A small number of respondents (19) appear to have remarried after a period of separation without having been divorced. This might possibly be due to a failure to report the date of divorce and in any case it does not seem unreasonable to include these cases in the 'broken first marriages' sample. Overall, the 6,111 SCELI respondents can be subdivided into the 1,207 never-married respondents, 3,801 respondents with surviving first marriages, 157 respondents whose first spouses died before any marital dissolution had occurred, 943 respondents in the 'broken first marriages' sample, and 3 'problem cases' (whose recorded life histories merit their exclusion from any marriage-related analyses). Of the 943 respondents in the 'broken first marriages' sub-sample, the separation dates of about three-quarters were recorded to an accuracy of one month. The separation dates of the remainder of the respondents consisted simply of a calendar year, either because their separation was a *de facto* one derived from living arrangement histories, or because they were unable to recall their separation dates to the required accuracy.[1]

2. THE LITERATURE ON FACTORS INFLUENCING MARITAL DISSOLUTION

Previous research has shown that a very large number of factors affect the risk of a couple splitting up. These factors can be grouped into intuitively sensible categories such as personal factors, environmental factors, and temporal factors. For general sociological discussions of factors affecting the risk of marital dissolution, see Hart (1976) and Burgoyne *et al.* (1987).

Social-survey-based research on marital dissolution rarely allows assessment of the effects of personal attributes and attitudes on the risk of dissolution. It is clear, however, that religious beliefs affect the risk, and Kiernan (1986), in a study of teenage marriages, suggested that neuroticism might be associated with an increased risk. Kiernan also found that marital dissolution appeared to be 'transmitted intergenerationally', i.e. those individuals whose family histories include one or more marital dissolutions were at increased risk. Note that Kiernan's analyses were bivariate rather than multivariate.

Murphy (1985) emphasized the effects of demographic factors. Clearly, marriage cohort and birth cohort are important determinants of the risk of dissolution, given the rising trend in divorce rates since the turn of the century (see Burgoyne *et al.* 1987).

Perhaps the most important and well-documented factor affecting the risk is age at marriage, with the risk of dissolution being unusually high where the bride was a teenager. Burgoyne suggested that the high dissolution rate associated with teenage marriages may have been linked to housing, financial, and employment problems, but Murphy found that the effects of age at marriage persisted in multivariate analyses. A common-sense argument is that people who marry young are less likely to have adequately assessed their compatibility with their partners. However, there is little evidence that couples marrying young are less homogamous than other couples. Another argument suggests that people marrying young are not prepared for the stresses associated with marital relationships. The upturn in risk associated with late marriages is usually explained by one of a variety of common-sense arguments, e.g. it is the result of misguided marriages made 'before it is too late', or the result of marriages involving individuals who have unconventional attitudes towards marriage, or the result of marriages between individuals that 'nobody else wanted'.

The other set of demographic factors which have a well-documented effect on the risk of dissolution are factors related to fertility. Ermisch (1986) found a significant positive relationship between early childbearing and the risk of dissolution, while Kiernan found an increased risk attached to large family sizes. Murphy noted that it is difficult to differentiate between the effects of large numbers of children and the effects of early child-bearing since the two variables are highly correlated. He also suggested that the well-documented finding that premarital conceptions are positively related to the risk of dissolution is symptomatic of a broader relationship between the length of the interval between marriage and the first birth and the risk of dissolution.

Ermisch also found a significant positive relationship between childlessness and the risk of dissolution, which is consistent with the theory of 'marriage-specific capital' (Becker *et al.* 1977), which suggests that children can add to the 'value' of a marriage and hence act as a disincentive to dissolution.

One interesting finding common to all the above-mentioned authors is that social class and education appeared to have little effect on the risk of dissolution. The only notable class-related finding was made by Murphy (1985), who found support in a multivariate context for the observation made by Haskey (1984) that the divorce rate for men in Registrar General's Social Class V was particularly high.

However, variables relating to 'living conditions' *have* been found to be related to the risk of dissolution. In particular, both Kiernan (1986) and Murphy (1985) found household tenure to be of significance, with owner-occupiers having a lower risk of dissolution than those with other tenures. Furthermore Kiernan noted a relationship between low income and an increased risk of dissolution. These last two factors might also be considered in terms of 'marriage-specific capital'.

Finally, Ermisch examined in some detail the relationship between women's work experience and the risk of dissolution, and found that women with more work experience were more likely to divorce, possibly because they were less likely to be in a state of economic dependence on their husbands.

In order to obtain reasonably unambiguous results when examining the relationship between unemployment and marital dissolution, account needs to be taken of other relevant variables. Hence the results of authors such as Murphy (1985), Ermisch (1986), and Kiernan (1986) need to be borne in mind, and appropriate covariates need to be included in statistical analyses of the relationship.

3. APPROACHES TO MODELLING MARITAL BREAKDOWN

The main purpose of this chapter is to attempt to answer the question, does being unemployed at a particular point in time increase the risk of an individual separating from their spouse in the near future? In order to answer this question a modelling approach is needed which can assess the immediate or short-term effects of unemployment.

Two main modelling approaches have been used in recent literature examining the determinants of marital dissolution. One approach consists of the use of a set of 'static' logit models where in each model the probability of marital dissolution in a particular interval of time is specified as a function of a number of explanatory variables (Becker *et al.* 1977; Ermisch 1986).

The other approach consists of the use of a proportional hazards model (see Cox 1972). In a proportional hazards model the probability of marital dissolution at a specific point in time is equal to the product of a time-varying hazard rate common to all cases and an individual-specific factor. This constant factor is a function of the values for that individual of a set of covariates (Teachman 1982; Murphy 1985; Balakrishnan *et al.* 1987; Lehrer 1988). In other words, the risk of dissolution for any individual is equal to a general factor relating to how long they have been married multiplied by a specific factor relating to their specific characteristics.

A major limitation of examining dissolution by focusing on a particular interval and using a logit model is that no account can be taken of changes in covariates which occur during that interval. For example, a logit model focusing on the first five years of marriage could only include factors which pre-dated the marriage.

There are partial solutions to this problem; for example, by splitting marriage histories into five-year intervals starting at the date of marriage, Ermisch (1986) enabled time-varying aspects of women's work and fertility histories to be included as covariates in his models.

The above problem does not arise with proportional hazards models, since they can include covariates which change during the period of interest.

Ermisch's approach was also able to highlight variation between different durations of marriage in the effects of covariates. On the other hand, his choice of the intervals to be considered was arbitrary, and, by splitting the divorces in his data (the 1980 Women and Employment Survey) into several subgroups, Ermisch made it more difficult for himself to obtain statistically significant results if the effects of covariates *were* constant over time.[2]

Covariates with time-varying effects can still be accounted for in a proportional hazards model, but, as Murphy (1985) noted, the computational costs of including more than a very small number of such covariates may be high.

Overall, a proportional hazards approach seems more appropriate than a 'static' logit model approach to the examination of the relationship between unemployment and marital dissolution, since it allows the immediate or short-term effects of unemployment to be assessed (see also Lehrer 1988: 196–7).

There is much current research on the issue of unobserved heterogeneity or omitted variables (e.g. Crouchley and Pickles 1989; Davies and Pickles 1986; Gonul 1989; see also Davies *et al.* in Chapter 5). While this chapter makes no attempt to model for unobserved heterogeneity, one should at least be aware of its possible effects. The shape of the curve obtained by plotting divorce rates against duration of marriage (i.e. one where the divorce rate 'tails off' as duration increases; see e.g. Haskey 1988) is possibly partially the result of the 'early' divorce of individuals who have a higher than usual propensity towards marital dissolution for reasons which are unlikely to be adequately represented by the variables collected in SCELI or any other social survey. This form of unobserved heterogeneity, however, is relatively unimportant if one is primarily interested in the effects of covariates on propensity towards marital dissolution, and it is also not impossible that the shape of the curve *does* represent genuine changes with duration of marriage in the risk of dissolution.[3]

4. MODELLING THE EFFECTS OF UNEMPLOYMENT ON THE RISK OF MARITAL DISSOLUTION

In 943 cases (341 men and 602 women) SCELI respondents reported having divorced or separated from their first spouse. We do not know, however, whether the respondent's first spouse had previously been married.

At first sight the large disparity between the number of men in the sample whose first marriage ended in dissolution and the corresponding number of women is alarming. However, most of the disparity can be explained fairly simply. First, the number of female respondents in the SCELI sample is disproportionately large. Secondly, an examination of 1981 Census data roughly corresponding to the six SCELI areas confirms that the number of ever-divorced women in the SCELI age range in 1981 was noticeably larger than the corresponding number of ever-divorced men. This discrepancy probably reflects the average disparity of two or three years between husbands' and wives' ages.

However, a comparison of the current marital status distributions in the samples for the six areas with 1981 Census data suggests that the numbers of *currently* divorced men in the samples for some of the six areas were disproportionately low. This could be the result of respondents misreporting their marital status, but could also simply reflect a tendency for currently divorced men to be a difficult group to sample, since they are quite likely to be geographically mobile, even if only over short distances (see Goyder 1987: 100).

The issue of the geographical mobility of divorced people is an interesting one. The relationship between the 'outcome' of the SCELI respondents' first marriages and whether they were living in the same area as they had been at age 14 was briefly examined. Divorced or separated men had been slightly more geographically mobile in this respect than their female counterparts. When variables relating to residence at age 14 were included in the analyses performed later in this chapter, the results suggested that these men were more likely to have been geographically mobile than other married men or any married women, but the difference was not statistically significant (and the fact that the men may have moved before *or* after dissolution makes the analysis of dubious validity in any case).

The analysis reported below is based on 4,901 cases: the 943 respondents who had been divorced or separated, 157 cases where the respondent's first spouse died during the marriage, and 3,801 cases where the respondent's first marriage was still intact at the survey date. Note that many of these intact marriages may eventually have ended in divorce or separation.

The BMDP (1983) program P2L was used to fit proportional hazards models to the data. The lack of precision of the separation dates of some of the SCELI respondents meant that in some cases the dissolution event was only accurate to the level of calendar year. For this reason, and also to make the model-fitting process less 'expensive' in computer time, the basic unit of time considered was the calendar year. This reduced drastically the number of time points that the proportional hazards model had to consider, but it seems unlikely that the resulting increase in the coarseness of the data greatly obscured the relationship under examination.

The time origin for each case was the year of first marriage. As mentioned earlier, many of the respondents in marriages which were intact at the survey date may subsequently have been divorced or separated, hence there was a need to 'censor' these cases, i.e. to include implicitly in the analyses only that part of their marriage histories which pre-dated the survey. Therefore, those cases in which the marriage did not end in dissolution were censored at either 1986 or the year of the spouse's death for those who were widowed (i.e. any respondent whose first spouse died while the marriage was still intact was treated as being 'at risk' up until the year of their spouse's death). The year in which the *de facto* dissolution of each dissolved marriage occurred was used to mark the 'death' of that marriage.

The modelling approach initially used was to add relevant covariates or sets of covariates to the model until a stage was reached at which it was felt that the model would serve as an adequate 'base' model to which unemployment-related covariates could be added. This 'base' model is henceforth referred to as the 'Basic Model', and its parameter estimates are given in Table 9.1. (It should be noted that the modelling approach taken means that some of the changes in risk mentioned in the next few sections correspond to models containing fewer covariates than the Basic Model.)

Note that unemployment might indirectly affect the risk of dissolution by being causally related to some of the covariates in the Basic Model. Therefore, the final results are likely if anything to be an underestimate of the gross effects of unemployment.

The next few sections discuss the covariates that were considered for inclusion in the Basic Model.

4.1. Areas, Marriage Cohort, and Age at Marriage

Dummy variables were included in all the models fitted to take account of any differences in the risk of dissolution between the six study areas. (A dummy variable for sex was also included, to take account of the fact that the inclusion of sex-specific covariates and/or covariates which have different effects for the two sexes removes the natural equivalence of the hazard rates for the two sexes.)

In fact the inclusion of this group of dummy variables significantly improved the fit of the Basic Model, indicating that there may be underlying differences in the dissolution rates of the different areas. An examination of 1981 Census data corresponding to the six areas seemed to provide some support for the observed differences, though interpretation of these differences is difficult. It is possible that different geographical communities foster different attitudes towards the social acceptability of marital dissolution, but it is more likely that the between-area differences in the risk of dissolution reflect other differences between the areas, such as religious or cultural differences.

Beyond this it was clearly necessary to take account of the

increase in the rate of marital dissolution over time; the inclusion
of marriage cohort as a covariate was found to do this job well.

Both in the UK and the USA a low or a very high age at marriage is related to an increased risk of marital dissolution (for
women at least). It would have been possible to have included a
set of dummies relating to various ages at marriage to take
account of this effect, but the approach used here was to include
two covariates, one being age at marriage itself and the other
being the square of age at marriage minus 25. The second of these
covariates was designed to take account of any curvilinearity, for

TABLE 9.1. *Parameter estimates for the Basic Model*

Variable	Parameter estimate	Parameter estimate/ standard error	% change in risk
Marriage year	0.061	13.6	6.3
Age at marriage	−0.108	−10.3	*
(Age at marriage −25)^2	0.004	4.0	*
Female	−0.120	−1.5	−11.3
Coventry	0.318	2.6	37.4
Kirkcaldy	0.152	1.2	16.4
Northampton	0.414	3.5	51.3
Rochdale	0.402	3.3	49.4
Swindon	0.190	1.5	20.9
Pre-marital birth	0.467	3.1	59.5
Pre-marital conception	0.321	3.3	37.8
Male graduate	−0.689	−2.3	−49.8
Woman, father's occupation missing	0.290	2.6	33.6
Local authority, etc.	0.260	3.1	29.7
Private rented	0.180	2.1	19.7
Hotel/hostel/b. & b. etc.	0.632	3.3	88.2
Asian	−1.078	−3.5	−66.0
Job insecure at marriage	0.396	3.8	48.6
Job in armed forces at marriage	0.446	2.2	56.2
Birth of first child	−0.439	−4.2	−33.5
First birth interval	−0.044	−2.0	−4.3[a]

* Change in risk varies according to age at marriage.
[a] Per year.

example a higher risk of dissolution among both those who marry early and those who marry late. Both covariates significantly improved the fit of the models, and the parameter estimates were consistent with the frequently observed U-shaped relationship between age at marriage and dissolution rates, with high rates for young ages at marriage and the rates decreasing with age to a minimum somewhere between the late twenties and late thirties. There were too few late first marriages in the SCELI sample for this paper to confirm the increased risk of dissolution that other authors have found for this group.

Somewhat unusually in this context, the data examined here were for both sexes and one should consider the possibility that the effect of age at marriage is sex-dependent. As it happens, when this was investigated, little difference was found between the sexes in the effect of age at marriage on propensity to marital dissolution.

4.2. *Education, Occupation, and Social Origin*

While previous research suggests that educational qualifications, occupation, and social origin did not seem to be particularly strong influences on the risk of marital dissolution, the SCELI data allowed us to examine in detail the relationship between these variables and marital dissolution, and to separate the effects of these variables from unemployment-related effects. In fact, the SCELI data also showed the effects of these variables to be limited.

The three factors were initially operationalized in considerable detail (see Lampard 1990). In the first instance, the gross effects of education, occupation, and social origin on the risk of dissolution were examined, and then the effects net of the effects of the other covariates included in the model were examined. It transpired that most of the gross effects of the three stratification-related variables were better explained by other variables. Overall, social-stratification-related variables seemed to have little relevance in the study of factors affecting the risk of marital dissolution, once one had taken account of the effects of age at marriage and of factors such as housing, fertility and unemployment.

Once account had been taken of other factors, the only two

statistically significant effects (at the 5 per cent level) were a decreased risk of dissolution for male graduates and an increased risk of dissolution for women whose fathers' jobs when they were aged 14 were not given. This latter effect probably has more to do with the intergenerational transmission of marital instability (see e.g. McLanahan and Bumpass 1988) than it does with social stratification. The lack of a parallel effect for men may possibly be the result of the mechanism by which intergenerational transmission occurs being sex-specific (see Kiernan and Eldridge 1987, who relate women's ages at marriage to their mothers' ages at marriage).

4.3. Fertility

Four variables included in the model related to the respondent's fertility history. The first two were dummy variables relating to whether the respondent had fathered or given birth to a premarital child or had conceived a child premaritally, the latter variable being based on the birth of a child within the first eight months of marriage (arguably too long a period; see Ermisch 1986). The third variable was a time-dependent dummy variable switching to one at the year following the birth of the respondent's first child. All three of these variables were highly significant, with premarital births and premarital conceptions increasing the risk of dissolution by nearly 55 per cent and about 35 per cent respectively, but the birth of a first child decreasing the risk by about 40 per cent. These results are reasonably consistent with those of Murphy, who in addition found that children subsequent to the first had no appreciable effect on the risk of dissolution, and that the negative effect of premarital conceptions was largely removed on the addition of a dummy variable relating to whether the marriage ceremony had been a religious ceremony or in a register office (Murphy 1985: 450, 458).

No information was collected in SCELI on the fertility histories of the respondents' ex-spouses, and it was not therefore possible to take account of the effects of spouses having children by anyone other than the respondents.

Murphy also found that the length of the first birth interval (i.e. the interval between marriage and first birth) was negatively correlated with the risk of dissolution. To replicate this, a fourth fertility-related variable was included: a time-dependent covariate which took the value 0 until the year following the first birth and a value equal to the length of the first birth interval thereafter. The parameter estimate for this variable was negative, indicating a decreasing risk of dissolution with increasing length of first birth interval. The inclusion of this variable only slightly reduced the magnitude of the effect due to the birth of the first child, and only reduced the magnitude of the parameter estimates for pre-marital births and premarital conceptions by about 20 per cent.

The effects of premarital births and conceptions might have been expected to vary over time, but parameters introduced to allow for linear trends in the effects of these variables were found to be totally non-significant.

4.4. Premarital Cohabitation

The consensus of recent research is that premarital cohabitation is associated with an increased risk of marital dissolution (e.g. Balakrishnan *et al.* 1987 and Burnett *et al.* 1988, who respectively analysed fairly recent Canadian and Swedish data; see also Bumpass *et al.* 1989 and Hoem and Hoem 1988). Since the SCELI data contained information on its respondents' living arrangements since age 16 it was possible to set up a covariate relating to *de facto* premarital cohabitation (where cohabitation is simply defined as 'living with one's partner'). When this covari-ate (initially a simple dummy variable) was included in the model, its parameter estimate was found to be positive but not statistically significant, though if one took the estimate at face value there would be a 20 per cent increase in risk associated with premarital cohabitation.

However, the SCELI data allowed premarital cohabitation to be further divided into three categories: premarital cohabitation in the parental home of one of the spouses (which is not neces-sarily 'cohabitation' in the conventional sense of the word!), pre-marital cohabitation in the couple's *own* household, and finally premarital cohabitation elsewhere. The distinction between the last two categories is a subtle one (linked to the respondent's interpretation of the word 'own'); an examination of some of the completed questionnaires showed that the third category were probably mostly premaritally cohabiting in privately rented accommodation rather than (as might have been expected) in more unusual accommodation. When separate account was taken of these three categories of cohabitation, it could be seen that it was the first and third categories which were positively related to the risk of dissolution.

In fact this analysis provides no evidence that cohabitation in the way that it is usually defined (i.e. as a situation where two people are living as a couple in their own home in a 'marriage-like' relationship) is related to either an increased or a decreased risk of marital dissolution.

What the above results do suggest is that there may be a relationship between unusual or unsatisfactory living circumstances and the risk of marital dissolution. This brings us naturally on to the next important predictor of divorce or separation, household tenure.

4.5. Household Tenure at Marriage

Household tenure is an important factor in marital dissolution, since the loss of a valued 'home' might act as a deterrent against divorce or separation, whereas poor living conditions might reduce the value that an individual attaches to his or her marriage and increase the attractiveness of alternatives.

The highest risk of dissolution was found to belong to those respondents who lived in hostels, hotels, or bed and breakfast accommodation, followed at a distance by those renting public housing, and then by those who rented privately. These three groups had risks respectively about 80 per cent, 25 per cent, and 15 per cent higher than owner-occupiers. These results match those of Murphy (1985) in indicating the importance of tenure as a factor influencing the risk of marital dissolution.

However, tenure over time, and hence at the point of marital dissolution, might have been expected to be an even more relevant predictor than tenure at marriage. Furthermore, the distribution of household tenure at marriage has changed dramatically over the last few decades. There would seem to be scope for future researchers to examine in more detail the relationship between housing and the risk of marital dissolution.

One might hypothesize that owner-occupiers might have had 'more to lose' by dissolution than tenants, and that those who started their marriages in very 'unhomelike' circumstances were not starting their married life in conditions favourable to marital stability.[4]

4.6. *Other Covariates and a Summary of the Basic Model*

Two covariates were included in the Basic Model which have not been mentioned so far: first, a dummy variable corresponding to those of Asian ethnic origin was included, since these respondents had a low risk of marital dissolution; secondly, a dummy variable indicating whether or not respondents described their jobs at marriage as being 'insecure'. The parameter estimate for this variable was highly significant, indicating that those respondents with an insecure job at marriage were at a much increased risk of marital dissolution. Clearly job insecurity and unemployment are not unrelated, so the results for this covariate will need to be reconsidered in the light of the unemployment-related results produced below.

Ermisch (1986) included women's work experience in his models of the risk of marital dissolution, but he used a series of *static* logit models. Any attempt to take account of women's postmarital work experience within the framework used here would require the use of extra time-dependent covariates and was therefore ruled out to avoid an undesirable increase in the complexity of the model.

In sum, the Basic Model contained covariates relating to marriage cohort, age at marriage, study area, pre- and postmarital fertility, household tenure at marriage, ethnicity, job security at marriage, having a job in the armed forces at marriage, and two sex-specific covariates, i.e. a dummy variable for male respondents relating to the possession of a degree and a dummy variable for female respondents relating to their fathers' occupations not being recorded.[5]

4.7. *Premarital Unemployment*

It was not an entirely straightforward process to include unemployment-related covariates in the model, as it was necessary to distinguish between various types and durations of unemployment, and to take account of the form of the hypothesized effects of the unemployment. Initially the effect of premarital unemployment was investigated, as this might be expected to be qualitatively different from postmarital unemployment.

One might expect any increase in risk to be dependent on the duration of premarital unemployment, so linear and quadratic terms for the duration of premarital unemployment were included for each sex. The results for men and for women were not significantly different. The parameter estimate for the quadratic term was found to be negative, and that of the linear term positive, resulting in an estimated increased risk reaching a maximum at about two years' duration of premarital unemployment and returning to 0 at about four years' duration (which reflects the low rate of marital dissolution found among the small number of individuals with at least three years' duration of premarital unemployment: 3/41 or about 7 per cent, as opposed to 943/4,901 or about 19 per cent of the total sample, and 126/576 or about 21 per cent of those who had been premaritally unemployed). However, the dissolution rate for those with three or more years of premarital unemployment could easily be the artefactual result of the early censoring of the youngest marriage cohorts, since their marriages have coincided with a period of high unemployment levels.

4.8. *Postmarital/Pre-dissolution Unemployment*

Now we turn to the focus of the chapter, the relationship between unemployment *during marriage* and the risk of dissolution.

Two types of time-dependent covariate relating to unemployment were used. Firstly, one covariate was set up to represent approximately the effect of *current* unemployment on the risk of dissolution. In fact the actual covariate used was a dummy variable relating to the existence of an unemployment event at some point during the *preceding* calendar year, rather than in the current calendar year. This was necessary because of the possibility of an unemployment event in the calendar year of marital dissolution but subsequent to the dissolution. The parameter estimate obtained on the inclusion of this covariate was highly significant, indicating an approximately 75 per cent increase in the risk of marital dissolution in the calendar year following a calendar year including at least part of an unemployment event.

However, the occurrence of a postmarital unemployment event could simply be an indication that the respondent was the 'type of person' who was also susceptible to marital dissolution, rather than the unemployment event itself having any specific consequences. Another possibility is that a post-marital unemployment event might have a permanent and unchanging effect on the respondent's risk of dissolution (though this is perhaps a rather unconvincing hypothesis). If one is interested only in what happens *after* the postmarital unemployment event then these two possibilities are indistinguishable, since they both involve a characteristic of the respondent which is constant *after* the postmarital unemployment event.

To cope with these two possibilities a second related covariate (dummy variable) was created to represent the effect of *any* unemployment spell between marriage and marital dissolution. This second covariate was found to have a statistically significant effect on the risk of dissolution, indicating an approximately 30 per cent increase in risk, but the estimate for the first covariate was scarcely altered. This suggests that postmarital unemployment events have a dual significance, first, in terms of the specific consequences of being unemployed, and, secondly, in terms of acting as an indicator of an 'underlying tendency' towards marital dissolution.

Some confirmation for the latter hypothesis was found in the fact that when the second covariate was split into two according to whether the respondent had had a *pre*marital unemployment event or not, the parameter estimate in the former case was not significantly different from 0. Furthermore, the magnitude of the increase in risk associated with the second covariate was not dissimilar to that associated with premarital unemployment (as represented by a dummy variable).

The effect of postmarital unemployment was found to be the same for both men and women. However, the increase in risk was higher for female unemployment than for male unemployment, so it is possible that there is a greater risk attached to female events.

4.9. Final Results of the Survival Analysis

The parameter estimates of the Unemployment Model, which included all of the unemployment-related covariates, are given in Table 9.2.

TABLE 9.2. *Parameter estimates for the Unemployment Model*

Variable	Parameter estimate	Parameter estimate/ standard error	% change in risk
Marriage year	0.054	11.1	5.6
Age at marriage	−0.110	−10.4	*
(Age at marriage −25)^2	0.004	4.1	*
Female	−0.082	−1.0	−7.9
Coventry	0.264	2.1	30.2
Kircaldy	0.111	0.9	11.8
Northampton	0.374	3.1	45.4
Rochdale	0.372	3.1	45.1
Swindon	0.198	1.6	21.9
Pre-marital birth	0.443	2.9	55.7
Pre-marital conception	0.301	3.1	35.2
Male graduate	−0.648	−2.2	−47.7
Woman, father's occupation missing	0.297	2.6	34.6
Local authority, etc.	0.215	2.5	24.0
Private rented	0.154	1.8	16.7
Hotel/hostel/b. & b. etc.	0.599	3.1	82.1
Asian	−1.077	−3.5	−65.9
Job insecure at marriage	0.349	3.3	41.8
Job in armed forces at marriage	0.432	2.1	54.0
Birth of first child	−0.497	−4.7	−39.2
First birth interval	−0.040	−1.8	−3.9[a]
Pre-marital unemployed			
Duration	0.047	3.0	*
Duration^2	−0.001	−2.3	*
Unemployed during preceding calendar year	0.532	6.7	70.2
Post-marital unemployment (No pre-marital unemployment)	0.313	3.3	36.8
(Pre-marital unemployment)	−0.064	−0.3	−6.2

* Change in risk varies.
[a] Per year.

There was a little evidence of a slight reduction in the magnitude of some of the effects for the variables included in the Basic Model. The effect of an insecure job at marriage dropped slightly from 0.4 to 0.35, which was consistent with there being a correlation between job insecurity and unemployment.

Overall, however, the unemployment-related effects had an effect on the risk of dissolution which was largely over and above the effects of the variables traditionally considered as predictors. Indeed, unemployment seemed to have a relatively independent effect. The exclusion from the model of all the other variables except area, year of marriage, the two age-at-marriage covariates, and sex altered the parameter estimates for the unemployment-related covariates only slightly.[6]

4.10. Constructing an Index from Dissolution-Related Factors

The preceding analyses demonstrated that a number of factors increased the risk of separation or divorce. However, the analyses did not show whether or to what extent the effects of the various factors were cumulative.

An index was therefore constructed, with respondents scoring one point for each characteristic from the following list which applied to them:

1. Respondent fathered or gave birth to a child born *before* his or her marriage.
2. Respondent or respondent's partner premaritally conceived a child which was born *after* their marriage.
3. Respondent married at age 19 or less.
4. Respondent's household tenure at marriage was 'unusual' (hotel, hostel, bed and breakfast, etc.).
5. Respondent's job at marriage was insecure.
6. Respondent's job at marriage was in the armed forces.
7. Respondents had a period of unemployment at some time before his or her marriage.

Since (1) and (2) were constructed to be mutually exclusive, the theoretical maximum of the index was 6. In fact no respondent had a score of greater than 4. Almost half of the respondents had a score of at least 1, with about a sixth of the respondents having a score of 2 or more. Table 9.3 shows the results of a propor-

TABLE 9.3. *Parameter estimates from a proportional hazards model using an index-constructed from dissolution-related factors*

Covariate	Parameter estimate	Standard error	% of sample
Year of marriage	0.054	0.004	
Coventry	0.237	0.123	
Kirkcaldy	0.229	0.121	
Northampton	0.426	0.119	
Rochdale	0.331	0.121	
Swindon	0.222	0.123	
Index = 1	0.585	0.077	32.5
Index = 2	1.083	0.089	13.1
Index = 3	1.200	0.162	2.8
Index = 4	2.206	0.296	0.4

Note: Aberdeen and Index = 0 were used as base categories.

tional hazards model including year of marriage, study area, and the five levels of the index constructed above as covariates.

It appears that the effects of the various factors of which the index is composed were more or less cumulative, with the risk of dissolution being nine times as high for the small number of respondents with a score of 4 as that for respondents with a score of 0. In fact, of the 21 respondents with a score of 4, the marriages of 13 had ended in dissolution, including the marriages of 6 out of the 7 respondents married in 1975 or earlier.

5. MODELLING THE EFFECT OF MARITAL DISSOLUTION ON AN INDIVIDUAL'S UNEMPLOYMENT HISTORY

5.1. The Immediate Consequences of Marital Dissolution

It is likely that the most disruptive effects of a marital dissolution occur at the time of separation or immediately afterwards. Table 9.4 shows the number of unemployment events occurring to SCELI respondents in the calendar year of a marital dissolution and in the calendar years preceding and following that year. Table 9.5 shows the number of SCELI respondents who were

TABLE 9.4. *Unemployment events of 896 respondents whose first marriages dissolved in the calendar year of dissolution and the years preceding and following it* (year C = calendar year of dissolution)

Event in year (C – 1)	Event in year C	Event in year (C + 1)	Frequency
Yes	No	No	18
No	Yes	No	33
No	No	Yes	27
Yes	Yes	No	3
Yes	No	Yes	1
No	Yes	Yes	4
Yes	Yes	Yes	0

TABLE 9.5. *Periods of unemployment in the years preceding and following the year of marital dissolution for 896 respondents whose first marriages ended in dissolution*

Year	No. unemployed during year
Calendar year –3	54
Calendar year –2	52
Calendar year –1	52
Calendar year	71
Calendar year +1	85
Calendar year +2	79
Calendar year +3	95
Calendar year +4	93
Calendar year +5	93

unemployed at some point during the calendar year for the period from three years before the year of dissolution to five years after it. (Both tables are based on 896 SCELI respondents; the 47 respondents whose first marriages had dissolved but who were sampled because they were unemployed at the survey date are excluded. It should be noted that the tables are affected by trends in unemployment and the right-censoring of the respondents' life histories by the survey.)

The two tables suggest that marital dissolutions precipitate unemployment events in the calendar year of dissolution and the year following it. If attention is restricted to those respondents for whom the month of separation is known, the timing of some of these events can be seen more clearly. Table 9.6 shows the pattern of unemployment events falling within a year of the date of separation. There is some evidence that an unusual number of events occur in the month of dissolution and the six months following it.

Overall, there seems to be sufficient evidence for one to conclude that marital dissolution causes an unemployment event at or almost immediately after the point of separation, albeit in a relatively small proportion of cases.

5.2. A 'Case–Control' Study of the Effects of Marital Dissolution on the Risk of Unemployment

Prima-facie evidence for the immediate effects of marital dissolution on the likelihood of unemployment having been found, attention is now turned to the more general effects of marital dissolution.

One approach to examining the effects of marital dissolution on unemployment, similar to both the approach used by Ermisch (1986) and that used by Payne (1989) to examine the relationship between family formation and unemployment, would be to construct a binary dependent variable according to whether a respondent was unemployed a fixed number of years after his or

TABLE 9.6. *Unemployment events in the twelve months preceding and following the month of marital dissolution for respondents whose month of marital dissolution (m.o.d.) was recorded*

Period	No. of events
12–7 months before m.o.d.	7
6–1 months before m.o.d.	10
Month of dissolution	7
1–6 months after m.o.d.	15
[1 month after m.o.d.	5]
7–12 months after m.o.d.	9

Note: Two respondents had more than one event during the period.

her marriage, and to model this binary dependent variable including among the covariates an explanatory factor whose first level corresponded to surviving marriages and whose other levels corresponded to marital dissolution after various durations of marriage.

A problem with this approach is that it focuses on only one point in time, which means that it only utilizes a fraction of the data available. However, it would not be impossible to perform an analysis which simultaneously examined the employment status of respondents after several durations of marriage.

There is an obvious symmetry between examining the effect of unemployment on the risk of marital dissolution and examining the effect of marital dissolution on the risk of unemployment. This suggests that one might adopt the same modelling approach as in Section 4, namely, the use of a proportional hazards model. The first postmarital unemployment event would in this case be the 'death' equivalent and marital dissolution would be a time-dependent covariate.

However, this approach also has drawbacks. Information relating to the dissolutions of respondents with postmarital but pre-dissolution unemployment events would not be utilized. The approach also restricts attention to the first postmarital unemployment event (unless one uses sophisticated software capable of modelling repeated events). One would also have to take account somehow of the notable increase in the risk of unemployment at the time of dissolution or immediately afterwards.

There is a third approach, described below, which allows one to utilize all the post-dissolution unemployment histories of those whose first marriages dissolved, and which is adopted in this chapter.

One way to conceptualize the effect of marital dissolution on an individual's subsequent unemployment history is to consider it as the difference between that individual's actual post-dissolution unemployment history and the counterfactual history that would have occurred had that individual's marriage not been dissolved. This can be approached by matching each SCELI respondent whose first marriage dissolved with a similar SCELI respondent whose first marriage had not ended by the survey date, and examining the differences in their respective unemployment histories subsequent to the marital dissolution of the first respondent.

Broadly speaking, this is equivalent to an epidemiological 'case–control' study.

Clearly the crucial element of such a procedure is the way in which cases are matched with controls. In the SCELI data there are fortunately several times as many potential controls as cases. The nature of case–control studies is such that matching each case with more than one control would not really increase the efficiency of the analysis sufficiently to make it worth while trying to find more than one control for each case.

5.3. The Matching Procedure

Two obvious variables to use in the matching process are sex and study area. Since unemployment is unequally distributed between social and educational strata, it seemed sensible also to match for appropriate stratification variables. Unemployment events previous to a marital dissolution are unlikely to be disconnected to unemployment events post-dissolution, so there was a necessity for matching with respect to previous unemployment. It also seemed sensible to match for age and for duration of marriage. Finally (for women only) it seemed sensible to match for number of births (0 versus 1+) by the time of the case's marital dissolution (as a crude measure of the extent of a woman's childbearing 'responsibilities').

The matching in the analysis carried out here was therefore with respect to sex, area, previous unemployment (a simple dummy variable), social class at marriage, highest educational level at time of survey, age at survey, and marriage cohort. Women were also matched according to number of births. Matching according to social class at marriage, highest educational level, age at survey, and marriage cohort was carried out as follows:

Social class at marriage. Matching was according to four categories: Goldthorpe classes 1 to 2, 3 to 5, and 6 to 7, plus a 'not elsewhere classified' category).

Highest educational level at time of survey. Matching was according to four categories: graduates, respondents with A levels, respondents with O levels, and respondents with none of these.

Age at survey and marriage cohort. Each control was chosen

TABLE 9.7. *Case–control study results, men*

Existence of an unemployment event after the case's marital dissolution
(All matched pairs, no. = 307)

	Neither	Case only	Control only	Both	Ratio	Chi-squared
	179	73	33	22	2.21	14.3

Matched pairs according to existence or absence of unemployment periods before the case's marital dissolution

	Neither	Case only	Control only	Both	Ratio	Chi-squared
Yes (no. = 73)	35	18	11	9	1.64	1.2
No (no. = 234)	144	55	22	13	2.50	13.3

Existence of an unemployment event during the first five calendar years after the calendar year of the case's marital dissolution

Matched pairs according to the existence or absence of unemployment periods before the case's marital dissolution

	Neither	Case only	Control only	Both	Ratio	Chi-squared
Yes (no. = 73)	44	14	9	6	1.56	0.7
No (no. = 234)	186	29	15	4	1.93	3.8

Existence of an unemployment event more than five calendar years after the calendar year of the case's marital dissolution

Matched pairs according to existence or absence of unemployment periods before the case's marital dissolution

	Neither	Case only	Control only	Both	Ratio	Chi-squared
Yes (no. = 35)	22	6	3	4	2.00	0.4
No (no. = 175)	123	31	14	7	2.21	5.7

Note: all the chi-square values are on one degree of freedom. The ratio given is the ratio of the number of case-only pairs to the number of control-only pairs.

so that its values for age at survey and marriage cohort minimized the weighted sum of squares of the two differences between the case and the control, with a larger weight being attached to marriage cohort.

Clearly there are straightforward criticisms that can be made both of the limited range of the above variables and of their operationalization, but the tentative argument put forward here is that the variables used in the form used should have removed most of the variation which was not due to the marital dissolution of the cases, or at least due to underlying factors whose best representation is the marital dissolution event.

5.4. *Analyses and Results*

In order to simplify the pre-analysis data processing, the same calendar year framework was adopted as had been used in the first analysis. For this analysis the respondents who belonged to the booster sample, and hence by definition were unemployed at the survey date, were excluded to simplify the statistical analyses.

The first set of cases considered consisted of 321 male respondents whose first marriages had dissolved by the time of the survey. The matching procedure (as described above) succeeded in finding controls for 307 out of the 321 cases. The matching procedure was implemented using a specially written FORTRAN program.

Table 9.7 shows that after their marital dissolutions and up until the time of the survey in 73 of the pairs the cases had had an unemployment event (in this case defined as the *start* of an unemployment period) but the controls had not, whereas only 33 of the controls had had one in pairs where the case had not during the same period. McNemar's test (see Breslow and Day 1980) showed the difference between these two numbers to be highly significant, as the chi-square test statistic was 14.3 on a single degree of freedom. When the 307 pairs were divided into those who had been previously unemployed and those who had not it could be seen that the bulk of the difference was due to the latter group (234 pairs; chi-square statistic = 13.3), while the difference for the former group was positive but not statistically significant (73 pairs; chi-square statistic = 1.2). It was more instructive to examine the ratios of 'case only' to 'control only' pairs in the two

groups which were 2.5 and 1.64 respectively. These ratios suggested that the difference between the two groups may not have
been large.

When the dependent variable was split into two (i.e. unemployment events in the first five calendar years following the year of
dissolution, and unemployment events thereafter) the difference
between the cases' and the controls' propensities to unemployment did not appear to change much with time. In each time
period, the ratio of 'case only' to 'control only' pairs was slightly
larger for the previously unemployed group.

Turning to the female case, the matching procedure succeeded
in finding controls for 544 out of 575 cases. Table 9.8 shows that,
as was the case for men, there was found to be a significant difference between the cases and the controls with regard to
whether they had experienced an unemployment event after the
case's marital dissolution (chi-square statistic = 29.5).

Dividing the pairs into four groups according to whether they
had been previously unemployed and whether they had had a
child before the case's marital dissolution, it could be seen that
the difference between the cases and the controls was almost
entirely due to those pairs who had not been previously unemployed (a 'case only' to 'control only' ratio of 4.8 as opposed to
a ratio of 1.09 for those who had been previously unemployed).

There also appears to have been little difference between the
two groups who had not been previously unemployed (ratios of
4.25 and 5), suggesting that the birth of a child before the marital
dissolution was of little relevance in this context. Splitting the
dependent variable in the same way as in the male case gave
results that indicate that the increased risk of unemployment
events for the cases over and above that of the controls may
diminish over time.

Remarriage can play an important role in the economic circumstances of divorced women (Ermisch and Wright 1989), so
the sample was further split into those pairs where the case
remarried within the calendar year of dissolution or the first five
calendar years following it, and those where the case did not.
Somewhat surprisingly, the difference between the cases and the
controls with regard to unemployment events in calendar years
six or more years after the calendar year of the case's marital dissolution did not seem to be smaller in the former group than in

the latter group (the 'case only' to 'control only' ratios for those pairs with no pre-dissolution unemployment were 4.33 (13/3) in the remarrying group and 3.38 (27/8) in the other group).

It should be noted that the case–control analysis excluded consideration of unemployment periods starting during the calendar year of dissolution.

TABLE 9.8. *Case–control study results, women*

Existence of an unemployment event after the case's marital dissolution (All matched pairs, no. = 544)

	Neither	Case Only	Control Only	Both	Ratio	Chi-square
	427	84	26	7	3.23	29.5

Matched pairs according to existence or absence of unemployment periods and to existence or absence of a birth before the case's marital dissolution

	Neither	Case Only	Control Only	Both	Ratio	Chi-square
No–No (no. = 112)	89	17	4	2	4.25	6.9
No–Yes (no. = 341)	274	55	11	1	5.00	28.0
Yes–No (no. = 14)	8	1	4	1	0.25	0.8
Yes–Yes (no. = 77)	56	11	7	3	1.57	0.5

Existence of an unemployment event during the first five calendar years after the calendar year of the case's marital dissolution

Matched pairs according to existence or absence of unemployment periods and to existence or absence of a birth before the case's marital dissolution

	Neither	Case Only	Control Only	Both	Ratio	Chi-square
No–No (no. = 112)	102	9	1	0	9.00	4.9
No–Yes (no. = 341)	304	33	4	0	8.25	21.2
Yes–No (no. = 14)	10	1	3	0	0.33	0.3
Yes–Yes (no. = 77)	64	7	5	1	1.40	0.1

TABLE 9.8. *Cont.*

Existence of an unemployment event more than five calendar years after the calendar year of the case's marital dissolution

Matched pairs according to existence or absence of unemployment periods and to existence or absence of a birth before the case's marital dissolution

No–No (no. = 86)	69	12	3	2	4.00	4.3
No–Yes (no. = 240)	203	28	8	1	3.50	10.0
Yes–No (no. = 6)	3	1	2	0	0.50	0.0
Yes–Yes (no. = 37)	27	6	3	1	2.00	1.6

Existence of an unemployment event more than five calendar years after the calendar year of the case's marital dissolution

Matched pairs according to existence or absence of unemployment periods and to existence or absence of a birth before the case's marital dissolution for two groups: one where the case has remarried within the first five calendar years after the marital dissolution and one where the case has not.

Remarried cases						
No–No (no. = 46)	38	4	2	2	2.00	0.2
No–Yes (no. = 105)	95	9	1	0	9.00	4.9
Yes–No (no. = 4)	2	1	1	0	1.00	—
Yes–Yes (no. = 10)	6	2	2	0	1.00	—
Not remarried cases						
No–No (no. = 40)	31	8	1	0	8.00	4.0
No–Yes (no. = 135)	108	19	7	1	2.71	4.7
Yes–No (no. = 2)	1	0	1	0	0.00	0.0
Yes–Yes (no. = 27)	21	4	1	1	4.00	0.8

Note: all the chi-square values are on one degree of freedom. The ratio given is the ratio of the number of case-only pairs to the number of control-only pairs.

5.5. *Conclusions Relating to the Effects of Marital Dissolution on the Subsequent Risk of Unemployment*

Unsurprisingly, it appears that unemployment sometimes occurs as a direct consequence of marital dissolution at a point in time close to the date of separation. In addition to this, the case–control study showed that even more than five years after the date of separation, the risk of unemployment was still higher for individuals whose first marriages have dissolved than for comparable individuals in surviving marriages. However, the assumption that the cases did not differ from the controls in any significant or systematic way at the point at which the cases' dissolutions occurred is unlikely to be an entirely reasonable one. This means that we cannot dismiss with any conviction the notion that the differences found by the case–control analysis were largely the result of some underlying factor, or factors, of which marital dissolution happened to be a good predictor. The fact that the difference between cases and controls was smaller when there had been a previous unemployment event suggests that this may have been at least partially the case.

6. OVERALL CONCLUSIONS

In examining the effects of unemployment on the risk of marital dissolution this paper distinguished between:

1. Premarital unemployment. The marriages of individuals who had been unemployed before marriage had a significantly higher chance of failing.

2. The immediate consequences of postmarital unemployment. A bout of unemployment during one calendar year raised the chances of dissolution during the following calendar year by approximately 70 per cent.

3. Other effects of postmarital unemployment. Individuals who had experienced unemployment after their marriage subsequently had a significantly higher risk of dissolution. However, this was only true for individuals who had never been premaritally unemployed.

4. Other indicators of economic insecurity. Job insecurity at marriage was also associated with a significantly higher risk of

dissolution, suggesting that there is a similarity either between the effects of unemployment and the effects of job insecurity or between the characteristics of unemployed and insecurely employed individuals.

In short, it appears that postmarital unemployment caused a significant number of marital dissolutions which would otherwise either not have occurred at all, or would have occurred at a later date. There also seemed to be a more general relationship between a history of unemployment and marital dissolution, suggesting that some individuals had characteristics making them prone to both unemployment and marital dissolution.

However, the causal relationship between unemployment and divorce was not all one-way. A number of individuals experienced unemployment episodes as a direct consequence of the dissolution of their marriages. More generally, an individual whose marriage had dissolved subsequently appeared to be at a greater risk of unemployment than a comparable individual who was still married. However, this higher risk only applied when the individual had not been unemployed before the dissolution. This suggests that separation or divorce may act as a good predictor of unobserved characteristics associated with an increased risk of unemployment.

In conclusion, some marriages appear to dissolve as a direct consequence of unemployment, and some unemployment events appear to be a direct consequence of marital dissolution, but there is also evidence that some individuals have characteristics (the nature of which are left to the reader's sociological imagination) which are associated both with a higher risk of marital dissolution and with a higher risk of unemployment. Clearly an important task of future research is to pin down some of these characteristics.

NOTES

1. It is worth noting that the boost sample of unemployed respondents poses a problem when one is analysing the relationship between unemployment and marital dissolution. A respondent who was unemployed at the survey date may have been through a marital dissolution *before* he or she became unemployed, in which case, though the

respondent would be classified as having been employed at the point of marital dissolution, the marital dissolution may have been 'caused' by unobserved variables which were also responsible for the respondent's current unemployment. In other words, the inclusion of the booster sample results in distributions of unobserved variables in the sample which are biased with respect to the population distributions of these variables in the six study areas. Values of these variables which are associated with an increased propensity towards unemployment are likely to be over-represented, and these values are likely also to be associated with an increased propensity towards marital dissolution.

There are three possible approaches towards dealing with the above problem. First, one could attach weights to the cases according to whether they were unemployed at the survey date so that in effect the proportion of respondents unemployed at the survey date was the same as actually obtained in the 'main' sample. Secondly, one could include in the analyses variables intended to account for the bias due to the booster sample, e.g. a dummy variable corresponding to a 'booster/rest of survey' dichotomy or a dummy variable corresponding to an 'unemployed at survey date/other' dichotomy. Thirdly, one could exclude the booster sample from the analyses.

In this case the first approach was impractical since the software used in the first analysis does not allow weights to be used and the use of weights would have made the results of the second analysis statistically more difficult to analyse. The second approach is neither easy nor necessarily technically adequate, so the approach taken in this research was to check whether the inclusion of the booster sample cases had any clear effect on the parameter estimates of particular models by fitting the models twice. In the analyses reported in this chapter, the inclusion of the booster sample had little effect on the parameter estimates.

2. It would not be impossible, however, to specify a single logit model which allowed some covariates to have time-varying effects while holding the effects of other covariates constant; see e.g. Morgan *et al.* (1988).

3. Another problem is the possibility that the categories of one of the explanatory variables used in a model of propensity towards marital dissolution may contain different distributions of an important unobserved variable, inducing spurious time-dependence in the relative effects of the different categories.

4. Tenure at marriage might be expected to be of decreasing salience as duration of marriage increases, not least because tenure will change over time in some cases. This hypothesis was crudely tested by the inclusion of time-dependent covariates set equal to the dummy

variable for each tenure multiplied by the duration of marriage. All three of the signs of the resulting parameter estimates were negative, and the magnitude of each estimate appeared related to the magnitude of the effect relating to the corresponding dummy variable. A lack of statistical significance, however, meant that no firm support was obtained for the initial hypothesis, and there is a further possibility that the results are due to unobserved heterogeneity.

Note that the effect of living in temporary accommodation would have been noticably stronger had not a parameter corresponding to a job at marriage in the armed forces been included in the model.

5. At this stage an examination of the effects of the inclusion of the booster sample on parameter estimates was made by the simple expedient of fitting the same model to the sample including and excluding the booster sample. There was in fact little change in the parameter estimates.

6. At this stage the effect on *all* the parameter estimates of the removal of those cases originating in the booster sample was examined. Fortunately all the parameter estimates remained virtually unchanged when the model was refitted to the reduced sample.

10

Labour Market Deprivation, Welfare, and Collectivism

DUNCAN GALLIE AND CAROLYN VOGLER

1. INTRODUCTION

Changes in labour market conditions over the last ten years have led to renewed speculation about the future of collectivist attitudes. In Britain, the most striking change has been the sharp rise in the level of unemployment. However, many commentators have also suggested that profound changes are occurring in the character of employment, in particular through the rise of more precarious types of work. On one estimate, fully a third of British employees could now be considered part of the 'flexible' work-force (Hakim 1987). Overall, there has been an increase in the level of insecurity and a marked accentuation of financial inequality.

There have been two broad interpretations of the implications of these changes for people's wider social attitudes. Some have emphasized the way that they have diversified labour market statuses, thereby fragmenting the work-force and undermining the basis for traditional solidaristic attitudes. Those in secure employment, it is argued, have enriched themselves during the 'recession' and have come to perceive a fundamental gulf between their interests and those of the disadvantaged. They have become increasingly conservative in their attitudes and indeed have come to resent the prevailing structure of welfare provision which they see as serving primarily the interests of others. The overall impact of labour market change, then, has been a growing polarization between social groups and a general decline in collectivism (Offe 1986; Golding and Middleton 1982). For other writers, the sharp increase in labour market deprivation in the 1980s is thought rather to have heightened people's awareness of the essentially 'social' character of poverty and disadvantage. Those that have directly experienced unemployment and job insecurity channel their frustrations into resentment about the inegalitarian nature of society. Moreover, the attitudes even of those that have been personally unscathed are profoundly affected by the knowledge of the effects of unemployment that they acquire through their families, their friends, and the community (Mack and Lansley 1985).

The objective of this chapter is to consider the plausibility of some of these arguments, using data from the 1987 Household and Community Survey (see the Methodological Appendix at the end of this book for details). This enables us to construct a typology of recent labour market experiences and then to look at the way in which these relate to people's experience of financial deprivation, their use of and attitudes to local welfare provision, and finally their commitment to collectivist values.

2. PATTERNS OF LABOUR MARKET EXPERIENCE

While labour market experience is frequently thought to be a major influence in moulding people's identity and structuring their social attitudes, there have been few attempts to distinguish groups empirically in terms of such experiences. Indeed, the criteria on which such distinctions should be made remain vaguely formulated. Perhaps the most influential attempt in recent years to spell out the critical differences between labour market categories has been that of segmentation theory. Yet the case-study literature has raised increasing doubts about the value of a relatively simple schema that divides the work-force into a generally privileged primary and a generally disadvantaged secondary sector. Is it really the case that the rapidly expanding work-force of low-paid female part-time workers is characterized by the type of chronic job insecurity that is crucial to the concept of the secondary sector? How are higher-paid workers who play the external rather than the internal labour market to be classified within such a schema? It is clear that the relationship between the two key dimensions of labour market experience—pay and security—needs to be treated as problematic and cannot be defined by theoretical fiat.

It is necessary to adopt a classification of labour market experiences that takes account of the theoretical centrality of pay and insecurity, but allows for variation in the way they are combined. Moreover, it is clear that the security of a person's labour market situation cannot be assessed simply from current employment status, but must take account of people's experience over time. The classification developed here is an exploratory one. The point of departure was to distinguish the currently unemployed from the employed, non-employed, and self-employed as categories with a fundamentally different type of relationship to the labour market. People were classified as unemployed if *either* they were registered as unemployed *or* they had been without work and looking for work in the previous four weeks. The next step was to subdivide the employed into four groups: the insecure low-paid, the secure low-paid, the insecure higher-paid, and the secure higher-paid. Low pay was defined in terms of the Low Pay Unit's threshold of hourly pay of less than £3.50 per hour. People were allocated to the insecure employment categories if they had experienced three or more months' unemployment in the previous five years or if they regarded their current jobs as insecure.

It also seemed important to distinguish between categories of the non-employed. It is arguable that the frontier between unemployment and non-employment can be very fluid, with non-employment representing a coerced withdrawal from the labour market of people (especially women) who have been unable to find work over a period of time. Alternatively, such withdrawal may reflect the pressures of the benefits system, with its sharp disincentives to female employment where the husband is unemployed. This type of non-employment might then be seen as representing a form of 'latent' unemployment, in view of the largely involuntary nature of withdrawal from the labour market. The non-employed were therefore divided into two categories—the insecure and secure—depending on whether or not the non-employed person had personally experienced three months or more of unemployment in the previous five years or was currently living with an unemployed spouse. The sample numbers here were too small to impose an income criterion that would parallel that of pay for the employed, but it is notable that the average standardized household income of the non-employed was below that of any category of the employed and indeed in the case of the insecure non-employed was slightly below that of the unemployed. Finally, for purposes of comparison, the self-employed were retained as a distinct category, since it was not feasible, given the sample size, to disaggregate it further.

It is clear from the data that the assumption that low pay and job insecurity cannot be treated as invariably linked was correct. Rather the use of the insecurity criteria created two substantial categories of the low-paid (Table 10.1). Overall, 27 per cent of respondents came in the low-paid employment categories, and of these approximately 32 per cent (or 9 per cent of the overall sample) were classified as being in an insecure labour market position. There was a similar division among the higher-paid: 25 per cent of all respondents were 'secure higher-paid' and 8 per cent 'insecure'. Most of the non-employed were in the secure category (15.8 per cent of the sample), leaving 3.6 per cent of the sample as insecure non-employed. The self-employed constituted 7.3 per cent of the sample and the currently unemployed 13.2 per cent.

TABLE 10.1. *Labour market experience*

Labour market experience	No.	%
Unemployed	736	13.2
Insecure low-paid	477	8.5
Secure low-paid	1,028	18.4
Insecure higher-paid	452	8.1
Secure higher-paid	1,397	25.0
Self-employed	407	7.3
Insecure non-employed	200	3.6
Secure non-employed	880	15.8
TOTAL	5,578	100.0

Source: The Work Attitudes/Histories, 1986, sample, from which the Household Survey respondents were drawn as a subsample (see Table 10.2).

A first point to note about these labour market categories is that there were important differences in their gender composition (Table 10.2). Among the unemployed, although there were substantial proportions of both men and women, the data revealed the usual pattern for Britain of a higher proportion of men (55 per cent). The insecure low-paid were divided roughly equally

TABLE 10.2. *Labour market experience and gender*

Labour market experience	Men		Women		All	
	No.	%	No.	%	No.	%
Unemployed	109	55	89	45	198	100
Insecure low-paid	92	47	103	53	194	100
Secure low-paid	80	24	249	76	328	100
Insecure higher-paid	104	80	25	20	129	100
Secure higher-paid	355	73	131	27	486	100
Self-employed	86	84	16	16	103	100
Insecure non-employed	12	19	51	81	63	100
Secure non-employed	41	16	216	84	257	100

Note: The relationship between labour market experience and gender was significant at the 0.001 level.
Source: The Household and Community Survey, 1987.

between men and women, while women dominated among the secure low-paid (76 per cent). In contrast, the higher-paid categories were clearly dominated by men. This was the case for 73 per cent of the secure higher-paid and for as much as 80 per cent of the insecure. The non-employed were again predominantly women. This brings out once more the very high level of gender segregation in the labour market, although it does not support the view that women's labour market experiences are marked by higher insecurity. Overall, 32 per cent of men were in an insecure category, compared with 25 per cent of women. Nor would female part-time work appear to be as heavily associated with insecurity as is sometimes asserted. Part-time women employees were less likely to be in an insecure category than men and marginally less likely than full-time women employees. The distinctive characteristic of women's labour market situation is not its insecurity (whatever the formal employment protection provisions), but rather that women are channelled so heavily into the low-paid sector.

Secondly, there is a clear relationship between labour market experience and class. Table 10.3 shows this with respect to the Goldthorpe class categories.[1] Although each class is composed of people in diverse labour market categories, the proportion of those in the more deprived categories increases sharply as one descends the class scale. Further, if their most recent occupation

TABLE 10.3. *Labour market experience and class*[a]

Labour market experience	Men (class)[b]					Women (class)				
	No.	1+2,	3+4+5,	6+7	Total	No.	1+2,	3+4+5,	6+7	Total
Unemployed	103	10	10	80	100	86	14	28	58	100
Insecure low-paid	92	13	11	76	100	103	15	39	46	100
Secure low-paid	80	14	14	72	100	249	11	34	55	100
Insecure higher-paid	104	52	10	38	100	25	32	47	21	100
Secure higher-paid	355	50	15	35	100	131	51	37	12	100
Self-employed	86	25	75	—	100	16	19	72	10	100
Insecure non-employed	11	3	9	88	100	46	12	28	60	100
Secure non-employed	35	28	16	56	100	198	17	24	59	100

[a] Goldthorpe class categories: respondents' a current or last class.
[b] The relationship between labour market experience, class and gender was significant at the 0.001 level.

is taken as defining the class position of an unemployed person, 78 per cent of unemployed men and 47 per cent of unemployed women come from the non-skilled manual working class. Similarly, 74 per cent of male and 34 per cent of female insecure low-paid employees are non-skilled manual workers. In contrast, among both men and women the majority of higher-paid employees, whether secure or insecure, are either in the service class or in the lower non-manual class.

Thirdly, the labour market experiences of those currently in employment were clearly related to differences in employment sector. Those in the higher-paid categories were notably more likely to be employed in the public sector than those in lower-paid work. Whereas some 44 per cent of both the secure and the insecure higher-paid were in the public sector, this was the case for only 34 per cent of the insecure low-paid and for 31 per cent of the secure low-paid. While the difference emerges for both sexes, it was very much more marked among women. Indeed, 67 per cent of secure higher-paid and 66 per cent of insecure higher-paid women were in the public sector compared to only 34 per cent of the secure low-paid and 35 per cent of the insecure low-paid. At the same time, those in the higher-paid categories were much more likely to be trade union members. Just over half of the higher-paid (51 per cent of the insecure and 54 per cent of the secure) were in trade unions, whereas, among the secure low-paid, membership fell to 41 per cent and among the insecure low-paid to 34 per cent. Again, the differences were more marked for women than for men—mainly due to the very low levels of trade unionism among low-paid women.

Finally, the prevalence of the different labour market categories varied considerably by labour market (Table 10.4). If the insecure labour market statuses are taken together (the unemployed, the insecure low-paid, the insecure higher-paid, and the insecure non-employed), there is a broad division between two types of locality. Forty-two per cent of the sample were in insecure categories in Kirkcaldy, 38 per cent in Rochdale, and 35 per cent in Coventry. In the more prosperous localities, the proportions were notably lower. Thirty-one per cent were in insecure positions in Aberdeen and 28 per cent in Swindon and Northampton. In good part this reflects the differences in the levels of unemployment. The wider definition of unemployment

TABLE 10.4. *Labour market experience by area* (%)

Labour Market Experience	Aberdeen	Northampton	Swindon	Coventry	Kirkcaldy	Rochdale
Unemployed	11	11	11	14	18	15
Insecure low-paid	7	8	7	7	10	12
Insecure higher-paid	12	7	8	9	8	6
Insecure non-employed	1	2	2	5	6	5
Subtotal	31	28	28	35	42	38
Secure low-paid	20	19	19	17	16	19
Secure higher-paid	28	28	26	23	23	23
Self-employed	5	10	10	8	4	7
Secure non-employed	16	15	17	18	15	14
TOTAL	100	100	100	100	100	100
No.	961	932	904	916	949	915

Note: The estimates are based on the Work Attitudes/Histories sample, 1986, from which the Household Survey respondents were drawn as a subsample. The relationship between labour market experience and area was significant at the 0.001 level.

Source: The Household and Community Survey, 1987.

used in this analysis shows the same general differences between localities that is revealed by the somewhat lower official unemployment rates. In Swindon, Aberdeen, and Northampton 11 per cent of the sample were unemployed. In Coventry the proportion rose to 14 per cent, and in Rochdale to 15 per cent, while the highest level of unemployment was in Kirkcaldy (18 per cent). Although there is little difference in the overall proportions of non-employed, the higher unemployment localities were also marked by a higher proportion of insecure non-employed, possibly supporting the argument that, in situations of high unemployment, there is a process of constrained withdrawal from the labour market.

3. LABOUR MARKET EXPERIENCE AND FINANCIAL DEPRIVATION

Labour market experience could be expected to affect collectivist attitudes through the way it structures people's sense of their needs and interests. Certainly the data show that it was quite clearly related to very different levels of perceived financial deprivation. The most general indicator of this was a question asking people how easy or difficult they found it to make ends meet. The group suffering the highest level of financial deprivation were the unemployed, of whom 61 per cent found it either very or quite difficult, followed by the insecure non-employed, with 58 per cent experiencing financial difficulty. These two groups were quite clearly differentiated from all categories of the employed, although it is notable that the insecure low-paid experienced considerably greater financial difficulty than any of the other employed groups. Whereas 32 per cent of the insecure low-paid found it either very or quite difficult to make ends meet, this was the case for only 15 per cent of the secure higher-paid.

A very similar picture emerges from a number of other indicators of material deprivation. For instance, the unemployed, the insecure non-employed, and the insecure low-paid were notably less likely than others to have had a holiday in the previous twelve months. Whereas 76 per cent of the secure higher-paid had had a holiday, this was the case for only 32 per cent of the unemployed. There was also a significant difference between the two low-paid categories: 58 per cent of the insecure low-paid, but only 36 per cent of the secure low-paid, had been without a holiday. There were similar differences in the proportions that saved regularly. Among the unemployed the vast majority (78 per cent) spent whatever money they had, whereas this was the case for only 34 per cent of those in secure higher-paid work.

To provide a more general picture of the experience of material deprivation, people were asked what actions if any they had had to take to make ends meet during the previous two years. As can be seen in Table 10.5, the overall pattern suggests that there are distinct levels of action that reflect rather different degrees of financial difficulty. The commonest items on which people cut back were social activities, clothing, and holidays. Much rarer were reductions in heating and expenditure on food, together with measures such as getting into debt and borrowing.

There was a very marked difference in the level of deprivation of people with different labour market experiences. In general, the most sharply deprived were the unemployed, the insecure non-employed, and the insecure low-paid. Labour market experience distinguishes quite clearly within the employed. The insecure low-paid suffered more than the secure low-paid and the insecure higher-paid more than the secure higher-paid. For instance, 73 per cent of the unemployed, 67 per cent of the insecure non-employed, and 61 per cent of the insecure low-paid had reduced expenditure on clothing, in contrast to only 36 per cent of the secure higher-paid. Taking the more severe measures, 46 per cent of the unemployed had cut down on heating, compared with 20 per cent of the secure higher-paid. Thirty-eight per cent of the unemployed had reduced expenditure on food, and 22 per cent had been forced to miss a meal, while this was the case for 12 per cent and 2 per cent respectively of the higher-paid.

To provide a rough summary index of the experience of financial deprivation, a score of 1 was given for each action that a person had taken to cope with financial difficulty (Table 10.6). The unemployed and insecure non-employed were notably higher than any other category, with index scores of 4.5 and 4.3 respectively. The insecure low-paid had a score of 4, the insecure higher-paid of 3.3, and the secure low-paid of 3. The least affected were the secure non-employed (2.9), the secure higher-paid (2.5), and the self-employed (2.5). In short, there can be little doubt of the close relationship between labour market experience and financial deprivation.

4. LABOUR MARKET EXPERIENCE AND HOUSING

Labour market experience was linked to more general social deprivation and to greater dependence on collective provision through its implications for people's housing situation. It is sometimes argued that housing tenure forms a distinct basis of economic interest that cross-cuts those deriving from people's work and labour market situations, thereby providing an independent basis for political alignment (Rex and Moore 1967; Saunders 1981; Saunders and Harris 1987). The data, however, point to the heavily cumulative nature of social disadvantage. Within the sample as a whole, 69 per cent of respondents were owner-occupiers, 26 per cent were council tenants, and 5 per cent rented privately. However, there was a considerable difference between those in different labour market positions. Just over half of the unemployed and 46 per cent of the insecure non-employed were concentrated in the state council housing sector, compared with 36 per cent of the insecure low-paid, 30 per cent of the secure low-paid, 14 per cent of the insecure higher-paid, and only 12 per cent of the secure higher-paid.

While one of the original objectives of the provision of council housing was to sever the link between labour market disadvantage and housing disadvantage, inadequate funding of the state sector has led to a marked association between types of tenure and quality of housing. Quality of housing was measured by asking respondents to assess the state of repair of their current house or flat on a 0 to 10 scale. Owner-occupiers were living in the best-quality housing (mean score 7.7), while the average score for council tenants fell to 6.1. (Those experiencing the worst quality of housing of all were the small proportion of private tenants, with a mean score of 4.7.) Moreover, not only were those in deprived labour market positions more likely to be in the poorer-quality council housing sector, but they would also appear to have been in inferior accommodation within that sector. These differences in housing quality were closely paralleled by differences in the level of

TABLE 10.5. *Labour market experience and financial deprivation. Percentage who had done each of the following during the last two years, when their households were short of money*

Action	Unemployed		Insecure low-paid		Secure low-paid		Insecure higher-paid		Secure higher-paid		Self-employed		Insecure non-employed		Secure non-employed		Significance
	No.	%	No.	%	No.	%	No.	%	No.	%	No.	%	No.	%	No.	%	
Missed a meal for yourself	43	22	16	8	20	6	8	6	10	2	6	6	11	17	23	9	0.01
Reduced spending on family meals	75	38	44	23	70	21	17	13	57	12	8	8	28	44	67	26	0.01
Turned heat down	92	46	66	33	82	25	38	29	96	20	22	21	32	51	84	32	0.01
Reduced social life	130	66	124	64	159	48	71	55	196	40	38	37	36	57	117	45	0.01
Gave up holiday plans	106	54	96	49	119	36	52	40	152	31	31	30	37	59	97	37	0.01
Cut back on buying clothes	145	73	118	61	162	49	54	42	174	36	32	31	42	67	123	47	0.01

Worked overtime	21	11	72	37	106	32	44	34	172	35	24	23	6	10	16	6	0.01
Taken any job going	24	12	38	20	23	7	8	6	9	2	11	11	7	11	8	3	0.01
Reduced savings	64	32	71	37	113	34	63	49	158	33	26	25	24	38	68	26	0.01
Got into debt	58	29	45	23	39	12	31	24	58	12	16	16	19	30	41	16	0.01
Financial aid from family & friends	71	36	45	23	44	13	14	11	58	12	18	17	13	21	45	17	0.01
Borrowed money from elsewhere	46	23	27	14	29	9	16	12	54	11	12	12	7	11	24	9	0.01
Other (incl. sold car, HP goods repossessed)	26	13	16	8	27	8	14	11	20	4	12	12	10	16	25	10	0.01
Total no. in each labour market situation	198		194		328		129		486		103		63		259		

Source: The Household and Community Survey, 1937.

TABLE 10.6. *Labour market experience and financial deprivation*

Labour market experience	Whole sample	Men	Women
Mean	3.2	3.0	3.3
Unemployed	4.5	4.3	4.8
Insecure non-employed	4.3	4.2	4.4
Insecure low-paid	4.0	3.9	4.1
Insecure higher-paid	3.3	3.3	3.4
Secure low-paid	3.0	2.7	3.1
Secure non-employed	2.9	3.2	2.8
Secure higher-paid	2.5	2.5	2.6
Self-employed	2.5	2.5	2.6
Significance	0.001	0.001	0.001

Source: The Household and Community Survey, 1987.

people's satisfaction with their housing. Council tenants were substantially less satisfied with their housing than owner-occupiers, and unemployed council tenants were more likely to be dissatisfied than council tenants in general.

There were, however, quite significant differences between the areas in the way in which the state housing sector mediated the relationship between the labour market and housing disadvantage. To begin with, the proportion of the unemployed living in council housing varied substantially—from 42 per cent in Rochdale to 72 per cent in Kirkcaldy. At the same time, there were marked differences in the composition of the council housing sector. For instance, in Kirkcaldy, which had a very large stock of council housing, only 21 per cent of council tenants were unemployed, despite this being an area of very high unemployment. At the other extreme, in Coventry, which had the lowest proportion of council tenants, the proportion unemployed was as high as 47 per cent. This was paralleled by clear differences between the areas in the quality of housing in the council sector. The two Scottish localities had substantially better council accommodation than any of the English localities. The average scores for state of repair were 7.2 in Aberdeen and 6.4 in Kirkcaldy. Among the English localities, the highest-quality council housing was in Northampton (5.8) and the lowest in Coventry (5.1). In short, there was no neat relationship between the level of unemployment in a locality and the extent of housing disadvantage. Rather, the association between labour market position and housing was heavily mediated by the nature of local provision, which would appear to be related to political rather than to labour market factors.

5. LABOUR MARKET EXPERIENCE, HEALTH, AND WELFARE PROVISION

Another way in which labour market experience might influence people's wider social attitudes is through its implications for their relationship to community services. This is particularly likely in the case of the health services. There is a well-established association between unemployment and ill health (both psychological and physical), and, at least for psychological ill health, research has increasingly pointed to labour market experience as the primary causal influence (Warr 1987; Cook *et al.* 1987; Fox and Goldblatt 1982). It seems plausible that a higher incidence of ill health among those in disadvantaged labour market positions is associated with a greater need for, and different experiences of, collective services.

Psychological well-being was measured using a four-item version of the standard General Health Questionnaire (GHQ) measure and our data clearly confirm the poorer psychological health of the unemployed (Table 10.7). What is particularly interesting, however, is the distinctiveness of the unemployed compared to any of the categories of the employed. While those in insecure low-paid and insecure higher-paid work were more likely to experience stress than the secure, they are far closer to the stable employed than they are to the unemployed. The only group that comes closer to the pattern of the unemployed are the insecure non-employed, which might be viewed as a 'latent' unemployed category. In short, the data provide clear evidence of the importance of employment *per se* for psychological health, even when those in low-paid and insecure positions are taken into account. The general patterns are very similar for men and women. In particular, unemployment appears to be as harsh in its consequences for men as for women. Similarly, their GHQ scores are almost identical when in low-paid work.[2]

TABLE 10.7. *Labour market experience and psychological well-being* (GHQ score)

Labour market experience	Whole sample	Men	Women
Mean	3.5	3.5	3.6
Insecure non-employed	4.5	4.5	4.5
Unemployed	4.3	4.3	4.4
Secure non-employed	3.6	3.8	3.6
Insecure higher-paid	3.6	3.7	3.1
Insecure low-paid	3.5	3.7	3.4
Self-employed	3.5	3.5	3.5
Secure low-paid	3.3	3.2	3.4
Secure higher-paid	3.2	3.0	3.6
Significance	0.001	0.001	0.001

Note: The higher the GHQ score the poorer the psychological adjustment and vice versa.
Source: The Household and Community Survey, 1987.

The available measures of physical health were of a relatively simple self-rated type. These, however, provide a picture that fits well with the evidence from more detailed studies. The most general measure asked people to rate their health on a 0–10 scale. Physical health was poorest among the non-active, particularly among the men of whom 68 per cent were suffering from a long-standing illness (Table 10.8). The unemployed had notably poorer physical health scores than people in employment. However, the more detailed categorization of labour market experience reveals that there is also a difference in health levels among the different categories of the employed. Most particularly, the insecure low-paid had health levels that were significantly lower than those of the secure low-paid; indeed, they were identical to those of the unemployed. The secure higher-paid were also those with the highest ranking on the health measure. Disadvantage in labour market status was then closely paralleled by disadvantage in health.

One consequence of this was that use of the health services varied markedly according to labour market experience. We have two measures of this: first, the number of visits that people had

TABLE 10.8. *Labour market experience and self-rated physical health*

Labour market experience	Whole sample	Men	Women
Mean	7.3	7.5	7.2
Insecure non-employed	5.9	6.7	5.7
Secure non-employed	6.5	4.8	6.9
Unemployed	7.3	7.3	7.2
Insecure low-paid	7.3	7.4	7.2
Insecure higher-paid	7.4	7.4	7.4
Secure low-paid	7.5	7.8	7.4
Self-employed	7.6	7.5	7.7
Secure higher-paid	7.8	7.8	8.0
Significance	0.001	0.001	0.001

Note: The higher the score the better the physical health and vice versa.
Source: The Household and Community Survey, 1987.

paid to their GP in the previous twelve months; secondly, the number of visits that they had made to a hospital outpatients department in the previous three years. As can be seen in Table 10.9, those with the poorest physical health—the non-employed and the unemployed—made much more use of both services than did the employed. Moreover, those in low-paid employment made more frequent use of the services than those in higher-paid work. The figures for women include visits with children, and the correlation between self-rated health and visits to both GPs and hospital outpatients is notably weaker for women than for men (0.34 and 0.25 for men and 0.29 and 0.19 for women). None the less, while there is a generally higher frequency of visits by women than by men, the general pattern of the relationship between labour market experience and use of local health services is the same for both sexes.

There is some evidence that more frequent use of the services was associated with greater dissatisfaction with their quality. This was only marginally the case with respect to the time that people had to wait to see their GP, but it was more marked with regard to their experience of hospital outpatient services. Those in the more disadvantaged labour market positions—the unemployed, the insecure non-employed, and the insecure low-paid—were less satisfied with the time that they had to wait before they secured

TABLE 10.9. *Labour market experience and use of health services GP visits in the last twelve months*

Labour market experience	Whole sample	Men	Women
Mean	4.5	3.2	5.9
Insecure non-employed	10.1	7.5	10.7
Secure non-employed	8.1	8.0	8.1
Unemployed	6.7	5.9	7.8
Secure low-paid	3.8	2.8	4.2
Insecure low-paid	3.5	2.3	4.6
Secure higher-paid	2.9	2.5	4.0
Insecure higher-paid	2.7	2.4	4.1
Self-employed	2.4	2.3	3.2
Significance	0.001	0.001	0.001

Hospital outpatient visits in the last three years

Labour market experience	Whole sample	Men	Women
Mean	3.6	3	4.2
Insecure non-employed	8.2	5.1	8.9
Secure non-employed	5.3	10.4	4.3
Unemployed	5.2	4.5	6.0
Insecure low-paid	3.2	2.0	4.3
Secure low-paid	3.1	2.4	3.3
Self-employed	2.7	2.4	4.4
Secure higher-paid	2.6	2.5	2.7
Insecure higher-paid	2.4	2.0	4.2
Significance	0.001	0.001	0.001

Source: The Household and Community Survey, 1987.

their initial appointment and with the quality of treatment they received when they were seen.

In short, the evidence supports the view that labour market experience was closely connected with the level of dependence on collective welfare provision. Those in more disadvantaged labour market positions had poorer psychological and physical health and made more frequent use of local health services. Further, there is some evidence that they had a less satisfactory experience of these services.

6. LABOUR MARKET EXPERIENCE AND COLLECTIVISM

We take collectivist values to be values that favour redistributive state spending and taxation. The major instrument of redistributive expenditure is welfare provision, but it is well recognized that the different components of welfare state expenditure have substantially different implications for redistribution. The middle classes may well be the primary beneficiaries of expenditure on education and health; the more clearly redistributive services are those that cater specifically for the poor—for instance, income support for the unemployed and state housing provision. Taylor-Gooby (1985) has shown that this distinction between types of provision is reflected in the general popularity of different forms of expenditure. Universal services such as the NHS and education receive much higher levels of support than services for the poor. In so far as there is a crisis of support for the welfare state, the central controversy would appear to centre around its redistributive aspects. Certainly, with respect to collectivist values, it is attitudes to redistributive welfare provision that are of central interest.

How did commitment to redistribution vary according to labour market experience? Attitudes to redistributive expenditure can be examined through two questions on people's views about the level of unemployment benefit and one on their views about government expenditure on council house building (Table 10.10). The first item on unemployment benefit gave people the choice between the options that 'benefits for the unemployed are too low and cause hardship' and that 'benefits for the unemployed are too high and discourage people from finding jobs'. The second asked people whether they thought that the government should spend more, less, or the same amount on unemployment benefit. The question on government expenditure on council house building followed the same format.

The level of insecurity in people's labour market experience had a clear impact on their views about unemployment benefit. The unemployed were more likely than any other category to think that unemployment benefits were too low (83 per cent) and were the most likely to favour a substantial increase in

TABLE 10.10. *Labour market experience and items in the index of collectivism*

Percentage claiming that	Unemployed		Insecure low-paid		Secure low-paid		Insecure higher-paid		Secure higher-paid		Self-employed		Insecure non-employed		Secure non-employed		Significance
	No.	%	No.	%	No.	%	No.	%	No.	%	No.	%	No.	%	No.	%	
Benefits for the unemployed are too low and cause hardship	157	83	117	62	168	57	81	65	273	59	41	45	48	78	141	61	0.01
The government should spend a great deal more on unemployment benefit	118	60	94	49	121	39	59	48	151	32	23	24	33	52	93	38	0.01
The government should spend a great deal more on council house building	132	68	128	70	169	53	74	58	224	47	33	33	37	63	119	50	0.01

Those with high incomes should pay most towards the cost of the welfare state	144	76	135	71	224	71	102	81	336	71	53	56	35	59	152	63	0.01
Increased state expenditure should be paid for by taxing the rich	123	64	121	64	187	58	70	54	256	55	44	44	29	50	136	55	0.05
Agree strongly that rich people should pay a greater share of taxes than they do now	86	44	71	37	112	35	48	38	135	28	20	20	25	42	71	28	0.01

Source: The Household and Community Survey, 1987.

government expenditure (60 per cent). However, the level of insecurity also differentiated within the employed. The insecure low-paid were more favourable to increased expenditure than the secure low-paid; and the insecure higher-paid were more favourable than the secure higher-paid. Finally, the insecure non-employed were more favourable than the secure non-employed.

Turning to people's attitudes to expenditure on council housing, there is a very similar pattern. The unemployed, the insecure low-paid, and the insecure non-employed are notably more likely to support an increase in expenditure than other categories. For instance, 68 per cent of the unemployed thought that the government should spend a great deal more on council house building, whereas this was the case for only 47 per cent of the secure higher-paid. It is notable that there is also a clear difference between the two categories of the low-paid. Whereas 70 per cent of the insecure low-paid wanted a substantial increase in expenditure, the proportion among the secure low-paid fell to 53 per cent.

If increased expenditure on welfare provision is to be truly redistributive, it must be financed through a progressive system of taxation. People were asked, at different points in the schedule, two questions related to this. The first, and most general, asked who should pay most towards the cost of providing the welfare state: those with high incomes, those with middle incomes, those with low incomes, or all equally. This showed that the unemployed were again more favourable to redistribution than any category of the employed other than the insecure higher-paid. Secondly, after a question about their priorities for extra spending on welfare, people were asked how they thought this increased expenditure should be paid for. The options lay between increasing taxes for most people, increasing taxes for richer people, reducing defence spending, or reducing some other area of government spending. Two choices were allowed. Overall the most popular first choice was reduced expenditure on defence (31 per cent), followed by increasing taxation for the rich (30 per cent). In all, 57 per cent gave taxing the rich as either their first or second choices. Comparing people by labour market experience, the unemployed and the insecure low-paid were the most likely to give this option (64 per cent in each case), while the proportion fell to 55 per cent among the secure higher-paid and to

44 per cent among the self-employed. In their views about the financing of the welfare state, then, the unemployed emerge on both measures as markedly more committed to redistribution than other categories.

Finally, a more general question was asked about attitudes to inequality which did not specifically relate to welfare provision. People indicated how strongly they agreed or disagreed with the view that 'rich people should pay a greater share of taxes than they do now'. Again the unemployed, the insecure non-employed, and both categories of the insecure employed were the most likely to agree strongly that the rich should pay a greater share of taxes than they do now.

The individual items on welfare expenditure, the financing of welfare provision, and more general attitudes to redistribution repeatedly suggest a link between the insecurity in people's labour market situation and their favourability towards redistribution. To provide a more robust measure of collectivism, an index was constructed by allocating a score of 1 to the collectivist response on each of the items above and then summing an individual's scores across the items. The mean scores by labour market category are given in Table 10.11. The unemployed have quite clearly the highest collectivism score (3.8), followed by the insecure low-paid (3.4), the insecure higher-paid (3.4), and the insecure non-employed (3.3). The lowest score is to be found among the self-employed (2.1), followed by the secure higher-paid (2.8) and the secure non-employed (2.8). Among the employed, the insecure low-paid again emerge as more collectivist than the secure low-paid, and the insecure higher-paid are more collectivist than the secure higher-paid.

The unemployed were clearly the most collectivist group. But it seems plausible that the circumstances that precipitate unemployment will influence people's reaction to it. Overall 42 per cent of the unemployed had become unemployed because of a decision taken by their employer, while the remainder had become unemployed either after taking the initiative to leave their job in search of better work or after a period out of the labour market. If those that became unemployed as a result of a decision taken by their employer are compared with those that became unemployed in other ways, there is indeed a very clear difference in the strength of collectivist values. Both groups of the unemployed

TABLE 10.11. *Labour market experience and collectivism*
(mean collectivism score)

Labour market experience	Whole sample	Men	Women
Mean	3.0	3.0	3.0
Unemployed	3.8	4.0	3.6
Insecure low-paid	3.4	3.5	3.4
Insecure higher-paid	3.4	3.3	3.5
Insecure non-employed	3.3	3.1	3.3
Secure low-paid	3.0	3.0	3.0
Secure non-employed	2.8	3.6	2.6
Secure higher-paid	2.8	2.8	2.9
Self-employed	2.1	2.1	2.3
Significance	0.001	0.001	0.001

Source: The Household and Community Survey, 1987.

have higher scores than any other labour market category, but
those that became unemployed as a result of their employers'
action have an exceptionally strong attachment to collectivism (a
score of 4.2 compared to 3.6 among the 'other' unemployed).
This general pattern emerges quite clearly for both men and
women, although it is even more pronounced for women. In
short, the experience of becoming unemployed as the result of
purely external constraints appears to encourage, particularly
strongly, a belief in the need for greater collective regulation of
social inequality.

7. CLASS, GENDER, AND LOCALITY

'Labour market experience' and 'class' (in the form of the
Goldthorpe schema) are both conceptually and empirically inter-
related. If the unemployed and the non-employed are classified in
terms of the class position of the last job that they held, there is a
clear association between class position and the level of collectivism (Table 10.12). The *petit bourgeoisie* (class 4) has the lowest
score (2.0) and manual workers (classes 6 and 7) the highest (3.4).
Among employees or former employees, there is a noticeable dis-
continuity between the average scores for the service and lower
non-manual classes on the one hand, and the lower technician

and manual working classes on the other. The service class is too homogeneous in terms of the labour market categories to contrast class and labour market experience effects meaningfully. In the intermediate classes (lower non-manual and lower technicians) and the skilled and non-skilled manual classes, the unemployed and the non-employed are likely to have lower collectivism scores if they are in lower non-manual class positions than if they are in the manual working class (Table 10.13). For *current employees,* however, class differentials disappear when labour market experience is controlled for. Moreover, it is notable that most of the previous effects of labour market experience persist within each class. Thus, in three of the classes the unemployed have the highest level of collectivism, while in the fourth (the skilled manual working class) they are the second highest after the insecure higher-paid. Among those in the lower non-manual, the skilled manual, and the non-skilled manual classes, the insecure low-paid are more collectivist than the secure low-paid, and the insecure non-employed more than the secure. While these patterns do not emerge for those in class 5 (lower technicians), the sample numbers here are so small that it is scarcely worth speculating about the reasons for the discrepancy. In general, it is clear that the labour market categories enable us to discriminate within class categories. Indeed the data suggest that among the employed the difference in 'class effects' may primarily reflect the different distribution of labour market experiences within classes.

Taken overall, there is no difference between men and women in their level of collectivism (Table 10.11). However, it would

TABLE 10.12. *Collectivism and class*

Class[a]	Mean collectivism score (sample mean 3.0)
Higher service	2.6
Lower service	2.8
Routine non-manual	2.9
Petit bourgeoisie	2.0
Lower technicians	3.3
Skilled manual workers	3.4
Semi- and unskilled manual workers	3.3
Significance	0.001

[a] Class is measured according to the Goldthorpe schema.

TABLE 10.13. *Labour market experience, collectivism, and class, mean collectivism score*

Labour market experience	Unemployed	Insecure low-paid	Secure low-paid	Insecure higher-paid	Secure higher-paid	Insecure non-employed	Secure non-employed
Routine non-manual	3.6	3.4	3.0	3.3	2.7	2.7	2.5
Lower technicians	3.8	3.4	3.5	3.2	3.4	2.4	3.6
Skilled manual workers	4.3	3.2	2.3	4.7	3.0	4.0	3.2
Semi- and unskilled manual workers	3.8	3.5	3.3	3.3	2.9	3.5	2.9

Note: The relationship between labour market experience, collectivism, and class was significant at the 0.001 level.
Source: The Household and Community Survey, 1987.

appear that the implications of certain labour market experiences differ by gender. For both men and women, the unemployed are the most collectivist category, but the scores for men are markedly higher than for women (4 compared to 3.6). Further, there is an interesting difference by gender among the non-employed. The higher levels of collectivism among the insecure non-employed in comparison with the secure is due to the difference between women in these categories, in particular to the strikingly low level of collectivism among secure non-employed women. Among men, the situation is reversed: it is the secure non-employed men that are most collectivist. This is perhaps attributable to the fact that the men in this category are exceptionally likely to be suffering from some type of physical disability. This was the case for 68 per cent of the secure non-employed men, compared with 27 per cent of the women. The men in this category, then, are likely to feel a strong dependence on the provision of adequate state provision and this is reflected in their more general social values.

Finally, it should be noted that the level of collectivism differed substantially between localities (Table 10.14). This cannot be accounted for simply in terms of the prevalence of unemployment, or indeed of insecure labour market positions more generally. It was the case that the lowest levels of collectivism were to be found in two of the more prosperous labour markets—Swindon and Northampton. Further, three of the four localities with the highest levels of collectivism were high unemployment areas (Kirkcaldy, Rochdale, and Coventry). But what is notable is that Aberdeen, with one of the more dynamic local economies, had a markedly higher collectivism score than the other low-unemployment areas, indeed higher than Coventry and Rochdale with their very much sharper problems of unemployment. The differences between the unemployed in the different localities are relatively narrow. The distinctiveness of Aberdeen in relation to the other prosperous labour markets reflects primarily the high degree of commitment to collectivist values among the employed, particularly those in insecure low-paid positions and in secure higher-paid positions. Indeed, there appears to be a distinct Scottish effect—with the level of collectivism substantially higher among the secure higher-paid in Aberdeen and Kirkcaldy than in any of the other labour markets.

TABLE 10.14. *Area, party preference, and collectivism, whole sample*

Area	Mean Collectivism score	Party preference (mean collectivism score)			
		Conservative	Labour	Other	Don't know or would not vote
Mean		2.0	4.1	3.1	3.0
Kirkcaldy	3.6	2.3	4.3	3.6	3.6
Aberdeen	3.2	2.2	4.3	3.4	2.8
Rochdale	3.0	2.1	3.8	3.0	3.1
Coventry	3.0	1.8	4.0	3.1	3.1
Northampton	2.8	1.9	4.1	2.9	2.9
Swindon	2.5	1.8	3.7	2.6	2.6

Note: Party and area were significant at the 0.001 level. The relationship between party, area, and collectivism was significant at the 0.001 level.

Source: The Household and Community Survey, 1987.

Within localities, the unemployed still stand out as the most collectivist in each area. However, the other differences of pattern in the aggregate data emerge less consistently at locality level. The insecure low-paid are more collectivist than the secure low-paid in five localities, but not in Kirkcaldy. The general tendency for those in insecure higher-paid positions to have higher collectivism scores than those in secure higher-paid positions disappears in Aberdeen. In general, it would seem that employees in secure labour market positions in the Scottish localities are unusually attached to collectivist values. This suggests that there are influences other than those of labour market experience that have a powerful bearing on the importance attached to redistributive social policies.

8. PARTY, LABOUR MARKET SITUATION, AND COLLECTIVISM

There has been a growing awareness in recent years of the importance of political factors in influencing people's attitudes to social inequality (Castles 1978; Gallie 1983). Political parties appear to act as major agencies of tertiary socialization that mould, over time, their supporters' perceptions of society and attitudes towards particular types of policies. Their ability to do this depends upon the intensity of their efforts at mobilization and their skill at linking their messages to people's lived experience (Nie *et al.* 1976). In cases where a party has access to governmental power over a substantial period of time its cultural influence extends well beyond its own adherents.

Overall, as can be seen from Table 10.5, party support differentiated sharply between levels of collectivism. The mean score for Labour supporters was 4.1, whereas among Conservative supporters it fell to 2. There was little difference among Labour supporters in the different localities and there were only minor differences by gender. The influence of party is itself related to much earlier processes of political socialization (Greenstein 1965). Those that were currently Conservative supporters came disproportionately from families where both parents had been Conservative voters when the person was young, whereas 79 per cent of current Labour supporters were from households where

TABLE 10.15. *Labour market experience, party preference, and collectivism* (mean collectivism score)

Party preference	Unemployed	Insecure low-paid	Secure low-paid	Insecure higher-paid	Secure higher-paid	Self-employed	Insecure non-employed	Secure non-employed
Mean	3.9	3.4	3.0	3.3	2.8	2.1	3.2	2.9
Conservative	2.9	2.5	2.5	2.0	1.7	1.3	2.3	1.7
Labour	4.3	4.1	3.6	4.8	4.2	3.4	4.5	3.8
Other party	3.6	3.5	3.1	3.1	3.0	2.2	3.4	3.1
Don't know or would not vote	3.9	3.3	2.9	3.0	2.8	2.1	2.5	2.9

Note: Party, labour market experience, and the two way interaction between party and labour market experience were all significant at the 0.001 level.

Source: The Household and Community Survey, 1987.

both parents had been Labour. Further, whatever their current party allegiance, those whose parental households were Labour had higher collectivism scores.

It is notable that the implications of labour market experience for collectivism vary considerably depending on the nature of people's political allegiances. In Table 10.15 it can be seen that, while Conservatives are less collectivist in each labour market category, labour market experience has a much stronger influence among Conservatives than it does among Labour supporters. Among Conservatives, the score for the unemployed is 2.9, whereas it falls to 1.7 among the secure higher-paid and to 1.3 among the self-employed. There is a very similar effect among third-party supporters, for whom the scores for the unemployed, the insecure low-paid, and the insecure non-employed are considerably higher than for all other categories. In contrast, among Labour supporters, there is very little variation indeed between the average scores for the different labour market categories. For instance, the score for the unemployed (4.3) is remarkably close to that for the secure higher-paid (4.2). Exposure to a political ideology of collectivism, then, appears both to heighten the level of collectivism and to generalize collectivist values across labour market situations. The effect of labour market experience is sharpest on those that have little exposure to more radical political ideologies.

An indication of the respective influences of party, parental socialization, labour market situation, class, gender, and area can be obtained from the least squares regression reported in Table 10.16. The two strongest influences are those of party. Even when these are controlled for, there is still a very significant influence that comes directly from parental political socialization. Those whose parents were consistently Labour supporters are more collectivist in their values. However, despite the strength of political factors, the influence of labour market insecurity still emerges quite clearly. Unemployment enters the equation directly after people's political allegiances and is highly significant.[3] The earlier finding that labour market experience has least effect among Labour supporters reappears in the interaction term of unemployment and the Labour vote. Further, whether or not people are in an insecure low-paid or an insecure higher-paid labour market position also continues to have a significant influence on their level of collectivism.

TABLE 10.16. *Regression on collectivism*

Variables	Beta	T	Significance
Conservative	−0.19	−8.4	0.0000
Labour	0.22	8.7	0.0000
Unemployed	0.20	8.0	0.0000
Parents Labour	0.13	5.9	0.0000
Class 4 (self-employed)	−0.07	−3.5	0.0005
Kirkcaldy	0.10	4.5	0.0000
Insecure low-paid	0.08	3.7	0.0002
Aberdeen	0.08	3.6	0.0003
Unemployment/labour interaction	−0.07	−2.6	0.0096
Rochdale	0.05	2.2	0.0281
Insecure higher-paid	0.05	2.1	0.0329
Constant	2.5		

$R^2 = 0.22$.

Notes: The remaining labour market and class categories, together with trade union membership, public/private sector employment, and father's class variables failed to enter the equation.

Source: The Household and Community Survey, 1987.

The results confirm that the crucial aspect of class experience for collectivism is labour market experience. Once labour market experience has been controlled for, there is only one detectable class effect left: the self-employed are likely to have lower levels of collectivism,[4] probably reflecting the individualistic ethos associated with direct ownership. Finally, there remain certain area influences that cannot be attributed to labour market experience, class composition, or traditions of party support. In particular, the two Scottish localities again stand out as distinctively more collectivist.

It was noted earlier that patterns of labour market experience among those currently in employment were associated with rather different employment sectors. The higher-paid—whether secure or insecure—were much more likely than the low-paid to be in the public sector and to be in trade unions. It would seem plausible that both employment in the public sector and the experience of trade union membership would heighten commitment to collectivist values. Could it be that the apparent effects of labour market experience are a result of differences in what

are really experiences of the employment relationship? In practice
neither employment sector nor trade union membership entered
the equation or affected significantly the coefficients for labour
market experience. It is labour market experience rather than
such aspects of the work situation that would appear to be
significant for collectivism.

The data confirm that, when other variables controlled for,
those who have experienced labour market insecurity—whether
currently unemployed or in employment—remain significantly
more collectivist than others. It was suggested earlier that labour
market situation might have this effect through its implications
for people's experiences of financial deprivation, for the type and
quality of housing to which they had access, and for their use of
and dependence upon collective health provision. If these factors
are entered into the regression, however, only financial deprivation and council housing have any clear impact on the association between the insecure labour market statuses and
collectivism. For instance, when the experience of financial deprivation and housing tenure are controlled for, the beta coefficient
for unemployment, while remaining highly significant, declines
from 0.20 to 0.16. The extent to which people make use of collective health provision makes no difference at all. Although labour
market situation influences wider social attitudes partly through
its severe financial implications and partly through the way it
leads to very different housing conditions, the experience of
employment insecurity still has a major direct effect in moulding
people's attitudes.

9. TOWARDS POLARIZATION?

The evidence supports the view that differentiation of labour market experience leads to rather different attitudes towards collective
provision among those in relatively deprived and relatively privileged positions. However, stronger versions of the thesis also suggest that there is a tendency towards divergence or polarization
that is likely to intensify conflict over issues of redistribution.
Much longer-term data is really required to assess this argument.
It is possible, however, to examine the way in which individuals
changed in their attitudes to redistributive expenditure over the

TABLE 10.17. *Changes in attitudes to redistributive expenditure, 1986–1987 (holding labour market experience constant)* (%)

Expenditure on council house building

Change in attitudes to redistributive expenditure 1986–7	Unemployed	Insecure low-paid	Secure low-paid	Insecure higher-paid	Secure higher-paid	Self-employed	Insecure non-employed	Secure non-employed
Changed to more (from less or same)	13	18	26	26	27	35	9	26
Changed to less or same (from more)	3	5	9	4	8	9	10	10
Consistent more	83	75	57	58	55	46	76	56
Consistent same	1	3	8	12	11	10	5	9
TOTAL	100	100	100	100	100	100	100	100
No.	113	85	217	72	349	83	26	176

Expenditure on unemployment benefit

Changed to more (from less or same)	15	33	32	30	32	32	31	31
Changed to less or same (from more)	3	8	11	8	10	6	5	10
Consistent more	78	47	39	55	36	27	65	42
Consistent same	3	11	18	7	23	35	—	17
TOTAL	100	100	100	100	100	100	100	100
No.	116	91	196	68	334	77	29	171

Note: Changes in attitudes were significant at the 0.001 level.
Source: Respondents interviewed in both the Work Attitudes/Histories Survey, 1986, and the Household and Community Survey, 1987.

period 1986 to 1987. In both years people were asked about their attitudes to the level of government spending on council house building and on unemployment benefit. If the polarization thesis were correct, there should be some sign of a growing difference between those with more insecure and those with more secure labour market experiences. In practice, however, as can be seen in Table 10.17, those in all labour market situations changed primarily towards an increased commitment to collectivism. Moreover, contrary to the expectations of the polarization thesis, this shift was particularly pronounced among those in employment. For instance, among those in secure higher-paid positions, 27 per cent moved from saying in 1986 that council house expenditure should be kept the same or reduced to the view in 1987 that it should be increased. At the same time, only 8 per cent moved in the opposite direction. With respect to spending on financial assistance to the unemployed, 32 per cent of those in secure higher-paid positions moved to favouring higher expenditure, while only 10 per cent had shifted away from this position. Thus, over the period, the difference in the commitment to redistributive expenditure between those in secure higher-paid employment and the unemployed diminished sharply: for expenditure on council housing the difference in those favouring increased expenditure fell from 24 per cent to 18 per cent, and for financial assistance to the unemployed from 41 per cent to 30 per cent. In short, while in both years there were marked differences in attitudes between those with distinct labour market experiences, these have diminished rather than increased over time. Overall, while differences in labour market experience would appear to create groups with rather different levels of attachment to collectivist values, there must be considerable doubt about the validity of any deterministic scenario that sees changes in labour market structure as leading inexorably to cultural fragmentation among the labour force and the decline of collectivism in its more privileged sectors. The data suggest that, over the recent period, collectivist values have grown stronger rather than weaker and that there has been some degree of convergence rather than divergence between different labour market groups.

10. CONCLUSION

This chapter has been concerned to examine the implications of labour market change for collectivist attitudes. In particular, it has focused upon the argument that these changes have generated a new form of social polarization. There are, in fact, two distinct issues at stake. The first is whether those who suffered from deprivation in the labour market were also deprived in other important areas of their lives, leading to a marked difference in life chances between the greater proportion of the working population on the one hand and a stratum that suffered from generalized disadvantage on the other. The second is whether the growth of such differences in objective life chances led to distinctive and diverging attitudes towards economic inequality and the public provision of welfare.

The evidence points strongly in the direction of a process of cumulative disadvantage. Those in insecure labour market positions suffered from a series of major disadvantages in terms of personal welfare. The unemployed, the insecure low-paid, and the insecure non-employed stood out from other groups in the degree of financial difficulty they confronted and in the extent to which they had been forced to cut living standards in recent years. Labour market insecurity was also closely linked to the type and quality of people's housing, although there was evidence that the nature of local government policies could affect the strength of this relationship. Finally, labour market experience had a clear association with people's psychological and physical health. Those in more disadvantaged labour market positions had poorer psychological and physical health and were obliged to make more frequent use of local health services. In short, the cumulative nature of social disadvantage affected not only the unemployed but also those in other insecure labour market positions.

Did this mean, however, that those in more privileged labour market positions were coming to have increasingly different social values with respect to redistributive state spending and taxation than those that experienced labour market deprivation, thereby undercutting traditional solidarities in the labour force? The unemployed and the insecure low-paid were certainly more collectivist than those in secure employment, in the sense of favouring government action to reduce social inequality. However, far from diverging over the period 1986 to 1987, the social attitudes of the different labour market groups became more similar, due to the growth of collectivism among those in relatively secure employment.

Overall, the fact that the deterioration in the labour market in Britain in the 1980s accentuated the cumulative character of social disadvantage did not imply growing polarization at the level of social values concerning economic redistribution. This casts doubt on the type of economic determinism that underlay such arguments. The evidence showed the importance of political factors in influencing attitudes to economic redistribution. This suggests that the effectiveness of political mobilization may be a crucial factor mediating the relationship between labour market change, social divisions, and wider social values.

NOTES

1. These figures are based on a collapsed seven-class version of Goldthorpe's original (1980) eleven-class scheme, in which personal service workers (class 3B) have been classified as part of class 7:

Goldthorpe's (1980) 11-category class scheme		Collapsed seven-class scheme	
Class		Class	
1	Higher service class	1	Higher service class
2	Lower service class	2	Lower service class
3A	Routine non-manual	3	Routine non-manual
3B	Personal service workers		
4A	Small proprietors without employees	4	Self-employed
4B	Small proprietors with employees		
4C	Farmers and smallholders		
5	Lower technicians/supervisors	5	Lower technicians/supervisors
6	Skilled manual workers	6	Skilled manual workers
7A	Semi- and unskilled manual workers	7	Semi- and unskilled manual workers (including class 3B—personal service workers)
7B	Agricultural workers		

2. The relatively large differences between men and women in the

two higher-paid categories were based on very small numbers of higher-paid women. Retesting on the much larger Work Attitudes Survey reduced the differences until they were no longer significant.

3. If the unemployed are divided into (1) those who became unemployed as a result of a decision taken by their employer and (2) those who became unemployed after leaving their job in search of a better job or after a period out of the labour market, both categories of the unemployed enter the equation. The beta coefficient for those thrown out by their employer was 0.18 (T 7.6, sig 0.0000) and that for the 'other' unemployed group was 0.13 (T 5.6, sig 0.0000).

4. See n. 1 above. These results have been checked using an alternative combination of the Goldthorpe class model in which class 3B is classified as part of class 3. The conclusions were found to be identical.

METHODOLOGICAL APPENDIX

The Social Change and Economic Life Initiative

DUNCAN GALLIE

---

1. INTRODUCTION

The Social Change and Economic Life Initiative (SCELI) focused on six local labour markets—Aberdeen, Coventry, Kirkcaldy, Northampton, Rochdale, and Swindon. These were selected to provide contrasting patterns of recent and past economic change. In particular, three of the localities—Coventry, Kirkcaldy, and Rochdale—had relatively high levels of unemployment in the early and mid-1980s, while the other three had experienced relatively low levels of unemployment.

In each locality, four surveys were carried out designed to provide a high level of comparability between localities: the Work Attitudes/Histories Survey, the Household and Community Survey, the Baseline Employers Survey, and the 30 Establishment Survey. The interview schedules for these surveys were constructed collectively by representatives of the different teams involved in the research programme. In addition a range of studies was carried out that were specific to particular localities. These were concerned to explore in greater depth a number of themes covered in the comparative surveys.

A distinctive feature of the research programme was that it was designed to provide for the possibility of linkage between the different surveys. The pivotal survey (and the first to be conducted) was the Work Attitudes/Histories Survey. This provided the sampling frame for the Household and Community Survey and for the Employers Baseline Survey. The Baseline Survey in turn provided the listings from which organizations were selected for the 30 Establishment Survey.

The field-work for the Work Attitudes/Histories Survey and for the Household and Community Survey was carried out by Public Attitudes Surveys Research Ltd. The Employers Baseline Survey was a telephone survey conducted by Survey and Fieldwork International (SFI). The interviews for the 30 Establishment Survey were carried out by members of the research teams.

TABLE A1. *The Work Attitudes/Histories Survey, 1986, achieved sample*

	Aberdeen	Coventry	Kirkcaldy	Northampton	Rochdale	Swindon	Total
Eligible addresses	1,345	1,312	1,279	1,400	1,350	1,321	8,007
Achieved sample							
Main sample	997	990	1011	957	987	955	5,897
Booster sample	48	23	—	65	18	60	214
Total interviewed	1,045	1,013	1,011	1,022	1,005	1,015	1,6111
Response rate (%)	78	77	79	73	74	77	76

2. THE WORK ATTITUDES/HISTORIES SURVEY

This survey was concerned primarily with people's past work careers, their current experience of employment or unemployment, attitudes to trade unionism, work motivation, broader socio-political values, and the financial position of the household.

Two pilot studies were carried out in the preparation of the Work Attitudes/Histories Survey, testing questionnaire items, the placing of the work history schedule, interview length, and the contact procedure. The main field-work was conducted between June and November 1986. The objective was to secure an achieved sample of 1,000 in each of the six localities. As can be seen in Table A1, the target was marginally exceeded, providing an overall sample of 6,111.

The sampling areas were defined in terms of the Department of Employment's 1984 Travel to Work areas (TTWA), with the exception of Aberdeen. In Aberdeen, where the TTWA was particularly extensive and included some very sparsely populated areas, the Daily Urban System area was used to provide greater comparability with the other locations.

A random sample was drawn of the non-institutionalized population aged 20–60. The electoral register was used to provide the initial selection of addresses, with probabilities proportional to the number of registered electors at each address. A half open-interval technique was also employed, leading to the identification of a small number of non-registered addresses in each locality. Doorstep enumeration of 20- to 60-year-olds was undertaken at each address followed by a random selection using the Kish procedure of one 20- to 60-year-old at each eligible address.

To provide sufficient numbers for analysis, it was stipulated that there should be a minimum of 150 unemployed respondents in each locality. A booster sample of the unemployed was drawn in the localities where this figure was not achieved through the initial sample. The booster sample was based on a separate random sample of addresses, with a higher sampling fraction in the wards with the highest levels of unemployment. As with the main sample, addresses were selected from the electoral register. But, for the selection of individuals, only the unemployed were eligible for inclusion. This booster sample was implemented in five of the six localities, producing a total of 214 respondents. Response rates for the combined main and booster sample were approximately 75 per cent in each of the localities, ranging from 73 per cent in Northampton to 79 per cent in Kirkcaldy (see Table A1).

Where appropriate, weights have been used to take account of the booster sample, using the estimates of the proportion of unemployed available from the initial sample. There are also weights to provide a Kish adjustment for household size and to correct for an over-representation of women in the achieved sample (3,415 women compared with 2,696 men). The sex weight assumes equal numbers of men and women in the relevant population, as is shown to be almost exactly the case by examination of census data.

The interview consisted of two major sections. The first was a life and work history schedule in which information was collected about various aspects of the individuals' labour market, family, and residential history over the entire period since they had first left full-time education. Information about family and residential history was collected on a year grid basis. Information about labour market history—including spells of unemployment and economic inactivity—was collected on a sequential start-to-finish date-of-event basis. In the case of 'employment events' further information was collected about *inter alia* the nature of the job, the employer, hours of work, number of employees, gender segregation, and trade union membership. The second part of the interview schedule was a conventional attitudinal schedule, with a core of common questions combined with separate subschedules designed specifically for employees, for the self-employed, and for the unemployed and economically inactive.

While, for the greater part, questions in the schedules provide direct comparability between localities, some scope was given for teams to introduce questions that would be asked only in their own locality (or in a subset of localities). This usually involved teams introducing a broader range of questions for investigating one or more of the themes covered in the common questions.

3. THE HOUSEHOLD AND COMMUNITY SURVEY

In 1987 a follow-up survey was carried out involving approximately one-third of the respondents to the 1986 Work Attitudes/Histories Survey. This focused primarily on household strategies, the domestic division of labour, leisure activities, sociability, the use of welfare provision, and attitudes to the welfare state. The survey was conducted in each of the localities, with the field-work lasting between March and July. The survey produced an achieved sample of 1,816 respondents, of whom 1,218 were living in partnerships and 588 were living on their own. Where applicable a range of questions was asked of partners as well as of the original respondents.

The sampling lists for the survey were generated from computer listings of respondents to the Work Attitudes/Histories Survey who had agreed to being reinterviewed. To ensure that a sufficiently large number of the unemployed respondents from the Work Attitudes/Histories

Survey were reinterviewed, it was decided to specify that, in each locality, approximately 75 of the households in the follow-up survey would
be from households where the respondent was unemployed at the time
of the Work Attitudes/Histories Survey. For sampling, the lists were
stratified into four groups, separating the unemployed from others and
people who were single from those with partners. The sampling interval
was the same for those of different partnership status, but different sampling intervals were used for the unemployed and for others to obtain
the target numbers of people who had been unemployed at the time of
the first survey.

   In the event, 87 per cent of respondents (ranging from 84.8 per cent in
Coventry to 89.7 per cent in Aberdeen) had indicated that they were
willing to co-operate in a further phase of the research. Since the sampling areas were once more defined in terms of local labour markets,
there was a further attrition of the original eligible sample due to people
leaving the area (between 7 per cent and 9 per cent, depending on the
locality). Response rates (for those that had agreed to be reinterviewed
and were still in the area) were 75 per cent or better in each locality,
ranging from 75 per cent in Rochdale and Northampton to 77 per cent
in Kirkcaldy. The structure of the achieved sample is given in Table A2.
It should be noted that the table describes respondents with respect to
their characteristics at the time of the Work Attitudes/Histories Survey,
1986, since this was the relevant factor for the sampling strategy. The
economic and partnership status of a number of respondents had
changed by the time of the second interview. For instance, while 1,223
of these respondents were classified as having had partners in 1986, the
number with partners at the time of interview in 1987 was 1,218.

   The questionnaire for this survey consisted of three sections: an interview schedule including questions of both respondents and partners, a
respondent's self-completion, and a partner's self-completion. There was
a shorter separate schedule for single people. The questionnaires
included an update of the life and work histories of the original respondent and a full work history was collected for partners interviewed. The
self-completion for respondents and partners was used at different points
in the interview to collect independent responses from partners where it
was thought that issues might be sensitive or that there was a danger of
contamination of responses. The respondents and their partners filled in
the relevant sections of the self-completion in the presence of the interviewer, but without reference to each other. The great majority of questions were common to all localities, but, again, a limited number of
locality specific questions were allowed.

   The *Time Budget Survey*. The data available through the Household
and Community Survey interview was extended through a linked time

TABLE A2. *The Household and Community Survey, 1987, achieved sample by characteristics at time of Work Attitudes/Histories Survey*

	Aberdeen	Coventry	Kirkcaldy	Northampton	Rochdale	Swindon	Total
Total issued	390	400	399	404	402	394	2,389
Achieved sample							
Employed/non-active with partner, 1986	153	162	167	163	155	175	975
Employed/non-active single in 1986	68	54	62	60	68	48	360
Unemployed with partner in 1986	42	42	40	40	45	39	248
Unemployed single in 1986	41	44	40	38	32	38	233
Total interviewed	304	302	309	301	300	300	1,816
Response rate (%)	78	76	77	75	75	76	76

budget survey. This project was directed by Jonathan Gershuny of the University of Oxford. The final five minutes of the Household and Community Survey were devoted to introducing the time budget diaries to the individual or couple present. The diaries were designed to cover a full week starting from the day following the household interview. They required natural-language descriptions of the diarist's sequences of activities to be kept on a fifteen-minute grid, for the whole week, together with any secondary (i.e. simultaneous) activities and a record of geographical location and whether or not others were present during the activities carried out. Interviewers left behind addressed, reply-paid envelopes for return of the diaries at the end of the diary week.

Forty-four per cent of those eligible (802 of the original 1,816 respondents and 533 of their 1,218 partners) completed usable diaries for the whole week. This low rate of response, though not unexpected from a postal survey, raises the issue of the extent of non-response biases. In anticipation of this problem, a number of questionnaire items were included in the original Household and Community Survey interviews which were intended to 'shadow' or parallel evidence from the diaries (i.e. questions about the frequency of participation in leisure activities and about the distribution of responsibilities for domestic work). An analysis of the two sources of data showed that the distribution of frequencies of the questionnaire responses of those who failed to complete diaries was very similar to the distribution of questionnaire responses for those who did keep diaries. From this we may infer an absence of bias at least with respect to estimates of these leisure and unpaid work activities (for a fuller account, see Gershuny 1990).

4. THE EMPLOYER SURVEYS

The implementation of the Baseline Employers Survey, which was a telephone survey, was the responsibility of Michael White of the Policy Studies Institute. The schedule was drawn up in collaboration with a working party of representatives from the different teams involved in the SCELI programme.

The survey involved a sample of establishments. The major part of the sample was drawn from information provided from the Work Attitudes/Histories Survey about people's employers. Each of the 1,000 individuals interviewed in each locality was asked, if currently employed, to provide the name and address of the employer and the address of the place of work. The sample was confined to esablishments located within the travel-to-work areas that formed the basis of the research programme. Approximately 12 per cent of establishments initially listed could not be included in the sample because of insufficient information

TABLE A3. *The Baseline Employer sample*

	Aberdeen	Coventry	Kirkcaldy	Northampton	Rochdale	Swindon	Total
Sample from survey	345	280	229	287	233	273	1,647
Booster sample	52	54	32	51	55	39	283
Sample out of area	1	30	16	27	11	4	89
Eligible	396	304	245	311	277	308	1,841
Interviews	308	203	174	209	177	240	1,311
Response rate (%)	77.7	66.7	71.0	67.2	63.9	77.9	71.2

or closures. The sample covers all types of employer and both the public and the private sectors.

This method of generating a sample differs from a straight random sample drawn from a frame of all establishments. The latter would have resulted in a very large number of small establishments being included, while there was considerable theoretical interest in medium-sized and large establishments as key actors in the local labour market. The method used in SCELI weights the probability of an establishment's being included by its size: the greater the number of employees at an establishment, the greater its chance of having one or more of its employees included in the sample of individuals (and hence itself being selected).

The above method is closely related to sampling with probability proportional to size (p.p.s.); however, there are generally too few medium-sized and large establishments to generate a true p.p.s. sample. To increase the numbers of these medium-sized and large establishments, an additional sample of private sector employers with fifty or more employees was drawn from market research agency lists, supplemented by information from the research teams. The booster consisted of all identifiable establishments in this size range not accounted for by the basic sampling method. The sampling method, then, was designed to be as comprehensive as possible for medium-sized and larger employers. In practice, 70 per cent to 85 per cent of the sample by different localities were provided through the listings from the Work Attitudes/Histories data, while only 15 per cent to 30 per cent were from the booster sample. The structure of the achieved sample is presented in Table A3. The sample so generated under-represents smaller, and over-represents larger, establishments, but provides adequate numbers in all size groups. It is also approximately representative of employment in each area, but it is possible to use weighting to achieve an even more precise representation of local employment. This was carried out using tables of employment by size group of establishment within industry group within each local labour market, from the 1984 Census of Employment (by courtesy of the Statistics Division, Department of Employment).

There were five stages of piloting over the summer of 1986, particularly concerned to develop the most effective contact procedure. The main field-work period was from October 1986 to February 1987. The overall response rate was 71 per cent, ranging from 64 per cent in Rochdale to 78 per cent in Aberdeen and Swindon.

The interview schedules focused particularly upon occupational structure, the distribution of jobs by gender, the introduction of new technologies, the use of workers with non-standard employment contracts, relations with trade unions, and product market position. Different questionnaires were used for large and small organizations, with fewer questions being asked of small organizations. There were also minor variations in the schedules for public and private organizations, and for different industries. The four industry subschedules were: (1) manufacturing, wholesale, haulage, extractive, agriculture, (2) retail/hotel, catering/personal, and other consumer services; (3) banks, financial and business services, and (4) construction. These were designed to provide functionally equivalent questions with respect to product market position for different types of organization.

In each locality, there were follow-up interviews in at least thirty establishments—the 30 Establishment Survey—designed in particular to explore the motivation behind particular types of employer policy. While steps were taken to ensure that cases were included across a range of different industries, the composition of the follow-up sample was not a random one, but reflected team research interests. In contrast to the other surveys, the data from this survey should not be assumed to be generalizable to the localities.

REFERENCES

ALLISON, P. D. (1982), 'Discrete-Time Methods for the Analysis of Event Histories', in S. Lcinhardt (ed.), *Sociological Methodology 1982* (San Francisco: Jossey-Bass).

—— (1984), *Event History Analysis: Regression for Longitudinal Event Data*, Quantitative Applications in the Social Sciences (London: Sage).

—— (1987), 'Introducing a Disturbance into Logit and Probit Regression Models', *Sociological Methods and Research*, 15: 355–74.

AMIR, Y., and SHARON, I. (1984), '*Are Social–Psychological Laws Cross-culturally Valid?*', unpublished report, Bar-Ilan University; cited in G. Jahoda (1986).

ANDERSON, D. A., and AITKIN, M. (1985), 'Variance Component Models with Binary Response: Interviewer Variability', *Journal of the Royal Statistical Society*, B47: 203–10.

ANDERSON, E. B. (1970), 'Asymptotic Properties of Conditional Maximum Likelihood Estimators', *Journal of the Royal Statistical Society*, B32: 283–301.

ANWAR, M. (1979), *The Myth of Return: Pakistanis in Britain* (London: Heinemann).

ASHER, H. B. (1984), *Causal Modelling*, 2nd edn., Quantitative Applications in the Social Sciences (London: Sage).

ATKINSON, A. B. (1989), *Poverty and Social Security* (Hemel Hempstead: Harvester Wheatsheaf).

—— and Micklewight, J. (1985), *Unemployment Benefits and Unemployment* (London: STICERD).

ATKINSON, J., and MEAGER, N. (1986), *New Forms of Work Organisation*, Institute of Manpower Studies Report No. 121 (Brighton: Institute of Manpower Studies).

AXELROD, W. L., and GAVIN, J. F. (1980), 'Stress and Strain in Blue-Collar and White-Collar Management Staff', *Journal of Vocational Behaviour*, 17: 41–9.

BAKKE, E. W. (1933), *The Unemployed Man: A Social Study* (London: Nisbet).

—— (1940a), *Citizens without Work* (New Haven, Conn.: Yale University Press).

BAKKE, E. W. (1940*b*), *The Unemployed Workers* (New Haven, Conn.: Yale University Press).

BALAKRISHNAN, T. R., ROA, K. V., LAPIERRE-ADAMCYK, E., and KROTKI, K. J. (1987), 'A Hazard Model Analysis of the Covariates of Marital Dissolution in Canada', *Demography*, 24/3: 395–406.

BANKS, M. H., CLEGG, C. W., JACKSON, P. R., KEMP, N. J., STAFFORD, E. M., and WALL, T. D. (1980), 'The Use of the General Health Questionnaire as an Indicator of Mental Health in Occupational Studies', *Journal of Occupational Studies*, 53: 187–94.

BARRÈRE-MAURISSON, M., BATTAGLIOLA, F., and DAUNE-RICHARD, A. (1985), 'The Course of Women's Careers and Family Life', in B. Roberts, R. Finnegan, and D. Gallie (eds.), *New Approaches to Economic Life* (Manchester: Manchester University Press).

BARRON, R. D., and NORRIS, G. M. (1976), 'Sexual Divisions and the Dual Labour Market', in D. Barker and S. Allen (eds.), *Dependence and Exploitation in Work and Marriage* (London: Longman).

BEALE, N., and NETHERCOTT, S. (1985), 'Job Loss and Family Morbidity: A Study of a Factory Closure', *Journal of the Royal College of General Practitioners*, 35: 510–14.

BEAN, C. R., LAYARD, P. R. G., and NICKELL, S. J. (1986), 'The Rise in Unemployment: A Multicountry Study', *Economica*, 53, Supplement S1–S22.

BECKER, G. S., LANES, E. M., and MICHAEL, R. T. (1977), 'An Economic Analysis of Marital Instability', *Journal of Political Economy*, 85: 1141–87.

BERG, S. V., and DALTON, T. R. (1977), 'United Kingdom Labor-Force Activity Rates Unemployment and Real Wages', *Applied Statistics*, 9: 265–70.

BLACKBURN, R. M., and MANN, M. (1979), *The Working Class in the Labour Market* (London: Macmillan).

BLAU, P. M., and DUNCAN, O. D. (1967), *The American Occupational Structure* (Chichester: Wiley).

BLOSFELD, H. P., HAMMERLE, A., and MEYER, K. U. (1989), *Event History Analysis* (Hillsdale, NJ: Lawrence Erlbaum Associates).

BMDP (1983) *BMDP Statistical Softwear Manual* (London: University of California Press).

BODDY, M., LOVERING, J., and BASSETT, K. (1986), *Sunbelt City?* (Oxford: Oxford University Press).

BONNEY, N. (1985), 'On the Nature of the Universe', Working Paper, Department of Sociology, University of Aberdeen.

BOURDIEU, P. (1986), *Distinction* (London: Routledge & Kegan Paul).

BOWLEY, A. (1911), *Livelihood and Poverty* (London: Ratan Tata Foundation).

BRENNER, M. H. (1973), *Mental Illness and the Economy* (Cambridge, Mass.: Harvard University Press).

—— (1979), 'Mortality and the National Economy', *Lancet*, 2: 568–78.

BRESLOW, N. E., and DAY, N. E. (1980), *Statistical Methods in Cancer Research*, i: *The Analysis of Case-Control Studies* (Lyons: International Agency for Research on Cancer).

BUMPASS, L. L., MARTIN, T. C., and SWEET, J. A. (1989), *Background and Early Marital Factors in Marital Disruption*, National Survey of Families and Households Working Paper No. 14.

BURCHELL, B. J. (1989), 'The Impact on Individuals of Precariousness in the United Kingdom Labour Market', in G. Rodgers and J. Rodgers (eds.), *Precarious Jobs in Labour Market Regulation: The Growth of Atypical Employment in Western Europe* (Geneva: International Institue of Labour Studies).

—— and RUBERY, J. (1989), *Segmented Jobs and Segmented Workers: An Empirical Investigation*, SCELI Working Paper No. 13, Nuffield College, Oxford.

—— (1990), 'An Empirical Investigation into the Segmentation of the Labour Supply', *Work, Employment and Society*, 4: 551–75.

—— ELLIOT, B. J., and RUBERY, J. (1989), *Gender and the Structuring of Labour Markets*, SCELI Working Paper No. 15, Nuffield College, Oxford.

BURGOYNE, J., ORMROD, R., and RICHARDS, M. (1987), *Divorce Matters* (Harmondsworth: Penguin).

BURNETT, N. G., BLANC, A. K., and BLOOM, D. E. (1988), 'Commitment and the Modern Union: Assessing the Link between Pre-marital Cohabitation and Subsequent Marital Stability', *American Sociological Review*, 53: 127–38.

CALLENDER, C. (1985), 'Unemployment: The Case for Women', in C. Jones and M. Brenton (eds.), *The Year Book of Social Policy in Britain 1984–1985* (London: Routledge & Kegan Paul).

CARTER, I. (1979), *Farmlife in Northeast Scotland 1840–1914: The Poor Man's Country* (Edinburgh: John Donald).

CASTLES, F. G. (1978), *The Social Democratic Image of Society* (London: Routledge & Kegan Paul).

CATALANO, R., and DOOLEY, D. (1983), 'Health Effects of Economic Instability: A Test of Economic Stress Hypothesis', *Journal of Health and Social Behaviour*, 24: 46–60.

CHAMBERLAIN, G. (1985), 'Heterogeneity, Omitted Variable Bias and Duration Dependence', in J. J. Heckman and B. Singer (eds.), *Longitudinal Analysis of Labour Market Data* (Cambridge: Cambridge University Press).

CHAMPION, A. G., and GREEN, A. E. (1985), 'In Search of Britain's

Booming Towns: An Index of Local Economic Performance for Britain', University of Newcastle upon Tyne Centre for Urban and Regional Development Studies Discussion Paper No. 72.

CHAMPION, A. G., GREEN, A. E., OWEN, D. W., ELLIS, D. J., and COOMBES, M. G. (1987), *Changing Places* (London: Edward Arnold).

COOK, D. G., CUMMINS, R. O., BARTLEY, M. J., and SHARPER, A. G. (1982), 'The Health of Unemployed Middle-Aged Men in Great Britain', *Lancet*, 5:1290–4.

COOKE, K. (1987), 'The Withdrawal from Paid Work of the Wives of Unemployed Men: A Review of Research', *Journal of Social Policy.* 16/3: 371–2.

CORRY, B. A., and ROBERTS, J. A. (1970), 'Activity Rates and Unemployment: The Experience of the United Kingdom 1951–66', *Applied Economics*, 2/3: 179–201.

—— (1974), 'Activity Rates and Unemployment: The UK Experience: Some Further Results', *Applied Economics*, 6/1: 1–21.

COX, D. R. (1972), 'Regression Models and Life-Tables' (with discussion), *Journal of the Royal Statistical Society*, 74: 187–220.

CRAGG, A., and DAWSON, T. (1984), *Unemployed Women: A Study of Attitudes and Experiences*, Department of Employment Research Paper No. 47 (London: HMSO).

CROUCHLEY, R., and PICKLES, A. (1989), 'An Empirical Comparison of Conditional and Marginal Likelihood Methods in a Longitudinal Study', *Sociology Methodology*, 19: 161–81.

CURTICE, J. (1988), 'One Nation?', in R. Jowell, S. Witherspoon and L. Brook (eds.), *British Social Attitudes: The Fifth Report* (Aldershot: Gower).

DANIEL, W. W. (1981), *The Unemployed Flow*, 1st Stage of Interim Report (London: Policy Studies Institute).

—— (1983) 'How the Unemployed Fare after they Find New Jobs', *Policy Studies*, 3, part 4 (Apr.), 246–60.

—— (1990), *The Unemployed Flow* (London: Policy Studies Institute).

DAVIES, R. B. (1992), 'Sample Enumeration Methods for Model Interpretation', in B. Francis, P. G. M. van der Heijden, W. Jansen, and G. Seeber (eds.), *Statistical Modelling* (Oxford: Elsevier).

—— and Crouchley, R. (1986), 'The Mover–Stayer Model: Requiescat in Pace', *Sociological Methods and Research*, 14: 356–80.

—— and PICKLES, A. R. (1985), 'Longitudinal versus Cross-sectional Methods for Behavioural Research: A First-Round Knockout', *Environment and Planning*, A 17: 1315–29.

—— (1986), 'Accounting for Omitted Variables in a Discrete Time Panel Data Model of Residential Mobility', *Quality and Quantity*, 20: 219–33.

DENNIS, N., HENRIQUES, F., and SLAUGHTER, C. (1956), *Coal is our Life* (London: Tavistock).

DEPARTMENT OF EMPLOYMENT (1988), 'Ethnic Minorities and the Labour Market', *Employment Gazette*, Mar., 164–77.

DEX, S. (1988a), 'Destinations of those who Left the Long-Term Unemployed Register in 1986', report to the Department of Employment.

—— (1988b), *Women's Attitudes towards Work* (Basingstoke: Macmillan).

DILNOT, A., and KELL, M. (1987), 'Male Unemployment and Women's Work', *Fiscal Studies*, 8: 1–16.

DOERINGER, P. B., and PIORE, M. J. (1971), *Internal Labour Markets and Manpower Analysis* (Lexington, Mass.: D. C. Heath).

DOOLEY, D., ROOK, K., and CATALANO, R. (1987), 'Job and Non-job Stressors and their Moderators', *Journal of Occupational Psychology*, 60: 115–32.

EEKELAAR, J., and MACLEAN, M. (1986), *Maintenance after Divorce* (Oxford: Oxford University Press).

ELIAS, P. (1980), 'A Time-Series Analysis of the Labour Force Participation of Married Women in the UK, 1968–75', Manpower Research Group Discussion Paper No. 9, University of Warwick (mimeo).

ERMISCH, J. (1986), *The Economics of the Family: Applications to Divorce and Remarriage*, Centre for Economic Policy Research Discussion Paper No. 140 (London: Centre for Policy Research).

—— and Wright, R. F. (1989), *Employment Dynamics among British Lone Mothers*, Centre for Economic Policy Research Discussion Paper No. 302 (London: Centre for Economic Policy Research).

EVERSLEY, D. E. C. (1959), *The Victoria Country History of Wiltshire* (Oxford: Oxford University Press).

FAGIN, L., and LITTLE, B. (1984), *The Forsaken Families* (Harmondsworth: Penguin).

FEATHERMAN, D. L. (1971), 'A Research Note: A Structural Model for the Socioeconomic Career', *American Journal of Sociology*, 77: 293–304.

FINEMAN, S. (1983), *White Collar Unemployment: Impact and Stress* (Chichester: Wiley).

—— (1987), 'Back to Employment: Wounds and Wisdoms', in D. Fryer and P. Ullah (eds.), *Unemployed People: Social and Psychological Perspectives* (Milton Keynes: Open University Press).

FOTHERGILL, S., and GUDGIN, G. (1982), *Unequal Growth: Urban and Regional Employment Change in the UK* (London: Heinemann Educational Books).

FOX, A. J., and GOLDBLATT, P. O. (1982), *Longitudinal Study: Socio–Demographic–Mortality Differentials 1971–1975*, OPCS (London: HMSO).

FRASER, C. (1981), 'The Social Psychology of Unemployment', in M. Jeeves (ed.), *Psychology Survey No. 3* (London: Allen & Unwin).

FRESE, M. (1985), 'Stress at Work and Psychosomatic Complaints: A Causal Interpretation', *Journal of Applied Psychology*, 70: 314–28.

FRYER, D. (1986), 'Employment Deprivation and Personal Agency during Unemployment: A Critical Discussion of Jahoda's Explanation of the Psychological Effects of Unemployment', *Social Behaviour*, 1: 3–24.

—— and PAYNE, R. L. (1984), 'Proactivity in Unemployment: Findings and Implications', *Leisure Studies*, 3: 273–95.

—— (1986), 'Being Unemployed: A Review of the Literature on the Psychological Experience of Unemployment', in C. L. Cooper and I. Robertson (eds.), *International Review of Industrial and Organisational Psychology*, vol. 1 (Chichester: Wiley).

GALLIE, D. (1983), *Social Inequality and Class Radicalism in France and Britain* (Cambridge: Cambridge University Press).

—— (1988), *Technological Change, Gender and Skill*, Social Change and Economic Life Working Paper No. 4.

—— (1991), 'Patterns of Skill Change: Upskilling, Deskilling, and the Polarisation of Skills?', *Work, Employment and Society*, 5/3: 314–51.

GARCIA, J. (1989), 'Incentive and Welfare Effects of Reforming the British Benefit System: A Simultation Study for the Wives of the Unemployed', in S. Nickell, W. Narendranathan, J. Stern, and J. Garcia, *The Nature of Unemployment in Britain: Studies of the DHSS Cohort* (Oxford: Oxford University Press).

GERGEN, K. (1973), 'Social Psychology as History', *Journal of Personality and Social Psychology*, 26: 309–20.

GERSHUNY, J. (1983), *Social Innovation and the Division of Labour* (Oxford: Oxford University Press).

—— (1990), 'International Comparisons of Time Use Surveys: Methods and Opportunities', in R. von Schweitzer, M. Ehling, and D. Schafer, *Zeitbutgeterhebungen* (Stuttgart: Metzer-Poeschel).

—— MILES, I., JONES, S., MULLINS, C., THOMAS, G., and WYATT, S. M. E. (1986), 'Preliminary Analyses of the 1983/4 ESRC Time Budget Data', *Quarterly Journal of Social Affairs*, 2: 13–39.

GOLDING, P., and MIDDLETON, S. (1982), *Images of Welfare* (Oxford: Martin Robertson).

GOLDTHORPE, J. H. (1987), *Social Mobility and Class Structure in Modern Britain*, 2nd edn. (Oxford: Clarendon Press).

—— and HOPE, K. (1974), *The Social Grading of Occupations: A New Approach and Scale* Oxford: Clarendon Press.

GONUL, F. F. (1989), 'Comparison of Hazard Functions with Duration Dependence and Stayer–Mover Structure with an Application to Divorce', *Economics Letters*, 30/1: 31–6.

GOYDER, J. (1987), *The Silent Minority: Non-respondents in Sample Surveys* (Cambridge: Polity Press).

GREENHALGH, C. (1977), 'A Labour Supply Function for Married Women in Great Britain', *Economica*, 44: 249–65.

—— (1980), 'Participation and Hours of Work for Married Women in Great Britain', *Oxford Economic Papers*, 32: 296–318.

GREENHALGH, L., ROSENBLATT, Z. (1984), 'Job Insecurity: Towards Conceptual Clarity', *Academy of Management Review*, 9: 438–48.

GREENSTEIN, F. I. (1965), *Children and Politics* (New Haven, Conn.: Yale University Press).

GRICE, J. W. (1978), 'A Time-Series Model for Labour Supply', Treasury Working Paper, AP (78) 11 (mimeo).

HAKIM, C. (1987), 'Trends in the Flexible Workforce', *Employment Gazette* (Nov.), 549–60.

—— (1991), 'Grateful Slaves and Self-made Women: Fact and Fantasy in Women's Work Orientation', *European Sociological Review*, 7: 101–22.

HARLOE, M. (1975), *Swindon: A Town in Transition: A Study in Urban Development and Overspill Policy* (London: Heinemann).

HARRIS, C. C. (1987), *Redundancy and Recession in South Wales* (Oxford: Blackwell).

HART, N. (1976), *When Marriage Ends: A Study in Status Passage* (London: Tavistock).

HARTLEY, J. (1989), 'Organisational Decline, Job Insecurity and Industrial Relations', Paper presented to the Fourth West European Congress on Psychology of Work and Organisations, Cambridge.

HASKEY, J. (1984), 'Social Class and Socio-Economic Differentials in Divorce in England and Wales', *Population Studies*, 38: 419–38.

—— (1988), 'Trends in Marriage and Divorce, and Cohort Analyses of the Proportion of Marriages Ending in Divorce', *Population Trends*, 54: 21–8.

HEADY, P., and SMYTH, M. (1989), *Living Standards during Unemployment*, vol. 1 (London: HMSO).

HECKMAN, J. J. (1981), 'The Incidental Parameter Problem and the Problem of Initial Conditions in Estimating a Discrete Time-Discrete Data Stochastic Process', in C. F. Manski and D. McFadden (eds.), *Structural Analysis of Discrete Data with Econometrica Applications* (Cambridge, Mass.: MIT Press).

—— and SINGER, B. (1984), 'A Method for Minimizing the Impact of Distributional Assumptions in Econometric Models for Duration Data', *Econometrica*, 52: 271–320.

HENSHER, D. A., and JOHNSON, L. W. (1981), *Applied Discrete Choice Modelling* (New York: Wiley).

HOBSBAWM, E. J. (1968), *Industry and Empire* (Harmondsworth: Pelican).

HOEM, B., and HOEM, J. M. (1988), *Dissolution in Sweden: The Break-up of Conjugal Unions to Swedish Women Born in 1936–60*, Stockholm Research Reports in Demography No. 45, University of Stockholm.

HOFSTADTER, D. R. (1979), *Gödel, Escher, Bach: An Eternal Golden Braid* (London: Harvester).

HORRELL, S., RUBERY, J. and BURCHELL, B. (1989), 'Unequal Jobs or Unequal Pay?', *Industrial Relations Journal*, 20: 176–91.

HOUSE OF COMMONS (1980), Minutes of evidence taken before Industry and Trade Select Committee, HC367-ii, 1979–80, 23 Jan., 105.

IFF Research Limited (1988), *Vacancies and Recruitment Study*, research report prepared for the Employment Service (London: Department of Employment).

JACOBSON, D. (1987), 'A Personological Study of the Job Insecurity Experience', *Social Behaviour*, 2: 143–55.

JAHODA, G. (1986), 'Nature, Culture and Social Psychology', *European Journal of social Psychology*, 16: 17–30.

JAHODA, M. (1982), *Employment and Unemployment: A Social-Psychological Analysis* (Cambridge: Cambridge University Press).

—— (1989), 'Why a Non-reductionist Social Psychology is almost too Difficult to be Tackled but too Fascinating to be Left Alone', *British Journal of Social Psychology*, 38: 71–8.

—— LAZARSFELD, P., and ZEIZEL, H. (1972), *Marienthal: The Sociology of an Unemployed Community* (First pub. 1933; London: Tavistock).

JAMES, S. A., LACROIX, A. Z., KLEINBAUM, D. G., STROGATZ, D. S. (1984), 'John Henryism and Blood Pressure Differences among Black Men: The Role of Occupational Stressors', *Journal of Behavioural Medicine*, 7: 259–75.

JEFFERYS, J. B. (1954), *Retail Trading in Great Britain 1885–1950* (Cambridge: Cambridge University Press).

JOSEPH, G. (1983), *Women at Work: The British Experience* (Deddington: Philip Allen).

JOSHI, H. (1984), *Women's Participation in Paid Work: Further Analysis of the Women and Employment Survey*, Department of Employment (London: Department of Employment Research Paper No. 45).

KASL, S. V., COBB, S. (1982), 'Variability of Stress Effects among Men Experiencing Job Loss', in L. Goldberger and S. Breznitz (eds.),

Handbook of Stress, Theoretical and Clinical Aspects (New York: Free Press).

KELL, M., and WRIGHT, J. (1990), 'Benefits and the Labour Supply of Women Married to Unemployed Men', *Economic Journal*, 400, Supplement, 119–26.

KELLEY, J. (1973), 'Causal Chain Models for the Occupational Career', *American Sociological Review*, 38: 4.

KELVIN, P., and JARRETT, J. E. (1985), *Unemployment: Its Social Psychological Effects* (Cambridge: Cambridge University Press).

KIERNAN, K. E. (1986), 'Teenage Marriage and Marital Breakdown: A Longitudinal Study', *Population Studies*, 40/1: 35–54.

——— and ELDRIDGE, S. M. (1987), 'Inter- and Intra-Cohort Variation in the Timing of First Marriage', *British Journal of Sociology*, 38: 44–65.

KNOX, S. S., THEORELL, T., SVENSSON, J. C., and WALLER, D. (1985), 'The Relation of Social Support and Working Environment to Medical Variables Associated with Elevated Blood Pressure in Young Males: A Structural Model', *Social Science and Medicine*, 21: 525–31.

KOMAROVSKY, M. (1940), *The Unemployed Man and his Family* (New York: Octagon).

LAMPARD, R. J. (1990), *An Examination of the Relationship between Marital Dissolution and Unemployment*, ESRC Social Change and Economic Life Initiative Working Paper No. 17 (Oxford: Nuffield College).

LANCASTER, B., and MASON, T. (eds.) (1987), *Life and Labour in a Twentieth Century City: The Experience of Coventry* (Coventry: Cryfield Press).

LANCASTER, T., and NICKELL, S. J. (1980), 'The Analysis of Re-employment Possibilities for the Unemployed?', *Journal of the Royal Statistical Society*, 143: 141–65.

LANDSBERGIS, P. A. (1988), 'Occupational Stress among Health Care Workers: A Test of the Job Demands-Control Model', *Journal of Organisational Behaviour*, 9/3: 217–39.

LASH, S., and Urry, J. (1987), *The End of Organised Capitalism* (Cambridge: Polity Press).

LAYARD, R., BARTON, M., and ZABALZA, A. (1980), 'Married Women's Participation and Hours', *Economica*, 47: 51–72.

LEHRER, E. L. (1988), 'Determinants of Marital Instability: A Cox-Regression Model', *Applied Economics*, 20/2: 195–210.

LIEM, R., and LIEM, J. H. (1988), 'Psychological Effects of Unemployment on Workers and their Families', *Journal of Social Issues*, 44/4: 87–105.

LOCKWOOD, D. (1966), 'Sources of Variation in Working Class Images of Society', *Sociological Review*, 14: 249–67.

LOW PAY UNIT (1988), *The Poor Decade: Wage Inequalities in the 1980s* (London: Low Pay Unit).

MACK, J., and LANSLEY, P. (1985), *Poor Britain* (London: Allen & Unwin).

MCKEE, L., and BELL, C. (1985), 'Marital and Family Relations in Times of Male Unemployment', in B. Roberts, R. Finnegan, and D. Gallie (eds.), *New Approaches to Economic Life* (Manchester: Manchester University Press).

—— (1986), 'His Unemployment, her Problem: The Domestic and Marital Consequences of Male Unemployment', in S. Allen, A. Watson, K. Purcell, and S. Wood (eds.), *The Experience of Unemployment* (London: Macmillan).

MCKENNA, S. P., and FRYER, D. M. (1987), 'Perceived Health during Lay-off and Early Unemployment', *Occupational Health*, 36: 201–6.

MCLANAHAN, S., and BUMPASS, L. (1988), 'Sons, Daughters and the Risk of Marital Disruption', *American Journal of Sociology*, 94/1: 110–29.

MCNABB, R. (1977), 'The Labour Force Participation of Married Women', *The Manchester School*, 45: 221–35.

MARSDEN, D. (1975), *Workless* (2nd edn. 1982; London: Croom Helm).

MARSH, C. (1990), 'The Road to Recovery? Some Evidence from Vacancies in One Labour Market', *Work Employment and Society*, 4/1: 31–58.

—— and ALVARO, J. L. (1990), 'A Cross-cultural Perspective on the Social and Psychological Distress Caused by Unemployment: A Comparison of Spain and the United Kingdom', *European Sociological Review*, 6: 237–55.

MARSHALL, G. (1984), 'On the Significance of Women's Un-employment, its Neglect and Significance', *Sociological Review*, 32/2: 234–59.

—— ROSE, D., NEWBY, H., and VOGLER, C. (1988), 'Political Quiescence among the Unemployed in Modern Britain', in D. Rose (ed.), *Social Stratification and Economic Change*. (London: Hutchinson).

MARTIN, J., and ROBERTS, C. (1984), *Women and Employment: A Lifetime Perspective* (London: HMSO).

MARTIN, R., and WALLACE, J. (1984), *Working Women in Recession* (Oxford: Oxford University Press).

MARWICK, A. (1970), *Social Change in Britain* (London: Macmillan).

MASSEY, D. (1984), *Spatial Divisions of Labour: Social Structure and the Geography of Production*, (Basingstoke: Macmillan).

—— and MEEGAN, R. (1982), *The Anatomy of Job Loss: The How, Why and Where of Employment Decline* (London: Methuen).

References 357

MASSY, W. F., MONTGOMERY, D. M., and MORRISON, D. G. (1970), *Stochastic Models of Buying Behaviour* (Cambridge, Mass.: MIT Press).
MATTINSON, J. (1988), *Work, Love and Marriage: The Impact of Unemployment* (London: Duckworth).
MEAD, L. M. (1985), *Beyond Entitlement* (Glencoe, Ill.: Free Press).
MEADOWS, P., COOPER, H., and BARTHOLEMEW, R. (1988), *The London Labour Market*, Department of Employment (London: HMSO).
MILES, I. (1983), *Adaption to Unemployment?*, Science Policy Research Unit Research Report, University of Sussex.
MINFORD, P. (1983), *Unemployment: Cause and Cure* (Oxford: Martin Robertson).
MOLHO, I., and ELIAS, P. (1984), 'A Study of Regional Trends in the Labour Force Participation of Married Women in the UK, 1968–1977', *Applied Economics*, 16/2: 163–74.
MORGAN, S. P., LYE, D. N., and CONDRAN, G. A. (1988), 'Sons, Daughters and the Risk of Marital Disruption', *American Journal of Sociology*, 94/1: 110–29.
MORRIS, L. D. (1985), 'Renegotiation of the Domestic Division of Labour', in B. Roberts, R. Finnegan, and D. Gallie (eds.), *New Approaches to Economic Life* (Manchester: Manchester University Press).
—— (1988), 'Employment, the Household and Social Networks', in D. Gallie (ed.), *Employment in Britain* (Oxford: Blackwell).
—— (1990), *The Workings of the Household* (Oxford: Polity Press).
MOYLAN, S., MILLAR, J., and DAVIES, R. (1984), *For Richer, for Poorer? DHSS Cohort Study of Unemployed Men* (London: HMSO).
MUCKENBERGER, U., and DEAKIN, S. (1980), 'From Deregulation to a Floor of Rights: Labour Law, Flexibilisation and the European Single Market', *Zeitschrift fur auslandisches und internationales Arbeits und Socialrecht*, 3: 153–207.
MURPHY, M. J. (1985), 'Demographic and Socio-economic Influences on Recent British Marital Breakdown Patterns', *Population Studies*, 39/3: 441–60.
NEYMAN, J., and SCOTT, E. (1948), 'Consistent Estimates Based on Partially Consistent Observations', *Econometrica*, 16: 1–32.
NICKELL, S. J., NARENDRANATHAN, W., STERN, J., and GARCIA, J. (1989), *The Nature of Unemployment in Britain: Studies in the DHSS Cohort* (Oxford: Oxford University Press).
NIE, N., VERBA, S., and PETROCIK, J. R. (1976), *The Changing American Voter* (Cambridge, Mass.: Harvard University Press).
O'BRIEN, G. (1985), 'Distortions in Unemployment Research: The Early Studies of Bakke and their Implications for Current Research on Employment and Unemployment', *Human Relations*, 38: 877–94.

OAKLEY, A. (1974), *The Sociology of Housework* (Oxford: Martin Robertson).

OFFE, C. (1986), 'Democracy vs. the Welfare State?', Paper presented to the ESRC Symposium on Socioeconomic Change in the West, Cambridge.

OLIVER, J. M., and POMISTER, C. (1981), 'Depression in Automotive Assembly-Line Workers as a Function of Unemployment Variables', *American Journal of Community Psychology*, 9: 507–12.

OPCS (Office of Population Census and Surveys) (Social Survey Division) (1987), *The General Household Survey 1985*, Series GHS No. 15 (London: HMSO).

—— *Marriage and Divorce Statistics, Review of the Registrar-General of Marriages and Divorces in England and Wales 1987*, Series FM2 No. 14 (London: HMSO).

PAHL, J. (1989), *Money and Marriage* (London: Tavistock).

PAHL, R. E. (1984), *Divisions of Labour* (Oxford: Blackwell).

PAYNE, J. (1989), 'Unemployment and Family Formation among Young Men', *Sociology*, 23/2: 171–92.

PAYNE, R. L., WARR, P. B., and HARTLEY, J. (1983), *Social Class and the Experience of Unemployment*, Social and Applied Psychology Unit Memo No. 549, Sheffield University.

PENN, R., and SCATTERGOOD, H. (1989), *Corporate Strategy and Textile Employment*, ESRC Social Change and Economic Life Rochdale Project Working Paper No. 12, Department of Sociology, University of Lancaster.

POPAY, J. (1985), 'Women, the Family and Unemployment', in P. Close and R. Collins (eds.), *Family and Economy in Modern Society* (London: Macmillan).

REX, J., and MOORE, R. (1987), *Race, Community and Conflict* (Oxford: Oxford University Press).

RICHARDSON, K., and HARRIS, E. (1972), *Twentieth Century Coventry* (London: Macmillan).

ROSS, H. L., and SAWHILL, I. V. (1975), *Time of Transition: The Growth of Families Headed by Women* (Washington, DC: Urban Institute).

RUBERY, J. (1989), 'Precarious Forms of Work in the UK', in G. Rodgers and J. Rodgers (eds.), *Precarious Jobs in Labour Market Regulation: The Growth of Atypical Employment in Western Europe* (Geneva: IILS).

—— and WILKINSON, F. (eds.) (forthcoming), *Employers and the Labour Market* (Oxford: Oxford University Press).

—— (forthcoming), *Employer Strategy and the Labour Market* (Oxford: Oxford University Press).

SAMUEL, R. (ed.) (1977), *Miners, Quarrymen and Saltworkers* (London: Routledge & Kegan Paul).

SAUNDERS, P. (1981), 'Beyond Housing Classes: The Sociological Significance of Private Property Rights in the Means of Production', *International Journal of Urban and Regional Research*, 8: 202–27.

—— and HARRIS, C. (1987), 'Biting the Nipple? Consumer Preferences and State Welfare', Paper presented to the Urban Change and Conflict Conference, University of Kent at Canterbury.

SCHLOZMAN, K., and VERBA, S. (1979), *Injury to Insult: Unemployment, Class and Political Response* (Cambridge, Mass.: Harvard University Press).

SCOTT, A. M., and BURCHELL, B. J. (forthcoming), 'And Never the Twain Shall Meet? . . . Lifetime Segregation of Working Men and Women', in A. M. Scott (ed.), *Gender and the Labour Market* (Oxford: Oxford University Press).

SHAPIRO, E. G. (1977), 'Racial Differences in the Value of Job Rewards', *Social Forces*, 56/1: 21–30.

SIEGRIST, J., SIEGRIST, K., and WEBER, I. (1986), 'Sociological Concepts in the Etiology of Chronic Disease: The Case of Ischemic Heart Disease', *Social Science and Medicine*, Special Issue: Medical Sociology and the WHO's Programme for Europe, 22/2: 247–53.

SPILERMAN, S. (1972), 'Extensions of the Mover–Stayer Model', *American Journal of Sociology*, 78: 599–626.

SPSS Inc. (1988), *SPSS-X™ Users' Guide*, 3rd edn. (Chicago, Ill.: SPSS Inc.).

TAYLOR GOOBY, P. (1985), *Public Opinion, Ideology and State Welfare* (London: Routledge & Kegan Paul).

TEACHMAN, S. P. (1982), 'Methodological Issues in the Analysis of Family Formation and Dissolution', *Journal of Marriage and the Family*, 44: 1037–53.

THOMAS, G., WYATT, S., and MILES, I. (1985), 'Preliminary Analysis of the 1983/4 ESRC Time Budget Survey', Brighton: Science Policy Research Unit (mimeo).

TREW, K., and KILPATRICK, R. (1983), 'The Daily Life of the Unemployed: Social and Psychological Dimensions, Final Report to the SSRC.

UMS (Unit for Manpower Studies) (1977), *The Role of Immigrants in the Labour Market* (London: Department of Employment).

VEAL, A. J. (1986), *People in Sport and Recreation 1980: Summary of Data from the General Household Survey for England and Wales* (London: Centre for Leisure and Tourism Studies, Polytechnic of North London).

VOGLER, C. (1989), *Labour Market Change and Patterns of Financial Allocation within Households*, Social Change and Economic Life Working Paper No. 12, Nuffield College, Oxford.

WADE, D. C., COOLEY, E., and SAVICKI, V. (1986), 'A Longitudinal Study of Burnout' *Children and Youth Services Review*, 8: 161–73.

WARR, P. B. (1982), 'A National Study of Non-financial Employment Commitment', *Journal of Occupational Psychology*, 55: 297–312.

—— (1985), 'Twelve Questions about Unemployment and Health, in B. Roberts, R. Finnegan, and D. Gallie (eds.), *New Approaches to Economic Life* (Manchester: Manchester University Press).

—— (1987), *Work, Unemployment and Mental Health* (Oxford: Clarendon Press).

—— and JACKSON, P. (1985), 'Factors Influencing the Psychological Impact of Prolonged Unemployment and of Re-employment', *Psychological Medicine*, 15: 795–807.

—— and PAYNE, R. L. (1983), 'Social Class and Reported Changes in Behaviour after Job Loss', *Journal of Applied Social Psychology*, 13: 206–22.

WESTERGAARD, J., NOBLE, I., and WALKER, A. (1989), *After Redundancy* (Oxford: Polity Press).

WHITE, M. (1983), *Long-Term Unemployment and Labour Markets* (London: Policy Studies Institute).

WILLIAMS, R. (1976), *Keywords: A Vocabulary of Culture and Society* (London: Fontana).

ZABALZA, A. (1982), 'The CES Utility Function, Nonlinear Budget Constraints and Labour Supply Results on Female Participation and Hours', *Economic Journal*, 93: 312–30.

INDEX